TEACHING
WRITING
IN
SECOND
AND
FOREIGN
LANGUAGE
CLASSROOMS

The McGraw-Hill Second Language Professional Series

General Editors: James F. Lee and Bill VanPatten

Directions in Second Language Learning and Teaching

Primarily for students of second language acquisition and teaching, curriculum developers, and teacher educators, *Directions in Second Language Learning* explores how languages are learned and used and how knowledge about language acquisition and use informs language teaching. The books in this strand emphasize principled approaches to language classroom instruction and management as well as to the education of foreign and second language teachers.

Making Communicative Language Teaching Happen, Second Edition
by James F. Lee and Bill VanPatten, ISBN 0-07-365517-1

Translation Teaching: From Research to the Classroom
by Sonia Colina, ISBN 0-07-248709-7

Gender in the Language Classroom
by Monika Chavez, ISBN 0-07-236749-0

Tasks and Communicating in Language Classrooms
by James F. Lee, ISBN 0-07-231054-5

Affect in Foreign Language and Second Language Learning: A Practical Guide to Creating a Low-Anxiety Classroom Atmosphere
Edited by Dolly Jesusita Young, ISBN 0-07-038900-4

Beyond Methods: Components of Second Language Teacher Education
Edited by Kathleen Bardovi-Harlig and Beverly Hartford, ISBN 0-07-006106-8

Communicative Competence: Theory and Classroom Practice, Second Edition
by Sandra J. Savignon, ISBN 0-07-083736-8

Monographs in Second Language Learning and Teaching

The second strand in the series, *Monographs in Second Language Learning and Teaching*, is designed to provide brief and highly readable texts for beginners and nonspecialists that can be used as supplements to any of the books in the *Directions* strand or with other main texts. An additional goal of the *Monographs* strand is to provide an array of short texts that instructors may combine in various ways to fashion courses that suit their individual needs.

Input Enhancement: From Theory and Research to the Classroom
by Wynne Wong, ISBN 0-07-288725-7

Structured Input: Grammar Instruction for the Acquisition Oriented Classroom
by Andrew P. Farley, ISBN 0-07-288724-9

Teaching Writing in Second and Foreign Language Classrooms
by Jessica Williams, ISBN 0-07-293479-4

From Input to Output: A Teacher's Guide to Second Language Acquisition
by Bill VanPatten, ISBN 0-07-282561-8

Breaking Tradition: An Exploration of the Historical Relationship between Theory and Practice in Second Language Teaching
by Diane Musumeci, ISBN 0-07-044394-7

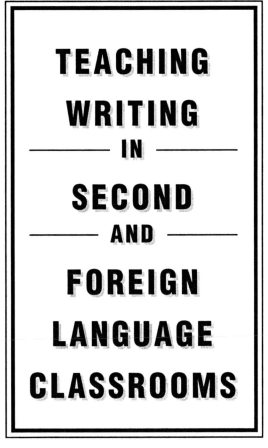

TEACHING WRITING IN SECOND AND FOREIGN LANGUAGE CLASSROOMS

Jessica Williams
The University of Illinois at Chicago

Boston   Burr Ridge, IL   Dubuque, IA   Madison, WI   New York
San Francisco   St. Louis   Bangkok   Bogotá   Caracas   Kuala Lumpur
Lisbon   London   Madrid   Mexico City   Milan   Montreal   New Delhi
Santiago   Seoul   Singapore   Sydney   Taipei   Toronto

Higher Education

This is an ⌐B⌐ book.

3 4 5 6 7 8 9 0 WDD WDD 12 11 10

ISBN-13: 978-0-07-293479-3

ISBN-10: 0-07-293479-4

Publisher: *William R. Glass*
Developmental editor: *Kate Engelberg*
Executive marketing manager: *Nick Agnew*
Project manager: *Jennifer Chambliss/Mel Valentín*
Senior production supervisor: *Richard DeVitto*
Design manager: *Violeta Díza*
Cover designer: *Violeta Díaz*
Interior designer: *Linda Robertson*
Compositor: *The GTS Companies/York, PA Campus*
Typeface: *Times Roman*
Printer: *Bookmart Press*

Library of Congress Cataloging-in-Publication Data

Williams, Jessica, 1957-
    Teaching writing in second and foreign language classrooms / Jessica Williams.
      p. cm. — (The McGraw-Hill second language professional series. Monographs in second language learning and teaching)
    Includes index.
    ISBN 0-07-293479-4 (softcover)
      1. Language and languages—Study and teaching. 2. Rhetoric—Study and teaching.
    3. Second language acquisition.   I. Title. II. Series.

P53.27.W55 2004
418'.0071—dc22

                                                            2004049852

http://www.mhhe.com

CONTENTS

CHAPTER 5   *RESPONDING TO SECOND LANGUAGE WRITING*   93

CHAPTER 6   *ASSESSING SECOND LANGUAGE WRITING*   119

CHAPTER 7   *THE EFFECTS OF PRODUCTION, INSTRUCTION, AND FEEDBACK ON L2 WRITING*   139

CHAPTER 8   *PROGRAM OPTIONS FOR SECOND LANGUAGE WRITING INSTRUCTION*   172

FOREWORD

An important aspect of learning to communicate in another language is developing *literacy*—the ability both to read and understand written texts and to write and compose in that language. How does a person become literate in another language? This question raises a host of additional questions and issues: What is the relationship of literacy to language acquisition more generally (by which we mean the creation of a linguistic system in the learner's head)? What role does literacy in the first language play in developing literacy in the second language? What kinds of tasks or task properties promote literacy in second language classrooms? How can literacy be assessed?

In this text, well-known applied linguist Jessica Williams explores various theoretical and practical issues in developing second language and foreign language writing abilities. Drawing upon her many years of experience teaching graduate courses in writing for both TESOL and foreign language teachers, Williams deftly handles topics such as the relationship of writing to second language acquisition, writing as a recursive process involving numerous subtasks, appropriate feedback and response to written production, approaches to the assessment of writers' work, program options for writing instruction, and many more. This highly readable text, designed for both ESL and foreign language contexts in which academic writing is a focus of concern, will be of use to teachers in training, curriculum developers, and administrators alike. We are very pleased to offer this volume in the McGraw-Hill Second Language Professional Series and believe it will find its rightful place on the shelves of professionals involved in second language teaching.

James F. Lee
Bloomington, IN

Bill VanPatten
Chicago, IL

December 10, 2003

PREFACE

Why write a book about second language writing? And how is this one different from others available on the market? I had several goals in writing this book and several ways in which I wanted it to be different.

First, I was interested in creating a short, accessible text that would be as useful as possible to ESL instructors, both new and experienced, charged with teaching writing to second language learners. In my 15 years as a professor in the TESOL program at the University of Illinois, I have been proud of the preparation we have given to ESL teachers. Yet our students are so busy, and there is so much for them to absorb in a short time—pedagogy, materials development, testing, second language acquisition theory and research, basic linguistics—that it is difficult for them to develop expertise in a specific area of the field. Our focus, and that of most second language teacher preparation programs, is on *language* teaching. In North America, at least in the last 25 years, this has meant *communicative* language teaching, which tends to favor instruction on spoken language. Some areas of academic language development, such as writing, must be covered in a few short weeks. Many recent graduates feel anxious and somewhat unprepared when they are assigned their first writing class, and like me, they learn on the job.

Yet acquiring advanced literacy skills is a high-stakes business, especially for second language learners here in North America. For those who don't acquire adequate writing skills, it can mean the difference between professional and economic success and failure. It is essential for second language professionals to be prepared to help learners toward their academic and professional goals. This book is designed to speak to this need—to help ESL teachers help their students become better writers. The book contains a combination of research results and practical advice and discussion, with an emphasis on findings that have direct implications for classroom writing teachers.

My second goal in writing this book was to provide resources for those who are interested in teaching academic literacy in foreign languages. The needs and motivations of foreign language learners may be quite different from those who are learning English in this country. There may be less economic pressure to acquire academic skills, yet the goals and needs of these students are no less important or real. Foreign language majors are also expected to do academic writing in their new language, and they, too, need instruction on how to do it. Throughout the book, I have used examples not just from ESL but also from commonly taught foreign languages, and I have taken into account the instructional needs of both ESL and FL learners and teachers.

My third goal in writing this book was to create a text that takes as its starting point the fact that our students are always second language learners. Even as we teach writing and other advanced literacy skills, our students continue to acquire language. Any instructional approach to second language writing ought to acknowledge the fact that this process does not end when writing instruction begins. Therefore, throughout the book, I have tried to tie writing instruction to research and practice in second language learning and teaching.

My hope is that many students and teachers will find this text useful. Specifically, it may be used

- as a supplementary text in a basic methods course;
- for a specific course on second or foreign language writing;
- as part of a preparation course for ESL or FL teaching assistants;
- as a text for continuing education courses for high school ESL teachers; or
- as an aid to practicing second language teachers who want more specialized preparation and instruction in teaching writing.

ORGANIZATION AND FEATURES

The book has eight chapters. Chapter 1 provides a basic introduction to the aspects of second language acquisition theory and research findings that are relevant to second language writing instruction. Chapter 2 explores the basic factors that affect learning to write in any language: the texts writers produce, the writers themselves, writing processes, and the writers' audience. The chapter pays special attention to the role of reading in developing writing skills. The third and fourth chapters are practical; they explore sequenced activities that have been shown to be effective in teaching second language writing. Chapter 3 is organized around writers' developing language proficiency, and Chapter 4 follows the stages of the writing process. Chapter 3 includes a special focus on writing instruction that exploits technology, and Chapter 4 has a special focus on in-class writing practice. Chapter 5 explores response to student writing, both by the teacher and by peers. Chapter 6 addresses evaluation issues, concentrating primarily on local assessment but also touching on large-scale institutional testing. Chapter 7 returns to the nexus of writing instruction and language acquisition introduced in the first chapter, this time focusing on the development of linguistic accuracy and feedback on error. Chapter 8 closes the book with an exploration of curricular alternatives in second language instruction, in particular, task-based and content-based approaches.

Following the model of other titles in this series, this book includes periodic "Pause to Consider" boxes. These boxes offer discussion points and activities designed to push students beyond the text—that is, to consider the implications of the issues presented in the text and to put some of the ideas into practice. The Pause to Consider boxes can be used for in-class discussions and activities or for at-home assignments. Key terms appear in boldface type in the text and are listed in the glossary at the end of the book with their definitions.

At the end of each chapter, resources are listed for those students who wish to explore the issues presented in the chapter further. To tailor the readings to students' specific interests, I have divided them into the subtopics addressed in the chapter. The most readily accessible readings are marked with an asterisk. I have also listed some websites that offer practical suggestions and activities that teachers can use right away. I have tried to include only websites with a stable track record that are likely to remain active and viable.

In addition to the glossary, there are two appendixes at the end of the book. Appendix 1 includes student texts in several languages to familiarize readers with typical learner production and to provide samples for practice in giving feedback. Appendix 2 includes examples of two widely used foreign language assessment instruments.

ACKNOWLEDGMENTS

I have many people to thank for helping make this book possible. My first thanks must go to Bill VanPatten and Jim Lee, without whom there simply would be no book. Before they approached me, the idea of writing this kind of book had never occurred to me. Bill's support and encouragement throughout the project have kept it and me on track. Valuable feedback and ideas have come from many quarters, including the reviewers of the original proposal: Maria Amores, Joanne Burnett, Anna Gemrich, Kimberly L. Geeslin, Jennifer Leeman, and Judith E. Liskin-Gasparro. Special thanks go to two friends and colleagues, Charlene Polio and Susanne Rott, who provided complementary perspectives and detailed reviews of the entire manuscript. The final product is infinitely better for their suggestions. For assistance on checking the accuracy of my non-English examples, collecting student writing samples, and sharing their expertise, thanks to Elisa Baena, Richard Cameron, Rebecca deWind-Mattingly, Leane Dostaler, Mohammed Errihani, Margaret Miner, Robert Romeo, Susanne Rott, and Andrew Young. Finally, I must thank the students in my Teaching Second Language Writing class, my guinea pigs, on whom I piloted much of the material that appears here. Their feedback and suggestions have resulted in many changes, additions, and a fair amount of material for the editing-room floor.

Thanks also to the McGraw-Hill team: William R. Glass, Publisher; Kate Engelberg, Developmental Editor; Jennifer Chambliss/Mel Valentín, Project Managers; Violeta Díaz, Design Manager; Rich Devitto, Production Supervisor; and Judith Brown, Copyeditor.

Second Language Acquisition and Second Language Writing: An Introduction

If both learning another language and learning academic writing are challenges, then learning to write in a **second language (L2)** can seem like an insurmountable task. In **foreign language (FL)** classes, many learners never move beyond composing single sentences or perhaps paragraphs. Yet language majors are required to read literature and other texts and then write critical responses and analyses, just as they might in their native language. In second language contexts, lack of writing proficiency can be a barrier to academic and professional success. Learning to write is an important part of second language education, particularly in academic settings; it is these settings that will be the focus of this text.

The term *second language learner* is often used to refer to those learning a new language in a country where that language is spoken; for example, a recent immigrant from Korea and a Brazilian learner on a student visa, both learning English in the United States, would be L2 learners. The term *foreign language learner* generally applies to a student of a language that is not spoken in that country, such as, learners of German at a U.S. high school, of Russian at a college in Canada, or of English in Japan. Sometimes this distinction can be important, and when it is, I use these terms to differentiate between the two kinds of learners. However, most of the time, I simply use the cover terms *L2 learner* and *L2 writer* to describe the learners and writers of a new language, regardless of the setting in which they are acquiring and using that language.

Most language teaching professionals feel reasonably well prepared for the classroom after they complete their training, if a little anxious about their first class. However, because much of their education may have been devoted to *language* teaching and learning—the acquisition of L2 grammar and vocabulary and the promotion of communication skills, especially speaking and listening—they may feel unprepared to teach composition in

1

2

CHAPTER 1
*Second Language
Acquisition and
Second Language
Writing: An
Introduction*

an L2. They may revert to their own experiences of learning to write in their first language, perhaps to their junior high or high school English classes. No doubt some of this reflection will be useful in their teaching; however, a central idea in this book is that learning to write in an L2 differs in important ways both from acquiring an L2, and from learning to write in one's native language.

Pause to consider...

the best way to learn to write well. Does it mean reading a lot? Writing a lot? Studying and following models of good writing? Following instructions about good writing (e.g., "Begin with a thesis statement.")? Do you think you learned to write in this way in your first language?

SECOND LANGUAGE ACQUISITION: SOME BASICS

Most textbooks on teaching L2 writing begin by exploring research and practice in writing in the **first language (L1)**. Indeed, most research into L2 writing has looked to L1-based studies for theory, insights, and techniques. We explore some of these important ideas in Chapter 2. We begin, however, with a brief exploration of L2 acquisition. This perspective is important because L2 writers are also still L2 learners; that is, they are still in the process of acquiring elements of a new language at the same time that they are mastering the skill of writing. L2 learners slowly build their knowledge of the sound system, grammar, and vocabulary in approximation of the new, target language. This approximation is often referred to as **interlanguage (IL).** The IL changes and develops over time, although most adult learners never achieve nativelike mastery of the target language. It is important for L2 writing teachers to acknowledge the ongoing nature of this process, because their students' IL knowledge will have a significant impact on their ability to compose in the L2.

We begin with an exploration of some of the generally (though not universally) accepted findings in L2 acquisition. We will refer back to these fundamental statements throughout the text. We will also explore how they apply specifically to the teaching and learning of L2 writing.

Statement 1: There Are Two Types of (Second) Language Knowledge: Implicit and Explicit

Not all IL knowledge is the same. This has implications for both learning and teaching. **Implicit knowledge** of an L2 is much like knowledge of a native language: It is tacit and abstract. It is knowledge on which a user can draw without thinking in order to produce or understand language. Indeed, users may not be able to explain what they know or be aware that there are rules for the use of a structure or specific words. Consider the following examples:

> (1) old, jewelry, wooden, little
>
>   Put these words in an order that describes the noun *box*.

If you were to compare your answers with those of other native speakers, chances are that most of you would come up with the following phrase: *little old wooden jewelry box.*

Consider another example. Compare the (a, b) pairs of sentences with the (c, d) pairs of sentences in (2).

> (2) a. It is certain that Roger will go.
>   b. It is likely that Roger will go.
>   a′. Roger is certain to go.
>   b′. Roger is likely to go.
>
>   c. It is probable that Roger will come.
>   d. It is clear that Roger will arrive soon.
>   *c′. Roger is probable to come.
>   *d′. Roger is clear to arrive soon.
>
> *This symbol means that the sentence is unacceptable.

Based on the pairs (a, a′; b, b′), you would be justified in thinking that c′ and d′ would be acceptable, but they are not. You know these things, of course, but do you know the rule? Do you know precisely why all native speakers will come up with this same answer? Probably not, and to be honest, who cares? This is knowledge that you use everyday but you never need to articulate—unless, of course, you are a teacher and you need to explain these things to a learner. The general reason for native speaker agreement on these examples is that native speakers all share much the same implicit knowledge of English. Implicit knowledge is the basis of our competence as native speakers.

I have often observed new teachers frustrated by exchanges such as the following:

> (3) T: (to a student) What's wrong with this sentence? *She didn't go back since the fire.* Can you correct it?
>   S: *She hasn't been back since the fire.*
>   T: Great! Why do we use *hasn't been?*
>   S: I don't know. It sounds better.
>   T: !!

The new teacher interprets the student's inability to respond to the question as a sign that she has not learned the material. On the contrary, she has learned it very well. In fact, her knowledge of the present perfect in English, like your knowledge of the examples in (2), is implicit. She doesn't know why the present perfect is appropriate; she can't articulate the rule for its use. In fact, her knowledge of this structure resembles that of a native speaker, and, after all, isn't that the goal of language teaching? Much of the knowledge used by proficient L2 learners is of this type, especially when they write.

There is another kind of IL knowledge that can be more readily articulated. This is referred to as **explicit knowledge.** Learners can provide rules and reasons for why and how a certain form is used, such as, "Use *a* for the

4

CHAPTER 1
*Second Language
Acquisition and
Second Language
Writing: An
Introduction*

first mention of a referent and *the* to mark the noun thereafter," or "Use *ser* for states of being and *estar* for impermanent states and locations." Frequently, FL classes emphasize the teaching of vocabulary and grammar rules like these. This kind of instruction can help learners develop their explicit knowledge of the new language. Most learners find this knowledge useful and refer to it often, especially when they are beginning their study of the new language. Perhaps you have had the experience of running through verb paradigms (*nous faisons, vous faites, ils font*) or adjective declensions (*ein alter Mann, einen alten Mann, einem alten Mann*) in your head as you search your memory for the proper form to use. It does not always come to mind quickly or easily, but learners can draw on this kind of knowledge when they do exercises and tests and, importantly, when they write. On the other hand, they may find it less useful if they become lost on the streets of Paris or Berlin.

There is considerable controversy in the field about whether these two knowledge sources are permanently separate and whether or how one influences the other. There are three main positions on this topic:

- Some believe that the role of explicit knowledge in L2 acquisition is relatively minor. Its primary function is to edit implicit knowledge. It can never change into explicit knowledge. The focus of L2 learning and instruction should therefore be on the development of implicit knowledge.
- Some maintain that with repeated use, explicit knowledge can be transformed into implicit knowledge. Implicit knowledge can also be acquired directly. The goal of language learning and instruction should therefore be the development of both types of knowledge as well as the conversion of explicit knowledge into implicit knowledge.
- Others claim that explicit knowledge remains separate from implicit knowledge; nevertheless, it plays an important role in structuring and shaping the development of implicit knowledge. The goal of language learning and instruction should therefore be the development of both types of knowledge, depending on the goals of the learner.

A full discussion of this issue is beyond the scope of this book, and it is not essential that we decide which one is correct. However, it is important to understand the distinction between the two types of knowledge, because L2 writers will have to develop and draw on both. In addition, different learners may be at different points in their development of these two types of knowledge, and teachers thus may need different instructional strategies.

Statement 2: Second Language Acquisition Takes Place Only in the Presence of Input—Usually Plenty of It

What is the source of learners' L2 knowledge? Some of it may come from rules that they read in books, but most implicit knowledge comes from the L2 data that are all around them, in a classroom or simply out in the real world, both in language that is addressed to them and in language that they read and hear as part of natural communication. All of the language that is available to learners through such exposure is called **input**.

The importance of input cannot be overestimated. Input is most useful for developing implicit knowledge when it contains meaningful messages rather than rules and information about language. It is a truism to state that L2 acquisition cannot take place without input, but sometimes we take it for granted. We assume that our learners are exposed to lots of it, especially if they live in the country where the target language is spoken. Unfortunately, this is not always the case, and we need to be sure that our classrooms are input-rich environments.

In general, though, learners in an L2 environment are more successful than those in FL classrooms. There may be a variety of reasons for this difference, but a major one is that there is limited input in FL contexts. For example, most English learners of Spanish have a difficult time learning the difference between the imperfect and the preterit tenses, or between *por* and *para*. For FL learners in the classroom, exposure to these forms is probably limited to what is in the textbook and what they hear from their teacher. Compare this situation to that of learners in an L2 environment. They may be surrounded by input, exposed to perhaps dozens of examples of this contrast every day. They have a rich storehouse of experience on which they may base their communicative choices. They may not even realize that they possess this knowledge; it may creep up incrementally as their exposure to relevant forms increases. Once this input becomes part of their implicit knowledge, the retrieval process is quick and automatic. The difference in how these two situations play out rests largely on differences in the quantity and range of available input, as well as opportunities for output.

We have explored the importance of input in L2 learning generally. But what is the significance of input in learning to write in an L2? In the writing classroom, the provision of input usually includes lots of reading. Reading is especially important because it provides L2 learners with exposure to vocabulary, spelling, structures, and usage that learners may not get from everyday conversation or even from lectures, thus improving the quality and range of input they get. It can also dramatically increase the amount of input they receive in the target language. Reading is important for native speakers as well: Skillful writers and writers with rich vocabularies are usually also extensive readers. This important connection is explored further in Chapter 2.

Reading takes on special significance as input because written language is not simply spoken language written down. Look at the following two examples of input. The first excerpt (4) is a spoken interchange between a writer and a writing tutor. (Each period represents a pause of .5 second.) The second excerpt (5) is an example of academic writing.

(4) K: Um... Well. This is uh.a paper I uh got back.from English and I discussed it with my teacher and she asked me to make some corrections and stuff. So I guess I I need some help with that.

   T: Do you have the paper assignment with you?

   K: Uh. No. It was just.she.just told us to pick one of the stories we read and do like a crit.critical review.

   T: So, you just want to work on the corrections the teacher suggested you should do?

6

*CHAPTER 1
Second Language
Acquisition and
Second Language
Writing: An
Introduction*

K: Yeah, cause she said it was a basically an OK paper. I mean, I got a B+ on it. There are just some things that I needed.needed to be like.sharpened.

T: OK, what are like the specific things your teacher wants you to work on?

K: um..the introduction and like.transitions.

T: OK, so what were.what were the things right now that you read that you remember talking about with your teacher and maybe possible suggestions..that she..made for you to do?

K: She just said like make the first paragraph stronger and.show her.the examples, not just tell her what happened…but show her them.

(5) Socioculture theory sees communication not just as a way of transmitting information, but as a process of jointly constructing new knowledge. Much of the work in this area draws heavily on Vygotskyan views of first language learning, in which learners first depend on **other-regulation,** that is, the guidance of more skilled individuals, to perform new and difficult tasks. Collaborative dialogue is a way for the novice to stretch current knowledge, as initial reliance on the expert yields to internalization of new knowledge by the novice and subsequent **self-regulation.** This is most likely to occur in the learner's **zone of proximal development,** the domain in which the learner is not yet capable of self-regulated activity, but can accomplish tasks under the guidance of experts. This zone is not simply a predetermined next stage of readiness. Rather, it is mutually constructed and can only be determined dialogically.[1]

Pause to consider...

the two excerpts (4) and (5). In what ways do they differ? What different kinds of knowledge about language and language use might an L2 writer gain from these two types of input?

It is easy to see immediately that the two selections are quite different. They differ in sentence structure and vocabulary, but they also differ in ways that transcend the sentence, at the level of *discourse.* **Discourse** is defined as a coherent sequence of connected spoken or written text. It is clear that written discourse, at least the academic discourse represented in (5), is structured quite differently from spoken discourse. No one carries on a conversation like this, at least not if they are interested in people actually listening to them. We will explore some characteristics of written discourse later. For now, the important point to remember is that L2 writers need to be exposed to a considerable amount of academic discourse as input as they learn academic writing. They need copious input to develop both their L2 proficiency and their writing skills.

Statement 3: L2 Acquisition Occurs as Both System Learning and Item learning

Thus far, we have assumed that the learning process is monolithic, that all L2 learning takes place in the same way. Although there are many things we still don't know about the process, it is certain that this is not the case. As suggested in Statement 3, some L2 acquisition is rule based (**system learning**) and some occurs one element at a time (**item learning**).

Many in the field of L2 acquisition believe that grammar is learned as a system, although some item learning may occur as well.[2] The German verb system provides an example of this. Learners may begin by learning individual verb forms separately, but once they figure out that the past tense is formed with an auxiliary verb plus *ge + verb* stem + *(e)t*, as in *Ich habe fünf Stunden gewartet (I waited for five hours)*, they no longer need to learn the form of each regular verb one by one. In essence, learners get the rest of the regular past tense forms "for free." Past forms for irregular verbs (e.g, *ist* → *war*), in contrast, need to be learned one by one, but even then, learners may discover patterns. For example, vowel alternations may be similar across sets of verbs; *finden* (find) → *gefunden* (found) is much like *trinken* (drink) → *getrunken* (drunk) and *singen* (sing) → *gesungen* (sung). These rules may be explicitly taught, but pattern knowledge can also be internalized without instruction or even conscious awareness. Any young English-speaking child can provide a similar example of this process. Ask her for the form of the irregular past verb *bring* and she will give you a blank look, but ask her, "Did your mommy bring you something from the store?" and she will happily answer, "Yes, she *brang* me a doughnut"! She has learned the rule for *ring-rang* and *sink-sank* and now applies it to *bring*. Later, she will inevitably figure out that the correct form is *brought*, but at no time is she consciously aware of the irregularity of either form.

Whereas we think of grammars as systems that can be acquired through the accumulation of rules, the tendency is to think of the acquisition of words as occurring through item learning, and this is probably the case. Learning one structure does not get you anything else "for free," as in the description of German past tense. When you learn the word *dog, chien,* or *perro,* you have just learned one new word, which refers to those furry, four-legged creatures. Words don't pattern in quite the same systematic way as grammar rules do, and thus they require a different strategy for acquisition. This is not to say that there is no systematicity in word use; as we will see, there is considerable patterning in the lexicon as well. Also, some structures seem to fall right in between the item learning associated with vocabulary and the system learning associated with grammar. Below are some French examples:

(6) a. *Il voulait Ø lire des romans français.* (He wanted to read French novels.)
    b. *Il s'est promis de lire des romans français.* (He promised himself to read French novels.)
    c. *Il a appris à lire des romans français.* (He learned to read French novels.)

It is apparent that in the English translation, the second verb in each sentence is in the infinitive, that is, *to* + verb; yet, in the French versions, sometimes the verb is introduced by *à*, sometimes by *de*, sometimes by nothing at all (Ø).

8

CHAPTER 1
*Second Language
Acquisition and
Second Language
Writing: An
Introduction*

You might think this is just a grammar rule (similar to, for example, the differences among the past tense forms in the three sentences), but the choice is controlled by the preceding verb (*want, promise, learn*), so it is also a vocabulary concern. We might say that a French L2 learner's "mental definition" of *se promêtre* should eventually include the fact that it is normally followed by the preposition *de* when used with an infinitive. The acquisition of these structures seems to involve elements of both system and item learning.

Even individual words have more regular patterns of (co-)occurrence than you might think. Fill in the blank for the following three examples:

(7) a. The candidate was eminently _____ for the position.
    b. The situation was fraught with _____.
    c. The children decided to dig a _____.

Your answers may not be the same as those of any other reader of this book. However, it is likely that your answers are something like (a) *qualified*, (b), *danger, problems, difficulty*, and (c), *hole, trench*. Why should your answers be so predictable? The answer is that there is patterning in the use of these words and, therefore, perhaps a certain degree of system learning in vocabulary acquisition. A large database of actual usage of English (called a **corpus**) would reveal that *eminently* often modifies *qualified*; they are almost a set phrase, much like *diametrically opposed*. In (b), your choice is obviously controlled by the word *fraught*. What do all of the words that seem to go with *fraught* have in common? In all likelihood, they are all negative. It is doubtful that anyone would offer *joy* or *laughter* as candidates to fill in this blank.

In (c), your choice is limited by the other content words in the sentence, primarily *dig*. What else can you dig besides a hole? A *grave* perhaps, but the word *children* would discourage that choice. Thus, we can say that *dig* and *hole* tend to pattern together (and perhaps are most easily learned together). This kind of patterning is all part of your implicit knowledge, which builds up after a great deal of exposure to the target input; it is the type of knowledge that L2 learners may have not yet developed. It is not even information they could easily get from a dictionary. If they looked up *fraught*, they would find something like *filled with* or *accompanied by*, encouraging them to use it in a wider and less appropriate sense, such as *The room was fraught with music*. You have gained this kind of implicit knowledge of words without thinking about it. It is essential to understand how these types of learning work because both system learning and item learning are part of developing L2 writing proficiency.

Pause to consider...

some other examples from the language that you teach in which

- learning one structure gets you something else "for free," that is, cases of system learning;
- elements have to be learned one by one, that is, through item learning;
- words tend to occur together.

Statement 4: Second Language Acquisition (and Use) Require Attention

We have discussed the importance of input and different types of learning, but we have omitted one important step. How does input get from the outside to the inside of the learner's head? In other words, many learners are surrounded by input, but what determines which bits of input are taken in and eventually become part of the IL? This is a complex question, but one crucial element of the process seems certain: **attention,** or concentration of mental focus.

Most researchers in the field of L2 acquisition believe that in order to learn something, you have to pay attention to it. This doesn't mean that, for Spanish, you have to consciously say to yourself something like, "Hey, that verb sounds funny. It must be some new variation of the third person plural of *venir*" when you hear *Espero que vengan temprano* (I hope they come early). It simply means that at some level, you notice the presence/novelty of the form *vengan*, perhaps storing it for future processing. It doesn't mean that you have learned it or that you can use it right away; this is just a first step.

Unfortunately, our attention is finite; we can't pay attention to everything. Often, there are many calls on our attention. Acquiring new linguistic knowledge requires attention, but accessing and using that knowledge can also be effortful, requiring considerable attentional resources as well. These two processes, acquiring and accessing, are not the same thing, as you will see later in this chapter. Learners may know, for instance, that certain verbs and expressions trigger the subjunctive in French or Italian, and they may even know the actual forms that they should use. Yet, during a spontaneous exchange, they may simply be unable to draw on that knowledge fast enough to use it. Their attention is split among too many different demands.

In writing, L2 learners have the benefit of extra time to consider their production and consciously direct their attention to specific forms or words. Yet the task of composing is itself challenging (even in the native language) and requires a significant amount of attention, drawing resources away from sentence-level language issues. If writers are concentrating on creating effective arguments, they may not be able to devote attention to grammatical and vocabulary choices. This is why even native speakers have to proofread; it's hard to stay focused on so many things at once. It is no wonder that L2 writers do things such as leave off the third person singular *s* in English or fail to include *iᶜraab* (word endings that mark mood and case) in Arabic. Neither of these is essential for expressing basic meaning, and writers may therefore pay little attention to them when they have more pressing concerns. Conversely, it is also possible for L2 writers to be so concerned with sentence-level accuracy that they are unable to pay sufficient attention to the effective communication of their ideas.

Statement 5: Having Linguistic Knowledge and Using That Knowledge Are Not the Same

We have already noted that even if learners have acquired L2 knowledge, they may not be able to use that knowledge easily. This is another central tenet of L2 acquisition. L2 learners draw on both implicit and explicit knowledge,

10

CHAPTER 1
*Second Language
Acquisition and
Second Language
Writing: An
Introduction*

depending on the context and task. Most spontaneous, real-time (meaning that there is no time to go back and edit or make corrections) activities, such as a conversation, require that users draw on implicit knowledge. Others, such as taking a test, may allow them to use explicit knowledge as well. Sometimes task demands are such that learners are simply unable to make use of everything they know. This is because they are not sufficiently skilled at deploying the knowledge that they have. For example, the student back in excerpt (3) seemed to have implicit knowledge of the present perfect in English. Yet it is quite possible that she would make an error in this same form if it were embedded in a particularly demanding task, such as a spontaneous response in a fast-paced conversation. Thus, learners must develop their linguistic knowledge as well as their skill in using it. These two aspects of L2 proficiency develop concurrently but in different ways. For written production, it can be hard to tell whether learner errors stem from lack of knowledge, lack of control over that knowledge, excessive task demands, or simple carelessness.

Statement 6: Practice Does Not Always Make Perfect in L2 Acquisition, but It Can Contribute to Skill Development

We have underscored the importance of input in the acquisition of linguistic knowledge, but we have said little about **output**—language that the learner produces. What role does output play in language development? In improving control of linguistic knowledge? Although it probably does not help learners to practice things they have not yet internalized, output does in fact have a number of important roles in the development of IL knowledge. It can

- help learners get access to more input. In spoken interaction, if they produce language, they are more likely to get a response;
- provide an opportunity for learners to test and get feedback on their hypotheses about how the L2 works;
- call their attention to things they don't know or can't do, perhaps prompting them to focus on these items in subsequent input.

All of these functions of output facilitate acquisition of linguistic knowledge, but output has an even more crucial role in the development of control of linguistic knowledge and of specific skills, such as writing. We will revisit the role of output in the development of L2 writing proficiency in Chapter 7, but here we consider output as a form of **practice,** defined as repeated engagement in an activity. Many scholars believe that language practice is most useful for helping learners access what they already know more quickly and accurately. Note, however, that practicing does not mean engaging in meaningless drills, in which there is no need to understand meaning, such as:

(8) a. *Ayer* _____ *(tener) Ramón un examén en matemática.*
    Yesterday Ramón _____ (have) a math test.
   b. T: Is the clock on the wall?
    S: Yes, it is.
    T: Yes. The clock is on the wall.

Practice should always involve the communication of meaning. Writing slot-and-filler drills (a) and answering mechanical questions whose answers are known to everyone (b) have little to do with authentic communication. If learners do a lot of slot-and-filler drills, it means they will probably get really good at slot-and-filler drills. However, it's not clear how useful that will be beyond the tests they might have to take in an introductory FL class. Thus, practice is more clearly associated with the development of fluency and control over knowledge than with the development of knowledge itself. Developing fluency and control is a form of **skill** building, and, as we will see, learning to write involves learning a skill. As in other skill development, practice is an important element. However, as we saw in (8), not all practice is equally useful. The same can be said of learning to be a good writer: Not all output activities are equally useful. We will explore different kinds of writing activities in Chapters 3 and 4.

Statement 7: Second Language Acquisition Takes a Long Time; for Many, the Process Never Ends

Finally, having realistic expectations is part of good teaching. What we teach is not always what is learned, at least not right away. Although it sometimes seems as if L2 students should have "already learned" some structure, rule, or word, it is frequently the case that L2 writers are still somewhere in the middle of the learning process, of adding to their IL knowledge as well as becoming more fluent or automatic users of that knowledge. Both of these processes take a long time. We tend to think that children learn all of this incredibly quickly in their first language, but consider again their rich environment, filled with input that provides them with thousands and thousands of examples of what they need to learn. In addition, the interactional demands on children are relatively modest. Adult L2 learners do not have these advantages, and teachers should not expect instant results.

On top of this challenge, L2 learners are asked to write, a skill that does not develop automatically even among native speakers and one that may place demands on the IL that learners simply cannot meet. An illustration of this point may be helpful. Academic writing in English often requires the use of the passive voice. Looking back at excerpt (5), you can see that the passive construction appears several times. Yet, the form, meaning, and use of the passive are complex and typically acquired late. L2 writers may simply not have this form available in their ILs. Thus, L2 writing classes have two goals: to enhance the language acquisition process and to help learners improve their effectiveness in written expression.

WHAT'S INVOLVED IN (ACADEMIC) WRITING?

Children master the grammar of their language (though they continue to acquire new vocabulary) relatively early in life. Grammar in this sense means the rules for how sentences and words are put together. Children obviously do this before they are asked to do much writing, certainly before they are

12

CHAPTER 1
*Second Language
Acquisition and
Second Language
Writing: An
Introduction*

expected to produce anything that approaches academic writing. They practice different kinds of writing throughout grade school and high school, receiving explicit instruction and exposure to appropriate models and input. L2 writers are at a considerable disadvantage in that they are expected to start producing complex, high-quality writing relatively quickly in a language they have not yet fully mastered. Of course, many L2 writers also have an advantage—most have already learned to write in their L1, some even to do academic writing. This experience can be helpful in learning to write in an L2, though it does not guarantee that it will be either easy or successful. We should also acknowledge there may be differences across cultures over what constitutes an acceptable style and standard of writing, so even a proficient L2 writer may have to learn new writing conventions and meet different kinds of expectations. This issue will be discussed at greater length in Chapter 2. In addition, not all L2 writers have well-developed literacy skills in their L1s. Many young immigrant learners in North America, for example, have had their L1 educations interrupted and therefore have not acquired these skills or have not done so completely.

Many researchers in the field agree that there are two major contributing factors to L2 writing proficiency: *L2 proficiency* and *L1 writing expertise*. What they continue to debate is exactly what role each factor plays and what the relative importance of each is. The significance of the first factor is the reason we have already spent so much time addressing L2 acquisition. We will continue to do so throughout the book.

So far, I have been using both the terms *composing* and *writing* in the discussion. *Writing* is a very general term, however, and can include the simple encoding of words on paper. Although I use this term throughout the book, what I am really talking about is **composing,** which has a more limited meaning: expressing meaning through writing. It is communication with a purpose rather than language practice. Composing is a complex process, involving a variety of skills and types of knowledge. L2 learners have to draw on all of these when they write. At a minimum, they need to build and consult implicit and explicit knowledge of their L2 and develop their skill as writers.

This kind of learning contrasts with the requirements of many "generic" L2 classes, in which the heaviest emphasis is often on developing implicit linguistic knowledge. In real-time communication, such as in a conversation, learners have to make quick decisions about production and interpretation; there is often no time to consult explicit rule knowledge or to consider specific word meaning. Therefore, L2 teachers often downplay the significance of explicit rule knowledge in their classes, instead stressing the importance of communicating meaning in authentic contexts.

Writing is different. Even in timed tasks, such as essay tests, learners have an opportunity to interpret texts and to consider what they want to express. Learners should be encouraged not only to draw on implicit knowledge, as the student back in (3) did, but also to consult their own explicit knowledge of rules, as well as other resources, such as dictionaries and handbooks. One of the most important roles of explicit knowledge is editing output, a process we will explore in Chapter 7. If L2 writers of French need to go back over a piece of writing and consider each past tense verb—should this really be in *passé composé*, or should it be in *imparfait?*—using explicit rules they have learned in the classroom, this practice should be encouraged. If they don't know these rules, consulting references can add to their explicit knowledge and improve the accuracy of their writing. In FL classes, the situation may be the opposite: The emphasis is placed on the development of explicit knowledge. For these L2 writers, the important point is that they not become so concerned with the linguistic accuracy of their texts that they ignore the central task, that is, the clear and persuasive expression of their ideas.

Writing clearly and persuasively is a skill that takes time to develop and involves much more than writing down spoken language. Written language, especially the kind of writing done in academic settings, has its own conventions and rules. It is quite possible to know an L2 very well, to be a fluent speaker, and to understand all that is going on, yet be an unsuccessful writer. This is certainly the case for native speakers, and there is no reason why this should be different for L2 learners. Furthermore, writing involves far more than just linguistic knowledge; it also entails gathering ideas and information, analyzing and organizing this information, and presenting it in a way that effectively communicates those ideas to the reader. Many linguists have compared the acquisition of an L1 to the development of teeth: Under normal circumstances, its appearance and use are inevitable. Virtually everyone learns a first language. It doesn't matter if a child doesn't like his "teacher" (usually a parent), or if he is motivated, or if his family is wealthy or poor or well educated or poorly educated. No child resists the process and says, "I don't think I want to do this language thing." And everyone ends up just about the same—as native speakers. Some of us have bigger vocabularies or are considered more eloquent speakers, and we all have different accents, but we all end up equal—as native speakers. This means that no one will accept a sentence like *Roger is clear to arrive soon*, and everyone knows that the plural of the word *brain* sounds like [braynz] not [brayns], even though it ends in *s*. In these things, we are all equal. Furthermore, it just happens; we are genetically programmed to develop language. Would that this were so with writing! Instead, writing is a skill that takes years and a good deal of effort to develop. Sadly—or happily—we do not end up the same. Some never get far in acquiring the skill; others develop it to a high level.

One of the ways in which a learner can become a better writer, as mentioned earlier, is by practicing writing. In L2 acquisition research, there is some controversy about the role of production, or output. How much does it help in the language acquisition process? Some argue that its role is minor compared to that of input. Again, we can contrast L2 writing instruction with instruction aimed exclusively at language development. Input is significant, no doubt, in L2 writing as well. Reading in particular is an important component of composition instruction, but here, the importance of output activities is also clear. To write well, one must write. It is a multidimensional skill that takes time and practice to master. At a minimum, a writer has to juggle the generation, analysis, and synthesis of ideas; the organization of discourse; the control of sentence structure; and vocabulary, spelling, and mechanics. It is difficult to learn to balance all of these things without attempting the task.

14

CHAPTER 1
*Second Language
Acquisition and
Second Language
Writing: An
Introduction*

One can learn all the strokes, kicks, rhythm, and breathing used in swimming, yet it's hard to become a good swimmer without getting into the water. In summary, then, in an L2 writing class, learners have to work on all fronts: the development and application of implicit and explicit linguistic knowledge and the development and application of their writing skills.

Finally, all acts of communication take place within a social context, and an academic setting is no exception. Even many native speakers feel as if they have entered a different world when they go to college. Scholars refer to the academic setting as a new **discourse community,** with a whole new set of rules, conventions, and expectations for generating and exchanging information. Until writers begin to understand and master those rules, they will not be considered successful writers. For instance, beginning writers are often confused about how much of their own voice they should allow into their texts. They complain that they receive double messages, that their teachers reject their "opinions" but then complain when they only report what they have read in other sources. They struggle with how much they need to lead readers through the argument presented in their texts and how much can be left for readers to infer. All of this knowledge comes with time, practice, lots of work, active reading, and, with luck, good teachers.

Pause to consider...

your own writing experience. Do you approach writing differently in your L2 and your native language? What did you learn (or were you taught) beyond language issues when you learned to write in your L2? What are the writing conventions or expectations of the discourse community in which you study and/or work?

CONTEXTS AND PURPOSES FOR SECOND LANGUAGE WRITING

As already noted, people learn to write in an L2 for a variety of reasons and in different contexts. These differences are likely to affect instructional choices. Students of English as a second language (ESL), students of English as a foreign language (EFL), and some FL students usually have significant practical goals for learning to write. Many of them hope to use their skills in their jobs. L2 students also have to write to complete their studies. There are some important differences between L2 settings and many FL settings, however, particularly in terms of goals, needs, and, certainly, motivation. For students of an FL, at least in the United States, learning to write in the L2 may simply be part of their academic career. Few learners will ever use these skills after they graduate. Nevertheless, FL majors are expected to achieve a high standard of writing and to carry out academic work in the L2. Many FL educators have noted that even students who have done well in basic language classes often struggle in upper division classes, in which they are expected to produce academic writing. This may be because in basic FL classes, often those included in an FL requirement, writing tasks tend to be quite simple—narration and description—if they are included at all.

For L2 learners intending to live and work in the target culture, L2 literacy can be crucial to academic and professional success. It is difficult to get through high school or college without writing, even for computer science majors or those in technical fields who claim that they "will never have to write." Engineers may think that all they will do is write computer code or interpret circuit diagrams, but if they are going to move beyond entry-level positions, they will have to use written communication extensively—whether informally, in emails, or formally, in reports and memos.

The type of writing required of learners will differ across purposes and genres. A **genre** is a particular type of text, such as a report, a memo, a newspaper story, a poem, or an academic paper, which has a characteristic format, features, and use. Learning to write involves mastering a variety of genres. Both on the job and in the classroom, learners will find that not all writing is alike. Writing a paper for a literature professor is quite different from writing up a chemistry lab report, which is different from writing an executive summary of a business report. The requirements of each task are determined by the social group, or discourse community, that uses the particular genre. Colleges and universities are large discourse communities, composed of many smaller ones (engineers, literature scholars, social scientists, doctors, and so on). They all have their own rules and conventions for sharing information through writing. Part of the job of a writing teacher is to introduce students to the practical reality of the discourse community they are attempting to join, that is, to facilitate their apprenticeship in writing.

This apprenticeship process is not unique to L2 learners; native speakers must go through it as well. Of course, native speakers do not have the additional burden of acquiring a new linguistic system at the same time. In addition, two groups fall in between native speakers and L2 learners. Many immigrants in North America come to writing classes speaking their L2 fluently but with no experience in L2 writing. Indeed, sometimes it is hard to tell what the L1 of these learners really is. For those learning to write in English, this group is often referred to as **generation 1.5.** Many of these students immigrated to North America sometime during their childhood or early teens. Their experiences are situated somewhere between what we think of as first and second generation. Some have had little literacy experience in their home language, over which they may have uncertain command. Their educational background and experience may overlap considerably with those of native speakers, as does their participation in popular culture. They may sound like native speakers, but the minute they begin to write, they resemble L2 writers. They face a dual challenge of mastering the written form of a "new" language and learning academic writing, perhaps for the first time.

Generation 1.5 has a counterpart among "foreign" language learners in the United States and Canada. These **heritage learners** may attend FL classes, sometimes simply to fulfill language requirements, sometimes in pursuit of cultural and linguistic roots, but the language they study is not foreign. Rather, it is often the language (e.g., Spanish, Chinese, Korean) they spoke or heard at home—from parents, grandparents, and friends. It may have been

16

CHAPTER 1
Second Language
Acquisition and
Second Language
Writing: An
Introduction

the first language that they learned, but it was quickly superseded by English. Heritage learners vary in their command of the oral form of the home language: Sometimes it is mixed with English or is in other ways unacceptable to purists or native speakers from the home country. Regardless of their oral proficiency, they frequently have had limited experience writing in that language. These heritage learners and their teachers also face a special challenge: adopting a more standard variety of a language they may already speak or understand and learning how to use it in academic writing.

Pause to consider...

what aspects of academic writing would be most challenging for foreign language learners? Generation 1.5 members? Heritage learners?

Teaching L2 writing requires that instructors have a foot in each of two fields: L2 acquisition, on the one hand, and composition, on the other. It involves two rather different types of learning: language acquisition and skill building, both of which require attention to the social context in which they occur. This chapter has provided an overview of the issues in second language acquisition that are relevant to L2 writing instruction and has outlined the many different challenges L2 writers and their teachers face.

SUMMARY

The goal of second language writing instruction is twofold: to promote higher L2 proficiency and to develop L2 writing ability. Both are essential. What we know about L2 learning can inform our instructional practices in the L2 writing classroom. The following seven statements summarize some of the generally accepted findings:

- There are two types of L2 linguistic knowledge: implicit and explicit. The first is unconscious and abstract, much like L1 knowledge. The second is knowledge *about* the language—rules and conventions. L2 learners need to draw on both types of knowledge as they write.
- Rich and copious input is crucial for L2 learning and for mastering L2 writing. Reading is particularly important for the latter.
- There are two basic kinds of language learning: system learning and item learning. The first is usually associated with the acquisition of the L2 grammar and the second, with vocabulary learning. This distinction is not always clear cut, however.
- In order to learn a new linguistic item or feature, a learner must pay attention to it, though it is not necessary for the learner to be conscious of noticing or to verbalize what has been noticed.
- Just because something has been taught does not mean it has been learned; just because something new has been learned does not mean

it will be used. Development of linguistic knowledge and development of the skill to use it are not the same thing; they occur concurrently.

- Practice is particularly useful is developing skills. Writing is a skill that requires considerable practice in both the first and second language.
- Acquiring a second language takes a long time. For many learners, the process never really ends.

There are many different kinds of L2 writers, and they write for different purposes and in different settings. They come to the task of L2 writing with different levels of L2 proficiency and expertise in L1 writing. The act of writing always takes place in a social context, which can vary widely. These differences should be considered in L2 writing instruction.

CHAPTER NOTES

1. From "Undergraduate Second Language Writers in the Writing Center," by J. Williams, 2002, *Journal of Basic Writing*, 21, 16–34. Reprinted with permission from the *Journal of Basic Writing*.
2. Not everyone agrees that learners form rules based on input. Some researchers favor the *connectionist* view, which holds that we internalize frequencies in the input and base our learning on those frequencies without ever making and testing hypotheses. What looks like rule-governed, systematic behavior is simply a reflection of the internalization of these input frequencies.

READ MORE ABOUT IT**

Second Language Learning

Gass, S., & Selinker, L. (2001). *Second language acquisition: An introductory course* (2nd ed.). Mahwah, NJ: Erlbaum.

Larsen-Freeman, D. (1991). Second language acquisition research: Staking out the territory. *TESOL Quarterly, 25,* 315–350.

*Lightbown, P., & Spada, N. (1999). *How languages are learned* (2nd ed.). Oxford: Oxford University Press.

*Pica, T. (1994). Questions from the language classroom. *TESOL Quarterly, 28,* 49–79.

*VanPatten, B. (2003). *From input to output: A teacher's guide to second language acquisition.* New York: McGraw-Hill.

Writing in a Second Language

*Campbell, C. (1998). *Teaching second language writing.* Boston: Heinle.

Ferris, D., & Hedgcock, J. (1998). *Teaching ESL composition.* Mahwah, NJ: Erlbaum.

**In this and all Read More About It sections, * indicates a reading that is accessible for beginning students.

18

CHAPTER 1
*Second Language
Acquisition and
Second Language
Writing: An
Introduction*

Harklau, L. (2002). The role of writing in classroom second language acquisition. *Journal of Second Language Writing, 11,* 329–350.

Kroll, B. (Ed.). (2003). *Exploring the dynamics of second language writing.* Cambridge: Cambridge University Press.

Silva, T., & Matsuda, P. (2001). *Landmark essays on ESL writing.* Mahwah, NJ: Erlbaum.

Writing in a Foreign Language

Reichelt, M. (1999). Toward a more comprehensive view of L2 writing: Foreign language writing in the U.S. *Journal of Second Language Writing, 8,* 181–204.

Reichelt, M. (2001). A critical review of foreign language writing research on pedagogical practices. *Modern Language Journal, 85,* 578–593.

Roebuck, R. (2001). Teaching composition in the college level foreign language class. *Foreign Language Annals, 34,* 206–215.

Scott, V. (1996). *Rethinking foreign language writing.* Boston: Heinle.

Writing for Generation 1.5

Harklau, L., Losey, K., & Siegal, M. (1999). *Generation 1.5 meets college composition.* Mahwah, NJ: Erlbaum.

Scarcella, R. (2002). Some key factors affecting English learners' development of advanced literacy. In M. Schleppegrell & M. C. Colombí (Eds.), *Developing advanced literacy in first and second languages* (pp. 209–226). Mahwah, NJ: Erlbaum.

Writing for Heritage Learners

Valdés, G. (1991). Bilingual minorities and language issues in writing: Toward profession-wide responses to a new challenge [On-line]. Available: http://www-gse.berkeley.edu/research/NCSWL/reportsnns.html.

CHAPTER 2

Factors and Processes in Second Language Writing

For the most part, L2 writing instruction has followed in the steps of writing instruction for native speakers. This practice is built on the assumption that L2 writers are much like native speakers in terms of how they approach writing. In the previous chapter, however, we noted that L2 learners differ from native speakers in important ways. In FL instruction, typically, writing is the last skill to be addressed. In some cases, especially outside of North America, it is not addressed at all, or it is viewed simply as a vehicle for language practice. In this chapter, we look briefly at the history of writing instruction for native speakers and its impact on L2 writing instruction. We also examine the factors that influence the teaching and learning of L2 writing. We look at these factors as they relate to four topics:

- The use of texts in teaching L2 academic writing
- The characteristics of L2 writers
- The processes involved in learning and teaching L2 writing
- The role played by the writer's readers—the audience—in L2 writing

THE USE OF TEXTS IN TEACHING L2 ACADEMIC WRITING

One way of looking at texts is to view them as decontextualized forms or vehicles for formal practice. In some language learning settings, particularly FL classes, writing may be viewed as an opportunity for students to practice structures and vocabulary that have been recently taught. Thus, for example, students may be asked to produce a narrative text about their weekend activities following instruction on past tense formation. Although we have established that output activities are an important part of L2 learning and L2 writing, such a view seems an unnecessarily narrow way of approaching L2 writing instruction, one that diminishes the importance of writing as a form of communication. This attitude is perhaps more common among teachers who see themselves as language teachers rather than as writing teachers. On the other extreme, some writing teachers may believe they have little responsibility for promoting their students' language acquisition and see their job instead as exclusively devoted to the teaching of writing. Chapter 1 presented arguments for why L2 writing teachers need to be both language and writing teachers. There can be no meaningful writing in the absence of language proficiency, but language proficiency is no guarantee of success in writing.

A more extended view of text production as language practice involves using texts as models of good writing. Within this approach, learners analyze authentic texts and produce their own versions, based on the models of various types of writing, such as descriptive, persuasive, or expository texts. This has been a common practice in teaching native speakers, one that may be familiar to you. This approach complements the view of L2 writing as language practice, with an emphasis on linguistic accuracy at all levels: sentence structure, word choice, spelling, punctuation, and rhetorical form. The influence of this approach on writing instruction is still pervasive today and underlies the widespread instruction of the five-paragraph essay in school-based or academic writing. It emphasizes required elements such as these:

- The opening paragraph must contain a thesis statement.
- The thesis should be supported by examples or statements of evidence, usually three.
- Each of the three should be presented in separate paragraphs, introduced by a topic sentence.
- All material in individual paragraphs should relate to the topic sentence.
- The final paragraph should be the conclusion, in which the thesis is restated in a somewhat different way.

Pause to consider...

the conventions of the five-paragraph essay. Do you recognize this form from your past experience? What are some positive and negative points of this kind of instruction and writing? What aspects of this approach do you think we should keep and what should we discard?

Features of Academic Writing

The clarity of this kind of writing is immediately evident, whatever it may lack in sophistication and creativity. Some wag once described this style as, "tell 'em what you're going to say, tell 'em, then tell 'em what you said." Clarity, or explicitness of expression, is generally prized in academic writing. This is one of the features that differentiates writing from speaking, a medium in which so many other aspects of the situation—gestures, tone, referents in the physical context, a listener's response—can help clarify meaning. One problem that new writers often have is making the transition from oral communication to written expression. Many teachers of high school and college freshman English comment that their students write the way they speak, and

TABLE 2.1 Features of Writing and Speech

Academic Writing	Conversational Speech
Usually one-way*	Usually two-way
Less context dependent	More context dependent
More complex syntax, such as subordination	More coordination
Reliance on mechanical (e.g., punctuation) and spelling conventions	Greater reliance on gestures and intonation
Tighter modification, such as relative clauses	Looser modification
Longer, denser, complete sentences	Hesitations, incomplete sentences, and interruptions
Lower frequency vocabulary	Higher frequency vocabulary
Off-line delivery**	On-line delivery

*Some may argue that writing is two-way as well. The meaning here is that writing is usually for an absent and perhaps unknown audience.
**Off-line means that writers have time to consider what they want to express and can go back and edit as needed. On-line speech, in contrast, is produced in real time, with little opportunity to edit.

indeed these writers need to learn a whole new set of conventions for writing. Table 2.1 shows some of the ways in which conversational speech and academic writing have been said to differ. It may help to look back at examples (4) and (5) in Chapter 1. Notice that the distinction is not just between speaking and writing but between particular kinds of speaking and writing. For example, when we talk about academic writing, we are not talking about making a speech, which can be very formal, or writing a quick email to a friend, which can look much more like a conversation.

What does all of this mean for L2 writers? It means that they will have to learn many new things beyond L2 grammar and words. They will have to consider an audience that they may not know and cannot see. They will have to assume a lot less and include a lot more; that is, they will have to provide a rich context so that their readers can interpret their meaning. Finally, they will have to learn all the conventions of academic writing, just as their native-speaking classmates will. However, on the plus side, they will not have to do this all on the spot, as they would in speaking. They will have time to consider what they want to say and how they want to say it. For L2 writers, this means they will be able to consult explicit, rule-based knowledge that they may have acquired in language class, something that is difficult to do in conversation because it happens too quickly.

We have been discussing a rather specific kind of writing—academic writing—which has its own rules and conventions that are unlike those for, say, short stories or newspaper articles. What is so special about academic writing? Why do native speakers have to learn it too? As we review the features that are generally characteristic of academic writing, keep in mind that they are just that—generalizations—and that, in fact, there is a considerable amount of variation in academic writing.

First, as indicated in the previous paragraphs, academic writing, at least in North America, tends to be quite explicit. It tends to place most of the responsibility on the writer rather than on the reader for communicating an effective message. It does not leave very much to the reader's imagination.

Second, academic writing tends to be in the form of an argument; writers make a claim or assertion and then provide evidence to persuade readers that their position is a correct one. Alternatively, writers may sometimes ask a question and build their way toward an answer, but even in this case, they are forwarding a claim; they are just presenting it in a different way. Contained in that argument we may find other types of rhetorical structures, such as explanations, descriptions, or reports, all to serve the author's central purpose.

Third, although writers are expected to express a view, we do not expect to find overt expressions of personal opinion, or emotional appeals, as in (1).

(1) a. I think that *Like Water for Chocolate* was a great movie.
b. We must help the children who are dying of starvation every day in Guatemala.

Instead, we expect writers to stand back and objectively review, evaluate, and present evidence that can substantiate their views. The statements in (2) are more likely to be found in academic writing.

(2) a. *Like Water for Chocolate* breaks new ground in cinematography.
b. More than 100 children die every month from malnutrition in Guatemala, and this number is rising.

Much of academic writing is written for scholars by other scholars. Of course, the writers in most L2 and FL classes are probably not scholars quite yet, but as writing teachers, we expect our students to start learning and using this style of writing. That is, we require that our students first demonstrate the knowledge they have gained as a result of some inquiry (reading a text, doing a laboratory experiment, conducting an interview) and then somehow apply it in the presentation of an argument.

In addition to these three basic characteristics of academic writing—it is explicit, it presents an argument for a claim or an assertion, and it excludes personal opinion, for the most part—academic writing also tends to be somewhat predictable in its structure. For example, as readers, we usually expect to be told early in the text what the topic of the text will be and what the writer will argue. In North America at least, readers expect to be able to follow the sequence of an academic text. Often, we expect the writer to provide us with a sort of "road map" of what to expect. Sometimes, a writer will signal this overtly, with expressions like the following:

(3) a. I will demonstrate how the events of September 11th have influenced policy decisions.
b. There are several ways in which oil can be recovered from underground reserves.

In (a), the reader is led to expect both a narrative and a demonstration of cause and effect. In (b), the reader expects that the text will enumerate and explain methods of oil recovery. If these elements do not appear in the text, the reader will feel misled. Conversely, if these elements appear without such introductory statements, the text will be considerably more difficult to follow.

Sometimes, different genres will have predictable, almost formulaic structures. For example, the research article has been shown to have a specific form.[1] Research scientists might begin an article by establishing the territory they wish to explore. They then display their knowledge of the field through a review of relevant background literature. The next step is to show that there is some gap or problem in current research, thus establishing a niche that their own research can fill. Thereafter follows a description of the method of research, findings, and finally, interpretation and relevance of those findings. This basic format is unlikely to vary much; it is what readers expect. Of course, we don't usually expect our students to do original research, but we do expect them to follow an accepted format. This is part of what they must learn in academic writing.

Of course, there are many other genres besides the research article. Other school-based genres might include the laboratory report or the critical summary. In fact, college students are required to write many different genres. As noted in Chapter 1, a genre is a category of texts that have a shared and recognized purpose. You may wonder why "shared?" Shared by whom? In the case of the research scientist, they are members of a community of scholars who share a body of knowledge, background experiences, and interests. This group is the scientists' discourse community. Indeed, one characteristic of a discourse community is that its members use the same genres for communication, as described in Chapter 1. When students come to college, they become members of a large discourse community of scholars, and we start expecting them to act the part. We even expect this in FL classes once learners have developed sufficient language proficiency. Learning academic writing is part of a socialization process, but it can be rather mysterious for those who are new to the discourse community. L2 learners, especially, need guidance.

Some studies suggest that the strong emphasis on the research essay in composition classes may be misplaced. In fact, it seems that most writing tasks in college are much shorter, more constrained, and often done in class. Furthermore, academic writing is not the only kind of writing, nor is it the only kind of writing done in school. Nonacademic genres include news articles, advertising copy, and literary forms such as short stories and poetry.

Pause to consider...

the discourse community. Do you see yourself as a member of a discourse community? How would you describe it? What kinds of genres have you been required to write? What kinds of genres do your students have to write? In your class? In other classes?

Yet another characteristic of academic writing is its use of certain kinds of language. For example, academic writing may contain more passives than other kinds of writing: *This view can be seen as a reflection of the experiences of those involved in the resistance.* Academic texts also tend to contain nouns bunched together (e.g., *perceptual analysis systems*) but fewer first and second person (*I* and *you*) mentions than other types of writing. For other specific characteristics of academic language use, refer to Table 2.1.

One difference that can be seen in language use between L1 and L2 writers is in vocabulary. This difference is clearly traceable to the fact that L2 writers are still learning the language. For example, L2 writers tend to overuse vague, higher frequency words (e.g., in English, *people, life, society, want, like*) compared to native speakers. Their texts also tend to be less cohesive than those of their native-speaker counterparts, in part because they do not use articles, pronouns, and other cohesive devices as effectively to establish connections across sentence boundaries. Instead, they tend to limit themselves to more superficial sentential transitions, such as *my first reason, therefore,* and *in conclusion.* Obviously, the texts of lower proficiency learners will be even more divergent in ways that may have little to do with differences in cultural orientation and are simply a reflection of their still developing language and writing proficiency.

Differences in Academic Writing Across Cultures: Contrastive Rhetoric

The features discussed so far may not be characteristic of academic writing everywhere. Some believe that both the rhetorical structure and the use of specific structures differ across languages and even across language varieties (e.g., British vs. American English). More important perhaps have been the claims that styles of writing, specifically in academic texts, vary across languages and cultures. This notion is referred to as **contrastive rhetoric.** This term is related to an earlier notion, **contrastive analysis.** Contrastive analysis was an attempt to predict and explain L2 learner errors based on a learner's L1. For example, some might claim that the reason that Spanish L2 learners of English have interlanguage (IL) forms such as *I no coming* or *I am living here two months* is that these are reflections of Spanish structures (*(yo) no vengo; hace dos meses que vivo aquí*). Similar claims are made in contrastive rhetoric, but in this case, they are made about writing style. For instance, it has been claimed that North American academic writing is linear: Writers state a claim and then provide evidence for it. In contrast, writers in other cultures (e.g., Chinese, German, Spanish) have been said to have a less linear form of argumentation, to lead the reader on a more meandering or indirect path to their conclusion, and to give the reader more responsibility for the interpretation of a text.

Culture no doubt has an influence on writing practices. Some cultures differ in the ways in which they prefer to structure their arguments and in what they choose as a source of authority. For example, writers in one culture may turn to scientific evidence and observation as the source of support for their claims, whereas those in another culture may refer to cultural or religious authorities or texts. Even in basic genres like the research article, some differences across cultures have been documented.

That said, there are several problems with how the contrastive rhetoric perspective is often presented in texts for writing teachers. First, any statement that characterizes "Asian" writers is bound to be a gross overgeneralization; it can unfairly construct identities and practices that may or may not apply to Asians. In fact, evidence shows that Asian high school students receive writing instruction much like that of Americans—a lot of emphasis on the five-paragraph essay! Second, the equation of writing style with culture can lead to insidious implications. If learners from certain countries or cultures write in a digressive or nonlinear manner, does this mean that they are less logical thinkers too, or maybe that the whole culture is a little illogical? Surely, we do not want to come to that conclusion! These kinds of comparisons tend to set up *us* versus *them*, East versus West, and North versus South oppositions that are not always productive. None of this is to say that culture has no influence in the classroom; on the contrary, its impact can be enormous, especially in the ways that it may guide interaction between learners and between learners and the teacher.

Finally, it is worthwhile to reiterate that many L2 writers are not so different from native speakers who are new to the discourse community. Novice native-speaker writing, too, may be digressive and appear illogical. It takes time to learn to write well, and clear instructions on what conventions are expected will be helpful to those unfamiliar with them, for both L2 and L1 novice writers.

Pause to consider...

how much influence you think culture has on writing. Is American writing more linear and explicit than writing in other cultures and languages?

CHARACTERISTICS OF L2 WRITERS

We have already begun to talk about writers. Culture is one important part of an L2 writer's profile. What other aspects of the writer's background are important? Two factors have often been mentioned as crucial elements in learners' growing expertise in L2 writing: their proficiency in the L2 and their background and ability to write in the L1. As mentioned earlier, writing is often the last skill to be taught in L2 instruction. This makes sense for two reasons: First, some learners may not need written language proficiency, and second, a significant level of linguistic knowledge is required before complex writing tasks can be effectively undertaken. The relationship between linguistic knowledge and L1/L2 writing proficiency is a complex one. There are two main, potentially opposing views on this relationship:

- We learn to write only once. Those who write well in their L1 can transfer these literacy skills to L2 contexts.

- L2 writing proficiency is rooted in L2 linguistic knowledge, which is acquired primarily through exposure to input. Extensive reading would therefore be expected to lead to proficient writing abilities. Writing, like other output activities, should await the development of substantial linguistic knowledge.

Most research on the notion of transfer of literacy skills from the L1 to the L2 has actually addressed reading. It has been a popular idea for some time that reading skills in the L1 will transfer automatically and easily to L2 reading tasks. In fact, however, recent research does not substantiate this perspective. There are so many factors that complicate the equation—the L1; L2 competence; background knowledge; social context; type of reading task—that researchers now take a considerably more conservative view of this process. Most now support some version of the **Language Threshold Hypothesis,** which states that learners must have sufficient L2 knowledge in order to tap into their L1 reading skills. Exactly how much is "sufficient" is not yet clear. What is clear is the importance of continuing to emphasize and build on L2 linguistic knowledge in reading and writing classes.

The Language Threshold Hypothesis pertains to reading. What about writing? It seems that there may be even less transfer of L1 writing skills than of L1 reading skills, at least at lower levels of language proficiency. The strong influence of L1 writing expertise in L2 writing performance is seen only in studies of more advanced learners. At these higher levels of language ability, L1 writing expertise seems to have an important influence on writers' composing strategies, including planning, making decisions, and solving problems encountered during composing. Incremental increases in L2 proficiency at this level seem to be merely additive; that is, they do not affect composing processes. In short, once a threshold of linguistic knowledge has been reached, the contributions of L1 writing ability and L2 language proficiency appear to be quite distinct.

Keep in mind, however, that many teachers will be working with writers who are considerably below this threshold. For such learners, the continuing labor of L2 acquisition should remain a significant component of any L2 writing program. Thus, the two positions on this relationship should not be seen as opposing. Rather, L2 writing teachers need to be aware of their students' L1 writing abilities and to encourage learners to use them whenever they can be helpful. However, teachers must also keep in mind that for many learners, the limitations of their L2 proficiency prevent them from tapping into this potentially rich resource.

A third factor influencing L2 writers—in addition to their L1 writing expertise and their overall L2 proficiency—is their reading proficiency in the L2. Several researchers in the field have noted that good writers "write like readers" and can "read like writers." One way in which teachers can help L2 learners to develop their writing skills is to show them how to be more critical readers. Some learners may already have some of these skills in their L1 but may not realize it. In this case, teachers can help them articulate and shape knowledge they already have. As an example, consider the excerpt shown in Figure 2.1. This is a piece of persuasive writing with a clear point of view. Learners need to discover how this point of view manifests itself in the

Chiropractors and Immunization

*Many chiropractors advise against immunization.** In 1992, 37%
of 178 chiropractors who responded to a survey agreed that
*"there is no scientific proof that immunization prevents infectious
disease"* and 23% said they were uncertain. Among the
"unproven" group, 24% were American Chiropractic Association (ACA) members and 65% belonged to the International
Chiropractors Association (ICA). Twenty-seven percent of the
respondents said their own families had not been immunized,
and 58% agreed with the statement "Immunization should
never be given to people over 60 years of age." Before filling
out the forms, the chiropractors were asked to read a 1979
American Public Health Association (APHA) policy statement
warning that 40% of American children under age 15 had
incomplete immunization against preventable diseases and
that severe complications can result. *Only* 14% agreed that
"the chiropractic profession should fully support the APHA
immunization policies for children and adults." Chiropractors
who graduated before 1980 tended to be more negative than
those who had graduated in 1980 or afterward. . . .

   In 1999, *Dynamic Chiropractic invited readers to state
whether they have immunized their children. This method is
not a precise way to collect such data,* but the answers were still
interesting. Of 140 responses, the results were:

- *My children have received absolutely no vaccinations: 59 (42%)*
- *My children received only some of the usually required
  vaccinations: 31 (22%)*
- *My children have received all of the usual required vaccinations:
  50 (36%)*

*Chiropractic's two largest organizations oppose compulsory immu-
nization.* The ACA has acknowledged "routine vaccinations
have been a proven and effective campaign in the control of
many diseases."

However, its current policy is:
   *The ACA supports each individual's right to freedom of choice
   in his/her own health care based on an informed awareness of
   the benefits and possible adverse effects of vaccination.* . . .
The International Chiropractors Association (ICA)'s current
policy states:
   *The International Chiropractors Association recognizes that
   the use of vaccines is not without risk. The ICA supports each
   individual's right to select his or her own health care and to be*

*Italicized sections are the subjects of the accompanying annotations.

- Thesis: chiropractors in general

- Quote contrasts with likely reader
  knowledge
- Quote marks show author attitude

- Statistical information provides
  objective evidence for argument

- Lexical choices show author
  attitude

- Reader must infer from font
  choice and following words that
  this is a periodical
- Author evaluation

- Statistical evidence of a more
  personal nature

- Thesis again: professional
  organizations

- Contrast marker implies hypocrisy

- Quotes from organizations' mission
  statements provide sense of objectivity

(continued)

27

made aware of the possible adverse effects of vaccines upon a human body. In accordance with such principles and based upon the individual's right to freedom of choice, the ICA is opposed to compulsory programs which infringe upon such rights. . . .

The ICA does not acknowledge benefit and *even* sells a book called *Vaccination: 100 Years of Orthodox Research Shows that Vaccines Represent a Medical Assault on the Immune System,* which contends that vaccines are ineffective and dangerous. . . .

- Lexical choices show author attitude
- Potentially inflammatory information

    State chiropractic licensing boards also support anti-immunization activities. In 2002, the boards in 40 states and the District of Columbia approved the awarding of continuing education credits for attending the Third International Public Conference on Vaccination, a meeting sponsored by the National Vaccine Information Center (NVIC), a group that is *rabidly* opposed to immunization.

- Thesis again: professional over-sight body

- Lexical choices show author attitude

    Chiropractors staunchly *opposed the use of the polio vaccine* in the 1940s and 1950s, and many still support that opposition, *saying that the incidence of polio is cyclical and would have declined without any vaccination program. The fact is* that since the vaccine's introduction, the incidence of polio has become extremely *noncyclical. The present rate of polio is less than one hundredth its lowest level before oral immunization programs began, and public health officials have predicted worldwide eradication by the year 2000. This is one of the most dramatic success stories in the history of medical science's struggle to reduce suffering and early death.* The same could be said of the vaccination program that rid the world of *smallpox*, a once prevalent deadly disease. *Chiropractors claim that somehow this would have happened anyway. That simply is untrue. . . .*

- Presentation of specific case
- Opposing argument
- Refutation presented as fact
- Lexical contrast
- Evidence to support refutation
- Emotional appeal
- Second specific example
- Opposing claim
- Refutation

FIGURE 2.1 Using texts to teach critical reading: An example of persuasive writing.

Note. From *Chiropractors and Immunization*, by S. Barrett. Reprinted from Chirobase (http://chirobase.org) with permission from Stephen Barrett, M.D. Retrieved October 24, 2003.

rhetorical and linguistic choices the author has made. It also has a clear organizational structure. They need to learn how this is made evident. Finally, readers must know certain things before they read the text in order to make sense of it. The notes running along the side of the text point to features that the teacher can bring out and discuss to show learners how to "read like a writer." In this kind of activity, the text should be sufficiently long and challenging to reflect the kinds of texts that L2 learners are likely to encounter.

    The role of reading in learning to write merits some more elaboration. To do this, we need to examine several issues:

- The role that reading has played in L2 writing instruction
- The various kinds of reading activities that can be used in the L2 writing classroom

- The benefits of reading for different aspects of the development of L2 ability, including linguistic knowledge, vocabulary, and writing proficiency

We have already seen that readings have often been used in the L2 writing classroom either as models to be emulated or as sources of new vocabulary or grammatical structures. This latter kind of reading has been called **intensive reading,** because each line is mined for new information about the language, primarily grammar and new words. In these uses of readings, form may be privileged over text meaning. This kind of reading is quite common in early levels of language instruction. Another frequent use of readings in L2 writing instruction is as a stimulus for discussion and subsequent composition, as a sort of springboard for a writing theme. These stimulus texts are often short, because the primary focus of the class is ostensibly on writing. In FL classes, the reading might be about the country or culture of the language being studied. In ESL classes, it is often on subjects of topical interest, such as youth culture, gender, or the environment. Topics generally change with each new writing assignment. One problem with this approach is that jumping around from topic to topic can make it difficult for writers to develop anything more than a superficial understanding of the subject or to become familiar with the vocabulary associated with it. Finally, in more advanced classes, readings have been used as source material for writing research papers.

More recently, however, readings have been seen in a somewhat different light. First, there is more emphasis on multiple readings around similar content. In this way, learners can develop deeper expertise and write with greater authority. This approach can also expose them to different perspectives and perhaps different genres and rhetorical stances on a single topic. Finally, it promotes the recycling of vocabulary that is necessary for successful lexical acquisition. As we will see, one frequent impediment to academic success for L2 writers is their limited vocabulary. Restricted vocabulary makes both reading and writing tasks difficult.

Another difference between traditional and current approaches is that reading choices are now more motivated by the goals of the writing assignment. For example, a particular reading might promote a discussion on how the author has used her knowledge of the audience to create a more effective argument. Another reading might illustrate a particular rhetorical structure that the author has used, how he has signaled stages of his argument, or ways in which he has referred to information outside the text that he expects his readers to know before they read the text. There are examples of these in the annotated text in Figure 2.1. Although this use of reading bears a passing resemblance to one mentioned earlier—models to be imitated—in fact, it is quite different. It is designed to get writers to start looking at texts as writers, rather than simply as readers of content. It is clear from educational research that reading and writing share general underlying cognitive processes. Most researchers believe that the two skills are interactive, with development in one promoting development in the other. It therefore makes sense to exploit reading processes in the writing classroom.

The kinds of readings teachers choose to assign may also depend in part on the pedagogical purpose they have in mind. We have noted the use of short intensive readings designed to promote writing goals. Such readings may be useful sources of information or points of departure for essays, but they are not always adequate as exclusive sources of input for language learning. Most L2 acquisition scholars recommend the inclusion of **extensive reading** in any reading/writing course. This kind of extended reading is often undertaken for pleasure and has been shown to be a rich source of input. It is claimed that this kind of reading can promote the development of linguistic competence, especially vocabulary. Some studies also indicate that extensive reading can lead to improvement in writing proficiency. Most of us would at least intuitively support the notion that good writers usually do a lot of reading. The main claim here is that reading is useful in facilitating L2 acquisition and, as noted several times already, L2 writing classes must promote both writing and language proficiency. A final pedagogical goal in reading may have little to do with improving language or developing skill. Some readings might be assigned simply to provide factual content. If students are writing about the history of public health, for example, they will need source material. This calls for a specific kind of reading, **reading to learn** (content, not language).

One last issue that needs to be addressed more fully is the development of L2 vocabulary. Limited vocabulary may cause difficulty in both reading and writing. Many L2 students are not fluent readers; rather, they read word for word, often missing the larger import of a text. Although it is true that for both native speakers and L2 learners, most new vocabulary words are learned incidentally, that is, without the intention to learn them, doing so requires a specific set of circumstances. For example, as native speakers, we learn many new words simply from reading. However, in order for readers to infer the meaning of new words from context (that is, without looking them up individually), they need to understand about 95–98% of the words in the surrounding text. Many L2 writers can't come close to this figure as they read new texts, which means they will either have to look up the new words in the dictionary or ignore them. It is estimated that a college freshman will need a vocabulary of about 17,000 words to undertake academic reading. It is likely that many L2 and FL learners are nowhere near that mark. What does this mean for L2 writers and their teachers? It means that teachers should

- be aware of the limits that restricted vocabulary places on the readings they can assign;
- assist L2 writers with vocabulary learning strategies[2]; and
- understand how restricted vocabulary can affect writing processes.

In terms of the last point, we have noted that many L2 writers have a narrow range of vocabulary from which to choose, often consisting of broad, high frequency words. For example, to express themselves precisely, native speakers of English might choose from among the following words as alternative to the verb *say: state, declare, maintain, tell, swear, mention, utter, comment, inform,* and so on. Similarly, native Spanish speakers might choose: *afirmar, sostener, expresar, hablar de, mencionar, contar,* or *informar* as alternatives to *decir.* An L2 writer, on the other hand, might have only *say/decir* at her disposal. Each of the alternative words has a slightly different meaning that can add clarity and sophistication to a writer's expression. Another problem is that L2 learners may simply not know the word in the L2 to express what they wish. They are then faced with using a word that may not really fit, neither sure of their selection nor satisfied with their limited lexical knowledge. Here is one more job for the L2 writing instructor—helping learners expand their vocabulary and access appropriate resources for doing so.

PROCESSES INVOLVED IN LEARNING AND TEACHING L2 WRITING

As noted in Chapter 1, researchers and educators in the field of teaching writing often prefer the term *composing*, because it emphasizes the importance of communication and the creative process that learners go through as they write. We know that composing is a complex and often lengthy process for both native speakers and L2 writers. As in most L2 writing research, examinations of composing processes have reflected prior work with native speakers. Early research focused on how writers plan, draft, revise, solve problems, and use a variety of strategies as they compose. For our purposes, the question is, Are the composing processes of native speakers and L2 writers the same, and if not, in what ways do they differ?

The answer to the first part of the question, not surprisingly, is yes and no. Investigations into L1 and L2 composing processes have found them to be generally similar, yet with some significant differences. For instance, L2 writers spend less time planning than native speakers do, evidently to their detriment. Obviously, they are also less fluent and accurate in their language production, that is, in word selection and syntactic choices. In fact, for them, all stages of composing are slower and more laborious. This slow pace may be due, in part, to the fact that many, or perhaps most, L2 writers use their L1 at some point during composing, making the process less automatic. It is also likely that many L2 writers experience a kind of overload when they write. Most psychologists agree that our brains have a limited capacity to process information and that we can only pay attention to a limited number of things at once. It may be that L2 writers, because they have to pay more attention to language issues as they write, are unable to devote as much attention to global planning of their writing. L2 writers also spend less time reviewing and revising their work, and they do so less deeply, compared to native speakers, attending more to sentence-level errors. Of course, these are generalizations, and not all L2 writers behave in the same way, any more than native speakers do. Nevertheless, these findings can provide insights into the challenges faced by L2 writers and suggest directions for L2 writing instruction.

Less proficient and less experienced L2 writers demonstrate the characteristics just described more regularly than both proficient L2 learners and those who have significant experience in L1 writing, reflecting the two factors—L2 proficiency and L1 writing ability—considered earlier. Like native speakers who are inexperienced writers, low proficiency L2 writers tend to fix on surface-level features, such as grammatical choices and mechanics, rather than on global issues such as rhetorical problems and audience awareness. One other important difference separates inexperienced writers from skilled (L1 and L2) writers. This distinction is between writing that simply retells information from other texts and resources and writing that somehow changes the information and creates something new from it. The texts of inexperienced writers usually display the first; yet academic tasks will eventually require the second. L2 writers who are still grappling with acquisition of L2 structures and vocabulary are often also limited to the first type of writing, perhaps because they do not have the linguistic resources to perform the second.

If some writers have more effective composing processes than others, then we must wonder if we can teach learners to be better composers. This is the goal of the **process approach** to writing. *Process approach* is a term that is used a lot, but not everyone is clear on what it means, or perhaps it is simply used in a variety of ways. Process approaches contrast with *product approaches*. The ideas in process instruction that have been incorporated into pedagogy are based on a variety of different theories of writing, which are informed in turn by fields such as psychology and linguistics rather than literature. The older product approaches to teaching writing tended to

- assume that writing is a linear process, with writers starting at the beginning of a piece and writing straight through to the end;
- assume that writing must be a solitary process;
- emphasize correctness of the final text;
- focus on the final product rather than the processes that lead up to it; and
- see the teacher's role as a judge and corrector.

In contrast, process-oriented pedagogy acknowledges that much of what is important in writing happens before the final draft; indeed, many of the ideas and even the text that is generated during the writing process may never even make it into the final product. Learners need time to generate and think through their ideas, to try them out, discard them, and revise them as needed. Novice writers may not be aware that this process is a normal and necessary part of writing. If they have been evaluated only on the correctness of their final drafts, they may have the impression that "good writers" (obviously not them) write perfect prose from the moment they begin writing. Process approaches attempt to dispel these notions and to actively help learners grapple with the composing process.

Thus, in process-oriented classrooms, learners might use a variety of techniques for generating ideas, together, in pairs, or on their own. Learners are encouraged to write multiple drafts—in practice, usually two to three—as they refine their ideas for what they wish to express. Between drafts, learners will often get feedback from their peers as well as their teacher. This feedback usually focuses initially on content and organization rather than simply on language form. Writers are expected to actively and thoughtfully revise content and organization based on this feedback, not just add a sentence here or change a word there.

This does not mean that no attention is paid to language form. Many writers attend to surface features of their writing throughout the writing process, editing for ungrammatical or awkward usage, though some teachers encourage their students to delay this part of the process until a later stage. The rationale for this pedagogical practice is that there is no point in editing passages that may not appear in the final draft and that early editing may unduly focus the writer on surface features. In summary, although there are many kinds of process approaches rather than a single one, they generally share these characteristics:

- emphasis on making learners aware of the processes they go through when they write
- acknowledgment of writing as an exploratory and recursive rather than linear, predetermined process
- focus on composing processes rather than on the finished product
- a view of writing as a learning and thinking process, suggesting that learners may discover what they think and mean as a result of composing
- focus on invention and discovery strategies in the early stages of composing
- a collaborative, supportive environment for composing, usually including the participation of peers
- intervention and assistance from the teacher at various points during the process rather than simply as an evaluator at the final stage
- reduction in the emphasis on rhetorical models, such as compare-and-contrast and cause-and-effect essays, and instead, a greater interest in issues such as planning, audience, purpose, and author's voice
- focus on the reader-writer relationship rather than on literary themes
- reduction in the importance of grammatical correctness and increased emphasis on the expression of meaning and personal voice
- evaluation in terms of audience needs, writer purpose, and task fulfillment

Instruction using a process orientation is now the norm in ESL composition classes, though its influence in EFL and FL classes in other languages has been somewhat less significant. Despite its widespread use, process-based instruction has not been without detractors. One concern is that this kind of instruction gives learners a false impression of what will be asked of them once they leave the composition classroom. As we saw in our discussion of academic needs analyses, authentic academic writing tasks are often timed and highly constrained. A second objection has been that process approaches ignore formal accuracy. It is certainly true that when these same learners take a history exam, for example, they will not have time to brainstorm, revise, and consult peers. Instead, they will be judged solely on product. However, if these learners can improve their writing in L2 writing classes, the hope is that their skills will become more automatic and transfer to other, less supportive settings. Indeed, timed writing tasks also require writers to go through a composing process—though perhaps a somewhat different one—that can be practiced in preparatory classes. Furthermore, it is not the case that process approaches have abandoned any attention to product; on the contrary, a process approach entails a product focus; it simply is not limited to a product focus. Correctness is always a concern, particularly with L2 writers, but it is not expected at all stages of the composing process.

A third, perhaps more serious problem with process approaches is how the theory behind them has been put into practice. Some educators have taken the surface features of these approaches and reduced them to a mechanical parody of the original conception. For example, some have claimed that the stages often mentioned in process instruction (i.e., prewriting, drafting, revising, and editing) have become reified such that process-based approaches have become as rigid as the product-oriented teaching that preceded them. In fact, the stages are not discrete and not necessarily always undertaken in the idealized order described. Writers go back and forth, revising ideas at all points in the composing process.

Pause to consider...

how much you know about your own writing processes. Do you begin with an outline? Notes? Do you begin at the beginning of a piece of writing (e.g., with an introduction), or do you start in the middle and add an introduction later? Do you revise as you write? Or do you write straight through and then go back and change things only after you have completed a first draft? If you revise during the drafting process, what do you change? Do you rearrange ideas? Cut things out and/or add new material? Change specific language? Punctuation?

THE ROLE OF THE AUDIENCE IN L2 WRITING

Most classroom writing tasks, in contrast to authentic writing tasks, are undertaken with the understanding that the teacher is the main audience. For L2 writers, it is often their language teacher. Later, when they finish their schooling, L2 learners will write for different purposes and different audiences. FL learners, on the other hand, may or may not use their writing skills after they have finished their academic careers, causing some FL educators to question the need for including writing in the FL curriculum. However, the direction of this apparent cause-and-effect relationship is not clear. If FL learners were to become proficient writers, perhaps there would be more opportunity for them to use their FL knowledge professionally. The current situation in the United States is that many FL majors, whatever their speaking skills, graduate without sufficient writing proficiency to use their FL in professional settings.

Much of the recent work in L2 writing has stressed the importance of authentic and relevant tasks for readers in a realistic social context. We explore tasks in Chapters 3 and 4, but here, the topic is readers. What should writers do to accommodate their readers? Here are some questions writers might ask themselves:

- Who are my readers?
- What is their social/educational/professional background? Is that important?
- What do they know about what I am writing about?
- What are their attitudes toward what I am writing about?

- What are they expecting? Are these expectations met as they read?
- How will they react to what I have written? Will they understand it? Is it clear? Will it provoke some emotion, such as anger or sadness?

All of these questions urge writers to write like readers, to anticipate what their audience needs to know and what readers will take from the texts that they write. The answers will influence how they structure their writing, how they present the content, and even the words they choose. One problem that novice writers often experience is a failure to take the needs of the reader into account. Readers are not blank slates; they come to the text with background knowledge, real-world experience, and experience with texts. For example, they may expect to be able to figure out in the first paragraph what the rest of the essay is going to be about. This knowledge helps readers to understand texts more easily and automatically.

It is easy for learners to assume that the reader is simply their teacher, but even this assumption requires that writers consider their audience. What the teacher knows may vary depending on the text. For example, if the assignment is a personal narrative, the teacher may have very little initial knowledge of the topic. Sometimes, this situation can work to the writer's advantage. I once had a student who turned in variations on a single paper—a narrative about his experiences in a Southeast Asian refugee camp—to at least half a dozen teachers and always got a positive response, whether or not it directly fulfilled the assignment. The teachers were so affected by the narrative's heavy emotional appeal that nothing else seemed to matter. He had sized up his audience well. If, on the other hand, the assignment involves responding to material that the whole class has read, the writer can assume that the teacher is already familiar with the content needed to understand the text and that he may not have to recapitulate all of the information. It also means that the writer will have to do more than simply display his own familiarity with the material. He needs to demonstrate that he can use the material to shape an argument.

Teachers are not just the readers of the text; they are also the final judges of it. Writers will therefore have to take this audience consideration into account as well. The role of the writing teacher is an ambiguous one, because the teacher is at once a reader and an evaluator of the text. It is often hard for teachers to balance these roles. Furthermore, because teachers are involved during the writing process in process-oriented classes, it can be even more difficult for them to distance themselves from the text and be authentic readers.

Another important audience in the writing classroom is the writer's peers. Frequently, in process-oriented classrooms, fellow learners are asked to read and respond to a writer's text. This practice increases the diversity of the audience and can direct the writer's attention to issues that might not have been addressed had the teacher been the only audience. In particular, it can increase a writer's awareness of audience expectations, helping the learner to write like a reader. The hope is that writers will start to become sensitive to their own readers' needs as they read texts produced by their peers. The kinds of questions they ask and responses they give regarding their peers' texts can eventually become the kinds of questions they ask of their own texts.

In addition, as the saying goes, "two heads are better than one." It is often the case that a task that one writer cannot accomplish on her own can become more manageable when undertaken collaboratively. This notion underlies the *collaborative* approaches to education that are widespread in K–12 settings. The value and techniques of peer response are covered at length in Chapter 5.

In order to improve as writers, however, it is beneficial for L2 writers to move beyond their classrooms in conceptualizing their audience. Good writers create a sort of space that is shared by the reader and the writer. They also anticipate the needs of their audience: when their readers will need more information, for example, or more evidence, and when they might be led astray. It may not always be possible to have learners write for an actual audience outside of the classroom, but there are ways to get writers accustomed to considering the needs of their audience. One way is to assign tasks that invoke a specific audience. For example, teachers may have their college students write for an audience of graduating high school students. Other teachers try to encourage their students to use their writing to change the community around them in positive ways. This might mean writing to school officials to convince them that certain policies should be changed. We consider this issue further in Chapter 3.

The purpose of this chapter has been to provide some background about the kinds of issues that are important in teaching L2 writers. For students in an L2 academic setting, academic writing can be particularly difficult because they may also be juggling other course work in the target language. For FL learners, the challenge may be in developing the motivation needed to develop writing proficiency at all. In the next chapter we explore tasks and activities that will help all learners improve their academic writing skills.

SUMMARY

This chapter examines the factors that influence the teaching and learning of L2 writing in terms of four basic topics: texts, writers, processes, and readers.

Traditionally, writing instruction has focused on the texts that writers produce. This approach is the basis of the school essay, sometimes called the five-paragraph essay. Texts are also used as models of good writing. This approach focuses on the important features of good writing—its structure and conventions. Clearly, there is more for L2 writers to learn than just a new language. Mastering the conventions and genres of academic writing is essential for becoming part of the academic discourse community.

Each L2 writer approaches the task of writing in an L2 with a specific background. Two of the most important aspects of this background are L2 proficiency and L1 writing ability. There is considerable controversy over how much each contributes to L2 writing proficiency, but it is clear that both are significant and that their relationship is complex. Because reading and writing share general underlying cognitive processes, reading ability in the L1 and the L2 also plays a vital role in learning to write. Better readers make better writers. Different kinds of reading activities contribute in different ways to building language and writing proficiency.

Studies of L1 and L2 writers suggest that their composing processes are similar but also differ in some significant ways. In some cases, L1 writing processes seem to transfer to writing in the L2. Most current approaches to teaching writing in both the L1 and the L2 focus on the writing process, in contrast to early instructional practice, which focused on the writing product. Process approaches stress the recursive nature of writing, writing as an act of communication, the importance of audience, and the benefits of collaboration.

Process-oriented instruction emphasizes the importance of accommodating readers, taking into account their background and what they know. L2 writers should write for a variety of purposes and for a diverse audience, not just for the teacher.

CHAPTER NOTES

1. *Genre Analysis*, by J. Swales, 1990, Cambridge: Cambridge University Press.
2. There are many excellent resources for this task. Two of them are *Learning Vocabulary in Another Language* by I. S. P. Nation, 2001, Cambridge: Cambridge University Press and *Vocabulary in Language Teaching* by N. Schmidt, 2000, Cambridge: Cambridge University Press.

READ MORE ABOUT IT

Reading and L2 Writers

Carson, J. (2001). Reading and writing for academic purposes. In M. Pally (Ed.), *Sustained content teaching in academic ESL/EFL* (pp. 19–34). Boston: Houghton Mifflin.

Carson, J., & Leki, I. (Eds.). (1993). *Reading in the composition classroom*. Boston: Heinle.

Grabe, W. (2003). Reading and writing relations. In B. Kroll, (Ed.), *Exploring the dynamics of second language writing* (pp. 242–262). Cambridge: Cambridge University Press.

Processes and Products of L2 Writers

Hinkel, E. (2002). *Second language writers' texts*. Mahwah, NJ: Erlbaum.

Hyland, K. (2002). *Teaching and researching writing*. Harlow, UK: Longman.

*Silva, T. (1993). Toward an understanding of the distinct nature of L2 writing: ESL research and its implications. *TESOL Quarterly, 27*, 657–675.

Genre/Academic Writing

Currie, P. (1993). Entering a disciplinary community. *Journal of Second Language Writing, 2*, 2–117.

*Accessible readings for beginning students

Johns, A. (1995). Teaching classroom and authentic genres. In D. Belcher & G. Braine (Eds.), *Academic writing in a second language* (pp. 277–291). Norwood, NJ: Ablex.

Johns, A. (2003). Genre and ESL/EFL composition. In B. Kroll (Ed.), *Exploring the dynamics of second language writing* (pp. 195–217). Cambridge: Cambridge University Press.

*Leki, I., & Carson, J. (1997). "Completely different worlds": EAP and the writing experiences of ESL students in university courses. *TESOL Quarterly, 31,* 39–69.

Spack, R. (1997). The acquisition of academic literacy in a second language. *Written Communication, 14,* 3–62.

Contrastive Rhetoric

Connor, U. (2002). New directions in contrastive rhetoric. *TESOL Quarterly, 36,* 493–510.

Leki, I. (1997). Cross-talk: ESL issues and contrastive rhetoric. In C. Severino, J. Guerra, & J. Butler (Eds.), *Writing in multicultural settings* (pp. 234–244). New York: Modern Language Association.

Spack, R. (1997). The rhetorical construction of multilingual students. *TESOL Quarterly, 31,* 765–774.

CHAPTER 3

Tasks and Activities for Second Language Writing

When learners are no longer just practicing language structures but are ready to communicate in writing, what should the course goals be? What kinds of activities will work best for different kinds of learners? Of course, the answers to these and related questions will depend on many things: who the learners are, how much of the L2 they know, what their own goals are, and so on. We start with some very general guidelines for developing classroom activities for L2 writers.

GENERAL GUIDELINES FOR DEVELOPING CLASSROOM ACTIVITIES

- *Learners should write a lot.* Chapter 1 outlined the argument for extensive input to L2 learners. However, we also saw that it is unlikely that L2 writers will improve their writing ability by simply being exposed to relevant input. They need to practice writing. They need to do different kinds of writing. And they need to do a lot of it. Writing is hard work, even in the L1 and even for those who write professionally. However, the process is generally even more difficult and laborious for those who do very little of it. Thus, it is important to include plenty of practice both in and out of class.
- *Writing tasks should reflect authentic purposes and genres.* Every writing task should reflect a principled decision about why such an activity will be beneficial. Learners are more motivated and do their best when they can see why they are doing something. Sometimes a task clearly reflects a task that learners will have to undertake later in their education—a research paper or a report, for example—though it is not always possible to give such an assignment. For low-proficiency learners, perhaps the goal of a task will have as much to do with language learning as communication. Even at higher proficiency levels, it is not always realistic to use target tasks in the classroom; nevertheless, the long-term pedagogical goals should always be clear. For example, learners might compare two proposed plans for future campus development, not because their views will be heard by university officials but because

they need to develop the analytical, rhetorical, and linguistic skills required to make such a comparison effective.

- *There should be guidance and scaffolding for all tasks and activities.* Nothing is more frustrating for learners than floundering, faced with a task they do not know how to complete. For all new writers, and for L2 writers in particular, it is crucial to provide the support and guidance needed for learner success. Such support can include breaking tasks down into simpler and smaller steps, providing preparatory analysis, modeling possible outcomes, encouraging peer assistance, and giving lots of feedback.

- *Content and activities should be recycled.* We rarely learn complex processes such as writing by doing them just once. If we design activities that incorporate content, language, rhetorical structures, and processes that have already been addressed in earlier classes, learners will become more familiar with the content and vocabulary and more comfortable with some parts of the writing tasks as they tackle new and more challenging ones. This approach also gives them a sense of accomplishment and success.

- *Expectations should be clear.* Designing activities and even writing test questions take time and thought. Learners appreciate clarity in instructions so that they know when they have accomplished tasks correctly. They need to know what a good job on a task looks like.

- *The course should reflect the dual goals of learning academic writing and improving L2 proficiency.* The course should balance the need to improve students' writing and the need to continue their language development. It is not necessary to view advanced language acquisition as a prerequisite for L2 writing; the two can develop together. Writing can assist in language development, and, clearly, continued language learning is crucial to the improvement of writing skills. Not every task needs to focus equally on both, however. Both of these processes take a long time, longer than the time frame of any single course.

DESIGNING TASKS AND ACTIVITIES FOR WRITING

As we have discussed several times already, neither learning a new language nor learning to write is a linear process. However, a class has to be sequenced in real time. Sequencing can be addressed in two basic ways: (1) in terms of learners' developing writing and language proficiency or (2) in terms of phases of the writing process. Most student writing textbooks are composed of units organized around phases of the writing process. We explore both approaches in this book, but we begin in this chapter by addressing activities based on proficiency level. We address the writing process itself in Chapter 4.

Writing and Composing

For most of this and the next chapter, we will be discussing writing activities as part of a communication process. Such writing activities are often referred to as *composing* in contrast to *writing*, which refers to any act of putting pen to paper (or fingers to keyboard), as described in Chapter 2. People write for a communicative purpose: to persuade, to present facts, to entertain, to express themselves. However, in beginning language classes, particularly in FL classes, writing is often incorporated into the curriculum before learners know enough of the new language to communicate effectively. What then, is the purpose of writing at all? In some classes, it is simply to practice a recently taught structure. Just about every beginning English, French, Spanish, or other language teacher has given an "If you won the lottery"–type assignment following instruction on the conditional form of the verb. Another example might be a descriptive writing assignment to practice case, number, and gender agreement in languages that require these features, such as a description of clothing items (*Ella lleva una falda amarilla; Sie trägt einen gelben Rock*). Writing might also be assigned to practice new vocabulary: weather phenomena, food items, and so on. Because writing tasks are so often assigned as a way to provide language practice, we should review the role of such output activities in terms of what is known about L2 learning before looking at examples of these activities.

Output activities cannot substitute for abundant input. Input provides the raw material that connects meaning to the forms learners read and hear. Some researchers have argued that output activities (in our case, writing tasks) do not help learners to establish these **form-meaning connections,** which are the first step in L2 learning. So why bother to assign output practice? One answer is that it can be helpful once initial form-meaning connections are made. The act of retrieval that is required when writers produce *s'il était prêt, nous commencerions* (*If he were ready, we would begin*) and *in einem alten Haus* (*in an old house*) helps learners to fix such forms in their long-term memory. Many psycholinguists also believe that doing something active with new knowledge (rather than just reading or listening) not only provides simple exposure but also helps learners to strengthen form-meaning connections. Writing is such an activity.

Of course, this assumes that learners will in fact retrieve those forms during the writing process, something they may not always do, especially once the focus is no longer on these specific structures. If learners have not developed any implicit knowledge of these forms, they may be forced to consult their explicit, rule-based knowledge in order to complete their writing assignment. As we have noted, there is still a great deal of controversy about whether repeatedly accessing explicit knowledge can result in any changes in the implicit linguistic system. We will not settle that question here. However, we can ask if there is any benefit in using explicit linguistic knowledge even if it does not result in permanent changes in the linguistic system. The answer to this depends on whether you think the accuracy of the written product is important. For most of us, it is. For example, my implicit and spontaneously accessible knowledge of the distinction between the noun and verb forms of *affect* and *effect* is a little shaky. Whenever I use one of these words, I have to consciously go through a rule recitation in my head. I go through this routine not because I think the distinction is ever going to become part of my implicit linguistic system (I have given up on that) but because I don't want people to laugh at my writing. The accuracy of my written product is important to me. It is part of my public face, and judgments are made about me based on how I write. Writers, especially L2 writers, whose mastery of the language is less than perfect, need to develop this practice of **monitoring** early on, that is, checking their production against their explicit rule knowledge. They will be evaluated on the basis of their writing, just as I am.

One other function of output tasks that we may not think of right away is the creation of need; that is, when students are given a written task—a description of their dorm room, a story about something that happened to them—the assignment may prompt them to realize that there are holes in their knowledge of the language they are learning. Maybe they realize they need the word for *bookshelf,* or they are not sure which classifier[1] to use with *bed* in Japanese. Many scholars and educators believe that learners are more likely to remember a word or structure when they establish the need for it them-selves, rather than when they read or hear it simply because it happens to be in the lesson. Once they have noticed this lack, they may be more likely to notice the word or structure in subsequent input. Thus, output activities can also play a role in making some aspects of input more significant and notice-able to learners.

In summary then, writing may facilitate language learning by

- strengthening form-meaning connections;
- promoting the application of explicit knowledge to spontaneous pro-duction through monitoring;
- creating communicative need that may stimulate subsequent noticing.

These are potential benefits of writing specifically for L2 development. Thus, in spite of the stronger role played by input in L2 acquisition, writing can play an important complementary role. Of course, facilitating L2 learning is only the first reason for learners to engage in L2 writing. It can also have a direct effect on their writing, a topic to which we turn later in the chapter.

Developing Tasks and Activities for L2 Writers: Design Considerations

As we have noted, writing activities are often aimed at giving students prac-tice in using language forms rather than practice in communicating ideas. This type of writing is often referred to as **controlled writing.** There are good rea-sons for using these kinds of activities, but they have limitations. When you are designing any instructional activity, it is a good idea to begin at the end. What should learners get out of it? Even if the goal is primarily the develop-ment of linguistic competence and fluency, the activity can be viewed in terms of *communicative goals* as well. For example, adjective clauses are an important and extremely useful structure for modifying nouns. Academic learners will need to use them extensively in their writing. One common use of adjective clauses in academic writing is extended definitions, as in a piece of writing containing advice to incoming students:

(1) A prerequisite is a class that you must take before you can take another class. For example, calculus is a prerequisite for introductory physics.

Here is another example, from a piece of writing about American pets:

(2) A ferret is a small mammal that belongs to the weasel family.

Writing contextualized, extended definitions is both a form of language practice and preparation for academic writing.

The following are questions teachers can ask themselves when they are designing writing activities (though not every activity will conform to all of them):

- Is the purpose of this activity primarily to recycle recent structures or vocabulary? If so, it is not really writing.
- Does it have a communicative purpose? What is it?
- Does it introduce writers to aspects of the composing process? Which ones?
- Does it allow writers to practice a specific genre? Which one?
- Is it likely to engage learners? Is it interesting?
- Does it integrate other skills and knowledge, such as reading or speaking?
- Do learners have a good chance of success with this activity? Is there enough support for it?
- Does it prepare learners for academic writing?

Writing Activities and Projects for Lower Proficiency Learners

We begin here by thinking about activities that can be used with learners whose L2 proficiency may not permit much extensive writing. These activities can facilitate continued language acquisition and promote the monitoring of output through the effective use of explicit linguistic knowledge. This does not mean, however, that they must be without communicative purpose. And although we are focusing on output (production) activities, I want to underscore, once again, that all learners need to be exposed to lots of input. It is particularly important that learners at lower levels of proficiency do a considerable amount of reading. Because reading is difficult for them, it is tempting to assign less of it. However, as we have seen in earlier chapters, both exposure to *new* vocabulary and rhetorical structures and *repeated* exposure to familiar language are crucial in the development of their language skills. Reading and analysis of written material are clearly an essential part of any L2 writing curriculum, but doing something *active* with some of the reading—taking notes, responding, summarizing, reformulating, or using thematic vocabulary—is just as essential. Material from the readings should be incorporated into subsequent output activities. Otherwise, much of what learners read may not remain with them for long.

Icebreakers

There are many getting-to-know-you activities that teachers often use in the first days of class. Often, these icebreakers are primarily oral activities, such as one in which learners have to find other learners with specified characteristics (e.g., *find a classmate with one sister and one brother, find a classmate who rides a bike to school*). These can easily be adapted to a written format, with students creating their own instructions following examples from the teacher. One-on-one interviews can also be useful: Learners interview a partner in order to answer a specified set of questions. In multilingual classes, such as in ESL settings, interviews may revolve around significant issues or events in the interviewee's country or culture. The interviewer then writes up the results, either in summary form or simply as a list of responses.

This kind of activity can be tailored to make it both a more appropriate preparation for academic writing and more communicative. First, the class might brainstorm about what questions to ask. What information might an audience want to know about class members? What vocabulary might be useful to describe them? Should the descriptions be unified with recurring themes, such as goals and aspirations or favorite haunts in the host city? What is the best way to take notes when another person is talking? In order to enhance the communicative purpose of the activity, the teacher may want to consider publishing the material in some way. If students are given a chance to revise and polish their interviews, their work might be collected in a class album or, if resources are available, published on a website. Providing an audience makes the task more real to the learners. Such activities clearly have a communicative goal. They can be quite simple or adapted to more complex tasks; for instance, learners might be required to summarize and synthesize interview material.

Familiar Genres

Controlled writing can be done effectively with familiar genres, such as children's stories and fairy tales. Learners begin with a skeletal story and, with specific instructions from the teacher (e.g., *add descriptive adjectives*), expand the story in a controlled manner. You can try this with a familiar story line, such as Little Red Riding Hood or The Three Little Pigs. Reduce the story line to about 10 to 12 simple declarative sentences, and then decide how students are to elaborate the story. This activity allows students to complete a task that is within their grasp and end up with a text that has relatively few errors.

Story Assembly and Completion Activities

The activities known as strip stories, chain stories, and story completion activities also work well with lower level learners. Strip stories depict separate stages in a series of events, either in pictures or in sentences (it is important that they represent a clear sequence of events). The sequence is chopped up, and learners have to reassemble the pieces and present the story in the appropriate order. If they only have pictures, learners will have to come up with their own language, a much more difficult task. However, the structural and discoursal features of a disassembled written text can also be exploited if the language is chosen carefully. If it is completely obvious from the content what the sequence is, a strip story will not be effective. The text should force learners to examine textual features as well. Here is an example of a short text in English. Although it is quite challenging—too difficult for beginning learners—it clearly speaks to readers' processes as they sort out temporal and causal relationships.

(3) Giselle is a high school student in Chicago. She always has a suntan, even in January. How does she do this? She doesn't go to the beach every weekend. Instead, she goes to a tanning salon once a week. She agreed to talk to us about her visits to the salon. However, she did not want to give her last name because she doesn't want her mother to find out about them. Her mother thinks Giselle's tan just comes from a bottle of tanning lotion. Using lotion is much safer for your skin than going to a tanning salon. Giselle knows tanning is not healthy for her skin. She does it anyway because all the other kids in her school do it.

Pause to consider...

the reading selection. What clues would readers use to figure out the sequence of the sentences if they were presented out of order?[2] Is there one unique solution? Could the sentences be ordered in any other way?

Chain stories and story completion activities operate in much the same way: They call on learners to read carefully and to make predictions. In chain stories, learners usually supply a short stretch of text and then pass it on to a classmate to continue with the next segment. This kind of activity can be entertaining but should be used with care with low-proficiency learners, who may supply illogical text, change the time frame, or offer non sequiturs. Therefore, it is important to monitor contributions, perhaps by putting them on the board, in order to control the story line. In story completion activities, the teacher usually supplies most of the text, perhaps a published story or newspaper article, and students, working either individually or collaboratively, must decide how the story should end. Finished stories are then shared.

These activities work well because they engage learners and call their attention to important textual features that they will need to be aware of as they become writers. The benefits of these kinds of activities can be increased if they are sometimes done collaboratively. When work is done together, learners often come up with solutions and knowledge that they could not have produced on their own. Finally, be aware that these story completion activities, in spite of their appeal and benefits, do not really represent a genre that is common in academic settings, and their communicative purposes are not terribly authentic.

Picture Responses and Descriptions

Writing activities that are generally more expressive than most academic tasks are picture responses and descriptions. For example, the teacher might provide a picture of a woman's face and ask students to write about what they think her life is like, what has happened to her, or what she is thinking. If several pictures are used, students can share their descriptions and guess which description belongs to which picture. In this way, they can gauge their effectiveness as communicators. Picture description tasks can also be useful for low-proficiency writers as language practice activity. If students need to practice contextualized use of modal verbs and other expressions of deduction, this might provide an appropriate opportunity. Using a photograph of a woman's face, they might respond with such sentences as these:

(4) She looks very happy.
   She must be having fun.
   Perhaps she got a good grade on her test.
   She might be going to a party tonight.

Other descriptive tasks include such well-worn assignments as *describe your room* or *describe a special place*. For imaginative or introspective learners, these kinds of tasks can be productive, but they also have some serious drawbacks. Often, lower proficiency learners do not have sufficient L2 knowledge, especially of vocabulary, to ensure successful completion of such tasks. Room descriptions can offer a way of practicing specific language structures (e.g., prepositions) and vocabulary (e.g., furniture), but they are not usually terribly interesting for learners. The "special place" type of assignment is an attempt to bring some critical thinking processes to the descriptive task: Why is it special for you? What does it represent? How does it reflect your present or past experiences? Again, the cognitive and imaginative abilities of these students may sometimes outstrip their linguistic proficiency such that the activity becomes frustrating.

In spite of the potential drawbacks, descriptive tasks can serve a useful purpose in the writing classroom. Description can be incorporated into other tasks that may be better preparation for academic writing. Descriptions based on close observation work particularly well.[3] For example, what do people do when they wait in line at the grocery store or when they are riding the subway? How could these situations be described to someone unfamiliar with them? Again, these tasks look ahead to academic writing tasks, in which learners have to use critical thinking skills to inform their observations (e.g., *Why does everyone avoid eye contact on the subway?*). It also forces them to take a more objective view of their own behavior and consider a new audience for their observations.

Giving Advice, Providing Instructions

One goal of academic writing instruction, as mentioned earlier, is to expose learners to a variety of writing genres that are important in an academic discourse community. Although many L2 writers aren't ready to join the community, it is not too early to work on appropriate genres, some of which don't revolve around the standard essay form. Tasks that involve giving advice and providing instructions require a variety of useful language and rhetorical forms. This kind of activity can be embedded in an authentic task, such as giving advice to future learners/visitors to their program or institution. What should visitors wear? What do they need to bring with them? What should they expect? And, like the observation-descriptions described above, this kind of activity can force students to view fairly simple and familiar procedures and objects in their own environment in a new light; for example, How do you navigate the bus or subway system in your city? How do self-service gas stations work? How would you give directions to someone totally unfamiliar with these processes?

> ## Pause to consider...
> what kinds of writing tasks of this variety would be appropriate for your group of writers; the difference FL versus L2 context might make in developing tasks for low-proficiency learners; how learners might use these genres later in their academic careers.

Journaling

The literature on L2 teaching contains many references to the value of journals. Journals are simply students' personal writing books (or electronic documents) in which they are free to write as they wish and, sometimes, about what they wish. Journals can be a place for writers to express their ideas freely. Most teachers do not grade journal entries, and they respond to the content rather than the form of the message. Having a context in which learners can write without risk is especially important for their continued language development. If all their writing is evaluated, learners are less likely to take risks and push their linguistic and writing abilities and resources to their limits. Journal entries can also be a source of writing ideas for more formal assignments if learners use their journals to explore topics of interest. Because it is a forum for expression that won't be judged, journal writing can be especially helpful with young or inexperienced writers or those who lack confidence in their L2 abilities.

Using journals also has drawbacks, however. First, if students are simply assigned open-ended personal writing, they may flounder, not knowing what to write about. It is better to tie these less formal journal writings to other activities or content in the course, such as a response to a reading, further exploration of a topic discussed in class, or a reflective consideration of a metacognitive topic (e.g., *What was the most difficult part of this project for you, and why?*). Second, journals represent a lot of reading for the instructor. If students are asked to write journal entries, they have every right to expect a response, and one with comments that are a little more engaged than "how interesting!"

Students' responses to journals vary considerably: Some enjoy the opportunity to write freely; others find the obligation burdensome. Some students may also write material that teachers don't feel comfortable reading. Many teachers introduce journals with a set of guidelines about appropriate topics to explore. Finally, in some classes students share their journals with one another. Teachers who plan to have students share should make this clear at the outset so that no one is uncomfortable or feels that his or her privacy is being breached.

The following are some guidelines for using journals in a writing classroom:

- Assign journal entries only if you or someone else is prepared to respond to them.
- Respond primarily to content.

- Respond to language problems when they prevent comprehension of the writer's meaning.
- Don't give grades on journal entries.
- Try to integrate journaling with other assignments and activities.
- Keep open-ended topics to a minimum.
- Provide guidelines for procedures and (in)appropriate topics.

Collaborative Projects

I have briefly mentioned the benefits of collaborative learning activities. Ideally, these are activities in which learners pool what they know and can do in order to achieve something each might not have been able to do individually. In addition, the oral interaction that takes place can facilitate linguistic development as learners negotiate meaning. If learner A does not understand learner B, learner A's signals of noncomprehension can tell learner B that his production is not targetlike. Learner B then has to make changes in his output in order to be understood. This process can be an important part of language learning. Thus, collaborative projects can weave together many of the skills that L2 writers need to develop.

Types of collaborative projects range from those narrowly focused on grammatical development, such as the dictogloss, described next, to much more ambitious projects. We explore a few of them here and others later when we discuss activities for higher proficiency learners. Although some require collaboration, others could also be adapted for individual work.

Dictoglosses   Dictoglosses resemble dictations, but dictoglosses differ in significant ways. The teacher reads a short, simple text, one to two paragraphs long, with mostly familiar vocabulary. The text is read once at a normal pace. Learners take notes but do not attempt to capture the text verbatim. The text may stress a specific grammatical structure that learners have not yet mastered, such as the contrast between the *pretérito* and *imperfecto* in Spanish. Then, in pairs (or somewhat larger groups), the learners attempt to reconstruct the passage as precisely as they can. It is up to the teacher whether students are given access to reference materials such as dictionaries. Because the text is short, learners can focus on its form as well as its message. And, because learners pool their knowledge, they can often jointly reconstruct what they could not do alone. This kind of activity pushes learners to achieve a level of precision in the linguistic output they might not otherwise manage. Research has shown that in these sessions, when learners discuss various grammatical and vocabulary options, there is clear evidence of learning: What is discussed and decided tends to be learned.

Scripts   Another activity that combines various skills, including reading and speaking, is script writing. Many students enjoy performing. For classes that involve reading fiction, groups might be asked to develop short skits based on readings. Although the original reading might contain some dialogue, students would have to flesh out the script with their own writing. One advantage of this kind of activity for lower proficiency learners is that much of the vocabulary is already in the text and simply has to be translated into dialogue form. This kind of recycling is an important part of vocabulary learning. The portions of the story presented should be relatively short so that learners do not have to wait too long to perform and the audience, however indulgent, does not have to sit through lengthy performances.

Exploring Proverbs   Some projects are just fun, whether they are done collaboratively or individually, regardless of their academic rigor. In heterogeneous classes (most likely L2 rather than FL classes), students often find it interesting and entertaining to share proverbs and colorful idioms from their countries.

Here are some examples, with their American equivalents in brackets:

- Pick up a sesame seed but lose sight of a watermelon. (Chinese) [You can't see the forest for the trees.]
- Some prefer carrots while others like cabbage. (Chinese) [To each his own. One man's meat is another man's poison.]
- An ass does not appreciate fruit compote. (Turkish) [Pearls before swine.]

This exercise could be just a short exchange in which students collect and share examples, or it could be a deeper exploration of the themes that proverbs encode. For example, most cultures have proverbs that extol the virtues of hard work, claim that wealth is not everything, warn that appearances can be deceiving, or acknowledge individuality. If students collect enough of these, either from classmates or by interviewing others, they can try to find these themes and explore why they seem to be pan-cultural. For FL students, this task might be adapted as a comparative activity, in which students collect proverbs in the target language and explore L1-L2 contrasts and similarities.

Analyzing Advertisements

Developing analytical skills is particularly important for inexperienced writers. Not every task in an L2 writing class has to involve academic texts. With simple texts, or even texts that are primarily visual, learners can begin to explore issues that are central to academic writing, such as the intended **audience** of a text. Advertisements are a ready source for this exercise: For whom is this lipstick advertisement designed? How about the ad with the luxury car parked in a sweeping driveway in front of a large house? Why have the advertisers chosen these particular words and images? How might their choices change if the ads were aimed at a different audience? With learners who have difficulty reading, and in classes in which time is limited, teachers can exploit visual material to encourage critical thinking.

Writing Activities and Projects for Higher Proficiency Academic Learners

Higher proficiency learners need to practice more authentic academic writing tasks. It is important that assignments reflect this need. In this section, we examine activities and tasks primarily from a product perspective, that is, in terms of what the final piece of writing should look like. In Chapter 4, we

TABLE 3.1 Authentic Academic Tasks

Summaries of outside sources, reports with analysis
Proposals or plans
Reactions to readings
Annotated bibliographies
Case studies
Application of theoretical concepts to data
Reviews and critiques

explore more systematically some of the steps involved in completing these tasks; that is, we examine writing from more process-oriented view.

The first question to ask is, What is an academic task? We might think of the five-paragraph essay or the research paper as being typical of the kinds of writing that will be required of college students. Indeed, these forms are common requirements in some classes, and it may be surprising to teachers that many students just out of high school have had relatively little experience with expository (essay) writing. It is especially important for L2 writing instructors to emphasize this type of writing if their students' primary experience has been with personal writing. For FL instructors, the need may be less pressing, as their students will probably receive separate academic writing instruction in English. However, any students majoring in a foreign language will soon find that they need to engage in expository writing in those classes as well. It is a good idea for instructors to find out about learners' writing needs. What we intuitively think they need and what their actual writing needs are may not be the same. Developing tasks with authentic goals in mind can help provide a context for assignments so that learners clearly understand why they are being asked to do them. A number of researchers have undertaken formal **needs analyses;** that is, they have investigated the needs of academic learners (mostly in English) and found that the research paper is only one form of required writing. Other frequently encountered, authentic academic writing tasks are listed in Table 3.1.

Remember that many L2 and FL writers are not yet able to do the kind of research that might be required in standard composition courses, in which learners must locate, compile, and analyze information from academic sources. They will probably work on those skills in other classes. Therefore, we begin here by exploring some less traditional genres that may nevertheless provide useful learning opportunities for L2 writers and prepare them for traditional writing assignments such as research papers. The kinds of activities we discuss require skills similar to those required in composition classes, yet they are more accessible to those with less extensive linguistic proficiency and writing experience. Therefore, in many cases, they are more appropriate for our target populations.

A first basic distinction we can make in considering academic writing activities is between those that require writers to *gather or generate information* and those that require them to *analyze and organize the information* they have collected or been given. Later, in Chapter 4, we talk more about the sequence that learners go through in these processes: developing a thesis, providing support, and so on. For now, we look at these tasks more generally.

Gathering and Generating Information

Personal Experience   Where can learners get the information they need in order to write? The easiest and most obvious answer is from their heads—from their own life experience. In fact, this is probably characteristic of most of the writing they have done in the past, when they were asked, *What do you think? What happened to you? Why did you like this?* There is nothing wrong with writing from personal experience; indeed, it has been argued that one problem learners encounter as inexperienced writers is that they have no real expertise on any topic that they can tap into and display. They often feel as if there are experts all around them and that they have little original to contribute. If there is one thing they are experts on, it is their own experience. For this reason, L2 writing instructors often begin a course by asking learners to consult their own experience in reference to something the class has discussed or a topic in their class textbook. For example, if the topic is intergenerational conflict, students may have a rich lode of experience they can consult in their writing. With personal writing assignments, there are two broad caveats to remember:

- Try to ensure that students do not simply tell a story. They are preparing to do academic writing, in which simply sharing stories is not generally acceptable. Try to get them to see their story as illustrative of some larger, more complex point. Why are they telling the story? What does it tell the reader about them? Their community? Their generation? The human condition?
- For international students studying in North America, some topics are by now so hackneyed that it is best to avoid them altogether. Examples of these might be *Describe a holiday in your country* or *Compare a city in your country to the city in which you are studying.* For immigrant students studying English, you can be relatively sure they have told the story of their journey to this country any number of times. For those who have attended high school in the United States, the usual suspects—gender roles, various topics under the general heading of multiculturalism—are also likely to be topics students have often addressed in earlier classes.

Surveys   From what other sources might students gather data for their writing? One place is other people's ideas and experiences. Survey and interview projects can be done individually or collaboratively and can integrate a variety of skills. These activities work well with students who still find the heavy reading loads in academic courses extremely challenging. They can practice the same skills of analysis and synthesis required in tasks that draw information from print and electronic sources. Written surveys are also less taxing for those whose oral skills are still developing.

What goes into making a survey? First, of course, the teacher and/or students need to decide on a topic of interest. Will it be about habits? Opinions? Past experiences? What topics will work? Here are some examples:

- The dining-out habits of local residents aged 18 to 50
- Views on a recent tuition hike
- Levels of awareness of specific international events among undergraduate students

When designing a survey, learners need to look ahead to the paper they will write and choose a topic that is sufficiently narrow that they will be able to treat it comprehensively but not so narrow that they will exhaust the topic in a paragraph. Perhaps there is a controversy at their university about whether a McDonald's franchise should be allowed on university property. The students might want to know how likely it is that such an establishment is needed or appreciated. There is thus a purpose to the information-gathering activity and, if publication is an option, an authentic audience as well.

Then learners need to write the questions. Teachers can facilitate the process with some pretask activities. What sort of vocabulary are the surveys likely to require? What grammatical structures will be needed? An obvious candidate is question formation. Another important aspect of the pretask phase is a discussion of the pragmatic appropriateness of the language students select: How can the questions be politely phrased? Even after the relevant vocabulary, grammar, and pragmatics have been addressed, writing questions is not as easy as it first appears. An initial attempt often results in questions like, *Do you eat at fast-food restaurants?* This kind of question will not yield useful responses (yes, no). Perhaps questions need to be asked in a multiple-choice format and couched in terms of frequency.

In short, the writing activity includes not just the final paper but the creation of the survey as well. It can also prime the issue of audience awareness, as students must put themselves in the shoes of the respondents who will answer their questions. For FL learners, respondents are harder to come by. Possibilities include other sections of the same class or more advanced learners, keypals (electronic pen pals), or even faculty.

Observational Projects Learners can also discover academic practices by engaging in the kind of research we usually associate with anthropologists: extended observation and analysis of observation data. They can use these techniques to learn more about the community they are entering. An FL classroom mini-ethnography is one example of this technique. Most language learners have sat in classes as passive receivers of new knowledge, but what would happen if they were to become more active observers? In such an activity, students might make several observations of lower level classes in the language they are learning, either repeatedly in the same class or in different classes. They might ask themselves the following questions:

- What is the ratio of student-to-teacher speech?
- What sorts of participant structures exist in the classroom, that is, what sorts of communication groups seem to be favored? Do learners work

together? Alone? Do they stay in their seats? Do they wait for the teacher to call on them? Is there more student-student interaction, or is student-teacher interaction the dominant mode?

- Is participation equally distributed? Do some students talk more than others? If so, how do those students seem to grab more turns at talk?
- How much is the L1 used in the class? How much of the L2? Are particular types of communication more likely to be in one language or the other?
- Does the teacher rely mostly on the textbook? On other materials?
- Does the teacher diverge from materials in response to student interest or questions?
- Do the students seem engaged? How can you tell?
- What kinds of language skills are stressed?

To round out the observations, students could interview participants and collect "artifacts." Interviews with students might include questions such as these:

- What are students' views of the class?
- Why are they taking the class? Is it a language requirement?
- What has been their past experience with FL classes?

Interviews with the teachers might include questions such as these:

- What are the teacher's views on effective language teaching?
- Why has she chosen this textbook? Or did someone else choose it for her?
- What are her views on the students?
- Is language teaching her area of professional expertise and interest, or does she pursue her own studies in another area, such as literature?

Artifacts would include copies of the textbook, workbooks, student homework, and tests.

Learners would then have to analyze the data they have collected and distill them in order to make general statements about language teaching at their institution. These statements might include the teacher's or department's perspective on language learning and instructional processes, the extent to which teacher beliefs match classroom processes, the consequences of requiring language study, and so on. Learners might also make recommendations based on their observations. In essence, the experience puts them in the position of becoming experts in one limited area, able to comment knowledgeably on what they have observed and learned.

Oral Histories and Interviews   Oral histories are a common assignment in history and sociology classes, and they also work well in language classes. It is likely that they will be best suited to ESL and heritage language classes because these are settings in which learners will have access to considerable numbers of target language speakers. As with the survey projects, learners will have to prepare a set of questions beforehand, but unlike the survey questions, these questions are posed orally, and students should feel free to follow their informant's lead and diverge from a prepared script. In addition, however, because of the oral and spontaneous nature of interviews, learners should practice by interviewing one another before they do so outside the classroom.

For these projects, it is useful to begin with an issue, even if is a fairly broad one, rather than a sort of "tell me about yourself" approach. Consider, for example, the issue of neighborhood gentrification, a possible project for heritage language classes. In many urban areas, immigrants from individual language groups have congregated in specific areas of the city. In some cases, this has occurred because new immigrants simply felt more comfortable living among their countrymen, and they gradually created a neighborhood where goods and services could be obtained in their home language, eventually resulting in ethnic enclaves. In other cases, immigrants have had little choice about where they line, with restrictive housing covenants and other more subtle forms of segregation effectively barring them from more desirable neighborhoods. In time, these enclaves often attract the interest of the wider public, with their stable populations and exciting restaurants and shopping. If the neighborhoods are in convenient locations, this can be enough to trigger gentrification: Wealthier, often white city residents move in and upgrade the housing stock, in the process attracting mainstream retailers. Taxes and rents rise, often squeezing out the original residents and shop owners and creating resentment toward the newcomers. Often there are some people still living in the neighborhood, usually older residents, who have seen it all happen and can tell the story—and are often eager to do so. Interviews with these informants can offer a rich glimpse into the history of the community.

Pause to consider...

how to adapt this kind of activity for an immigrant ESL population or an international student population. What sorts of changes would be necessary?

Analyzing and Organizing Information

So far, all of the activities for higher proficiency learners have involved generating or gathering information. Obviously, this is not the end of an assignment in a writing class. The next step is organizing and analyzing it. For example, in the oral history activity just described, learners need to do more than simply report what their informants have said. They must separate more important from less important information, they must summarize and make generalizations based on disparate information, and they must consider ways in which the stories the informants have told reflect themes that they should pursue in their writing. These analytical processes are common to most writing projects and reflect more traditional and perhaps typical academic writing activities learners will encounter later.

To explore tasks that ask learners to organize and analyze information, we return briefly to the list in Table 3.1. Academic tasks such as reports and proposals are macrotasks that even advanced learners may find daunting. In fact, these projects actually consist of a series of subtasks, each of which can be addressed individually. Some involve *analysis*, that is, the breaking down of a complex issue or topic into parts. An example of this might be the critical reading of a persuasive text provided in class; learners need to consider the separate points in the writer's argument. Other subtasks require *synthesis*, that is, the integration of a variety of sources into a coherent form. Examples of synthesis include comparing two writers' viewpoints on a single topic or assembling a series of examples to illustrate and provide support for a writer's point of view. Many academic writing tasks require both analysis and synthesis. Annotated bibliographies are an example of a writing task that involves the analysis of a series of articles on a selected topic as well as comparison (synthesis) across them. Finally, writers may be called upon to provide *evaluation* of the information they have gathered, that is, in effect, to insert their own voice into the conversation.

Many different subskills or subtasks may be involved in tasks that require learners to apply ideas, concepts, or theories to a set of data. "Data" might be in the form of literary material, scientific observations, or the kind of information collected in the oral history project described earlier. A literary example might be the story of Malinche, the Aztec woman who assisted Cortés in his invasion of Mexico. Her story has been used as a metaphor in discussions of North-South and male-female relations and has been reinterpreted in a variety of ways and contexts. A nonliterary example might address factors involved in immigrants' acquisition of English.

Pause to consider...

the two examples just given. If the "data" are short stories invoking Malinche, what subtasks would a writer have to complete in order to explore the use of the Malinche myth in modern Chicana literature? If data are graphs and charts based on census data reporting birthplace, schooling, and language(s) spoken in the home from the last 100 years, what subtasks would be involved in exploring this question?

Here are three other examples of real academic writing tasks:

- The oral history project on gentrification described earlier
- A research report on the history and status of French-based creole languages
- A persuasive essay on the use of plusses and minuses in grading college courses

Each of these writing tasks is quite different, but some subtasks are common across projects. Subtasks of these three projects are listed in Table 3.2. The lists are not exhaustive, and subtasks may vary depending on the specific assignment. What is certain is that academic writers will need to engage in all of these activities during their academic careers.

The first step for learners is to realize that they need to include these elements; only then can they go on to learn how to actually execute them in

TABLE 3.2 Subtasks of Three Academic Writing Projects

	Oral History	Research Report	Persuasive Essay
Topic	Gentrification	French Creoles	Pros and cons of grades
Target learners	Heritage learners	FL learners	ESL learners
Data collection	Collected orally from participants	Library research-print/electronic	Library research-print/ electronic/interviews
Possible subtasks	Summarizing Narrating Finding generalizations Exploring causes and effects Comparing and contrasting	Defining Classifying Exemplifying Comparing and contrasting	Summarizing Exemplifying Defining problem/ proposing solution Offering reasons Countering opposing views Evaluating

writing. For example, it may not be obvious to them that a report on French Creoles should begin with a definition of creole languages, that skillful and effective narratives are more than just stories, or that an argument for a grading system needs to present more than just the writer's opinions. Experienced writers may realize such essentials immediately, but this is not always the case with inexperienced writers. In fact, understanding the complexity of the tasks may be one of the more difficult aspects of learning academic writing. Once learners understand the task before them, learning how to put their ideas into writing becomes easier. Native speakers may take years to master some of these skills; it is even more challenging for L2 writers. Many student books offer advice on learning to encode these functions in writing. Most of the readily available textbooks of this kind are in English for learners of English but can be adapted to the teaching of writing in other languages. We explore a small selection of these subtasks next.

Defining Many types of writing require definitions. Writers of expository prose should always begin by asking themselves, Have I defined the terms I will be using? A definition may be the more familiar, formal, sentence-level definition, such as this one for *creole*: "A creole language is a pidgin language that has become the native language of a speech community." (Such a definition would then require a definition of a pidgin language.) Another type is an *extended definition*, such as this one, also for *creole*:

> Defined by specialists as, in a strict sense, a language that has developed historically from a pidgin. In the beginning the pidgin develops from trade or other contacts; it has no native speakers, its range of use is limited, and its structure is simplified. Later it becomes the only form of speech that is common to a community; it is learned increasingly as a native language, it is used for all purposes, and its structure and vocabulary are enlarged.[4]

Right away, two things are evident about these definitions. First, they may fulfill a variety of functions, that is, they may do more than tell literally *what*. Second, there are specific grammatical functions associated with them. The latter characteristic is particularly important for L2 writers. For example, in the extended definition of a creole language, we are given not only what a creole language is but a little bit of its history, its function, and a brief description. Exactly which threads of the definition should be included depends on what aspects of creole languages the writer chooses to pursue in the rest of the text.

The syntax of definitions provides an opportunity to show learners about grammar in context. Many learners may have been taught adjective (relative) clauses, for example, in a more artificial context, using sentence combining:

(5) The cat was in the tree.

The firefighter rescued the cat. → The firefighter rescued the cat that was in the tree.

Sentence combining is a largely mechanical approach to teaching adjective clauses. If this approach is paired with instruction on definitions, however, it becomes meaningful. In fact, it is difficult to write a succinct definition without using an adjective clause. Thus, the situation creates a communicative need, which is believed to facilitate L2 learning. In fact, although adjective clauses are indeed a way of combining short sentences with a common referent (in the preceding example, *the cat*), one of the most common discourse functions of relative clauses is complex modification. In English, simple modification is usually placed to the left of the noun, as in *artificial language*. Sometimes, however, we cannot squeeze everything into a one-word adjective, so we need more complex forms of modification. These forms are placed to the right of the noun in English, as in *a pidgin language that has become the native language of a speech community*. Thus the standard grammatical form for definitions in English is

X is a Y that zzz, where:

- X is the entity to be defined,
- Y is a more general class to which X belongs, and
- zzz is a descriptive clause that restricts the class of Y.

Most European languages operate in much the same way, with minor variations. Writing definitions is just one example of how rhetorical functions can be taught along with appropriate grammatical constructions.

Summarizing A task that poses a challenge for native speakers and L2 writers alike is summarizing. It requires a close reading of a text, the distillation of the ideas contained in it, and a reformulation of those ideas in a writer's own words. For L2 writers, the last part is particularly difficult because many feel they cannot possibly express the ideas as well as the original writer. There are other kinds of summaries as well, such as summaries of tabular or survey data. Like summaries of texts, these involve a distillation of information into one or two general ideas. A good summary should

- contain a clear topic sentence, expressing the main idea(s) of the original author or the main findings based on a set of data;

- include major supporting ideas and arguments;
- state the source;
- use different language than the original text;
- be shorter than the original text.

It should not

- include details;
- include the writer's opinions;
- distort the original author's meaning;
- use language of the original text.

The following excerpt is an example of an appropriate text for inexperienced learners to use to practice summary writing. It is short, simple, and has a clear point of view.

(6) Is Jim Crow Justice Alive and Well in America Today?

"Racial profiling" occurs when the police target someone for investigation on the basis of that person's race, national origin, or ethnicity. Examples of profiling are the use of race to determine which drivers to stop for minor traffic violations ("driving while black") and the use of race to determine which motorists or pedestrians to search for contraband.

Racial profiling is prevalent in America. Despite the civil rights victories of 30 years ago, official racial prejudice is still reflected throughout the criminal justice system. For people of color in cities large and small across this nation, north and south, east and west, Jim Crow "justice" is alive and well. Today skin color makes you a suspect in America. It makes you more likely to be stopped, more likely to be searched, and more likely to be arrested and imprisoned.

One of the ACLU's highest priority issues is the fight against the outrageous practice of racial profiling. Our recently released report Driving While Black: Racial Profiling On Our Nation's Highways documents this practice of substituting skin color for evidence as a grounds for suspicion by law enforcement officials.

Tens of thousands of innocent motorists on highways across the country are victims of racial profiling. And these discriminatory police stops have reached epidemic proportions in recent years—fueled by the "War on Drugs" that has given police a pretext to target people who they think fit a "drug courier" or "gang member" profile. We must put an end to the practice of racial profiling. That is why the ACLU has undertaken a major initiative to put an end to discriminatory police stops, including the launch of our Arrest the Racism campaign.[5]

A possible summary for this text might be as follows:

The ACLU claims that racial profiling, which is the practice of singling out individuals based on their race or ethnicity, is common in the United States. Although explicit discrimination is illegal, official prejudice occurs in less obvious ways. Nonwhites are suspected of illegal activities more often than whites, yet most of them are innocent. The ACLU argues that racial profiling is racist and must be stopped.

If we examine the summary more closely, we can see that it

- has a clear topic sentence that contains the main idea of the original text;
- preserves the perspective of the text's author;
- deletes a considerable amount of detail, such as illustrative examples;
- generalizes from multiple examples (e.g., "searched, arrested, and imprisoned" is generalized to "suspected");
- uses language different from that of the original text.

> *Pause to consider...*
>
> **grammatical structures to focus on when working with summaries. In the section on definitions, we noted that some specific grammatical constructions are naturally linked to that rhetorical function. What about summaries?**

Summarizing is a complex task that takes practice and patience, but instructors can structure and scaffold the task so that learners do not have to manage the whole task at once. **Scaffolding** is instructional support that helps learners to accomplish tasks that might otherwise be too challenging. How could the racial profiling summarizing task be simplified? Here are four options:

1. The easiest thing to do is to vary the difficulty of the text to be summarized, but this one is already quite simple.
2. Another possibility is to begin by having students put aside the text and try to write just one sentence containing the main idea in their own words (the process that is at the heart of any summary) or, if the text is long, one sentence per paragraph.
3. Another option is to supply students with parts of the summary and have them expand it. In example (a), the topic sentence and a conclusion are provided and students have to provide the support. In example (b), the supporting details are given and students have to provide the topic and concluding sentences.
   a. Topic sentence: The ACLU claims that racial profiling is common in the United States.
      Supporting details: _____
      _____
      _____

      Conclusion: The ACLU argues that racial profiling is racist and must be stopped.
   b. Topic sentence: _____
      _____

Supporting details: Although explicit discrimination is illegal, official prejudice continues in less obvious ways. Nonwhites are suspected of illegal activities more often than whites.

Conclusion: _____

_____

4. Finally, in a tightly structured approach, learners are instructed to write specific components of a summary:

A topic sentence containing the main idea and source: _____

One to two sentence(s) supporting the main idea: _____

One sentence expressing the author's view of the topic: _____

A Note on Plagiarism   One of the greatest difficulties for L2 writers is finding their own words to express the ideas in the original text. Remember, L2 writers are not just learning to write; they are still acquiring the L2 and therefore frequently cannot come up with equivalent expressions, at least not easily. It has often been noted that L2 writers are more likely than their native-speaking peers to engage in what their teachers view as plagiarism, perhaps for this very reason. As teachers, we need to look more closely at the situations in which learners are prone to "borrow" large chunks of text.

Consider the story of Sunhee (not her real name), a student in one of my graduate classes. I discovered that in a writing assignment, she had copied extended passages from one of her textbooks without attribution. The plagiarism was immediately obvious, and I gave her a rather stern lecture about the consequences of plagiarism and the need for attribution. She went home to rewrite the assignment. She came back the next week with a revised version. This one also contained extended passages from the text—many of the same ones—but this time, they were enclosed in quotation marks with references to sources. These passages were linked by a few of Sunhee's words, such as *and*, *but*, and *so-and-so says*. She thought she had solved the problem, and she might have been justified in believing that she had.

We often present the issue of plagiarism as one of academic honesty and express shock at the practice of "stealing" the ideas of others. We also frequently hear arguments made about cultural differences regarding attitudes toward intellectual property—that some cultures see this "borrowing" of ideas as an act of deference to and respect for the original author. Though cultural differences may indeed play a role, something more is involved here. In the case described here, Sunhee believed that her work was now "honest" by the standards I had outlined in my lecture. Yet it was clearly still unacceptable; it now contained what is often referred to as *patchwork plagiarism*. It is much harder to explain why this kind of work is unacceptable. She was not presenting the work as her own, so why then did I object? The problem is that the paper still contained nothing that was her own. But, she countered, the author said it much better than she ever could, and even if she put the ideas in her own words, the ideas would still not be hers, so what would be the point? Her argument was strengthened when she turned in her final version. It was indeed in her own words. However, because her command of written

English was shaky, it was filled with errors, many of which obscured her meaning. In fact, her second draft had been much clearer than the final draft, and her final grade reflected her problems in written expression. She was both disappointed and perplexed.

> *Pause to consider...*
>
> **Sunhee's situation. She was unhappy with her final grade and my explanation. Do you think her resentment was justified? What would you tell your students about plagiarism? What kinds of activities would help them to avoid patchwork plagiarism?**

One way to help students write better summaries is to have them learn new vocabulary. Unlike native speakers, L2 writers often cannot easily come up with another way of saying the same thing. Summary writing offers an opportunity to practice doing just that. Part of saying the same thing in a different way is finding the right words. This is an opportunity for contextualized vocabulary instruction. In the summary of the racial profiling text, note the words or phrases that are used as substitutes for those used in the text: *singling out, common, explicit discrimination, must be stopped.* Showing learners how to generate new vocabulary will help them avoid plagiarism. At the same time, however, it is important to stress that "your own words" does not mean simply substituting synonyms.

Comparing and Contrasting A final example of subtasks is one that comes up in all sorts of writing, including research papers, five-paragraph essays, technical and laboratory reports, response papers, and even journalistic pieces. Pick up any piece of writing and you are likely to find elements of comparison and contrast. We use comparisons and contrasts in metaphors, analogies, definitions, and descriptions. They make images more vivid, and they can help us understand new concepts. As rhetorical devices, comparing and contrasting offer a method of analysis that can make relationships among ideas clear.

Once again, the first step for learners is to decide that a comparison or contrast is the best way of expressing their ideas. Once a writer has decided on comparison/contrast, what is the next step? Let's return to our oral history project on neighborhood gentrification. Perhaps our writer has interviewed various residents of the neighborhood, both old-timers and those who have recently moved in. For the sake of simplicity, let's say that these two groups have generally different views of the changes in their neighborhood. Thus, a contrastive perspective makes sense. The general observation that the groups have different views says very little by itself, however. How can learners begin to make comparisons or contrasts that will lead to effective writing? One place to begin is **graphic organizers.** As learners sift through their interview notes or tapes, they need to look for recurring themes. These will become the criteria for contrast. On what do the two groups disagree? Increased resources? Rising rents?

TABLE 3.3 Graphic Organizer for Comparison Writing

Points of Comparison/*Contrast*	Perspective of Original Residents	Perspective of New Residents
Rents/assessments	*Higher prices forcing them out*	*Reasonable rents an asset*
New stores	<u>They like new supermarket</u> *Old café gone*	<u>They like new supermarket</u> *New latte shop*
Sense of community	*Feel it's disappearing; blame new residents*	*Do not have any*

Note. Items representing comparison are underlined; items representing contrast are italicized.

Better services? Once students have done some reviewing and brainstorming, they can create a chart that will form the basis for a subsequent paper. Table 3.3 presents a graphic organizer based on the gentrification example. It has been started, but other points of comparison/contrast could be added.

Once writers have charted their points of comparison and contrast, paragraph development comes more easily. Most academic writing books suggest two basic ways to organize such writing: either by separately examining each group (the old and the new residents) in terms of how they view each of the points that will be covered in the discussion, or by going over each of the points, one by one, discussing the two groups' perspective on each (Figure 3.1).

As with the previous two examples, defining and summarizing, it is valuable to introduce contextualized grammar instruction that matches the rhetorical purposes of students' writing, in this case, comparing and contrasting. Choices of structures for comparison will be language specific but will include ways of comparing single words (e.g., *as fast as*) as well as ideas. Most importantly for our purposes, students need to learn the linguistic devices for expressing these rhetorical functions. No matter what the language, such linguistic devices have semantic and syntactic restrictions, and writers need to learn them both. In the following example, we explore some of the linguistic devices for comparing and contrasting in English.

(7) a. The old and the new residents both appreciate some of the improvements that have come with gentrification.
b. There are many points of disagreement (between the two groups).
c. Older residents miss the old café.
d. New residents rave about the latte shop.

The pairs of sentences in (a) and (b) and those in (c) and (d) both express contrast, but the nature of the contrast is rather different. Let's try creating new sentences using the following linking expressions, all of which signal contrast: *however, nevertheless, in contrast, on the contrary, although*.

The old and the new residents both appreciate some of the improvements that have come with gentrification; *however*, there are many points of disagreement.

Two paragraphs:

Three paragraphs:

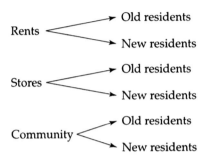

FIGURE 3.1 Comparison/contrast format for an essay

The old and the new residents both appreciate some of the improvements that have come with gentrification; *nevertheless,* there are many points of disagreement.

? The old and the new residents both appreciate some of the improvements that have come with gentrification; *in contrast,* there are many points of disagreement.

? The old and the new residents both appreciate some of the improvements that have come with gentrification; *on the contrary,* there are many points of disagreement.

The old and the new residents both appreciate some of the improvements that have come with gentrification *although* there are many points of disagreement.

Older residents miss the old café; *however,* new residents rave about the latte shop.

? Older residents miss the old café; *nevertheless,* new residents rave about the latte shop.

Older residents miss the old café; *in contrast,* new residents rave about the latte shop.

? Older residents miss the old café; *on the contrary,* new residents rave about the latte shop.

? Older residents miss the old café *although* new residents rave about the latte shop.

Clearly, not all the linking expressions, which are often called **logical connectors** or **transition words,** work equally well in the two sentences. Some are a little strange; others are downright wrong. Even some of those that are not marked with a ? don't sound quite right. For example, *however* works well with just about any two contrasting clauses, whereas *although* works best where the contrast is not absolute, as in (a) and (b). The two clauses do not present black-and-white alternatives as in the second set; rather, it's a case of "yes . . . but." In the more anomalous combinations, our expectations are actually contradicted. For example, in the second set about the old café, the connector *nevertheless* leads us to expect that we will be hearing something further about the old residents, something that is contrary to missing the old café, such as:

> Older residents miss the old café; *nevertheless*, they are flocking to the new latte shop.

On the contrary seems quite wrong in both sets in spite of the fact that it is a connector that marks contrast. Because we generally expect to hear *on the contrary* following a negative statement, which is then reversed and extended, this expression does not fit either context. A more likely context might be:

> Older residents don't miss the old café; *on the contrary*, they couldn't wait for the old firetrap to shut down!

Thus, although many L2 composition textbooks provide lists of these terms as if connectors that share one semantic feature (e.g., contrast) were all alike, these expressions are not interchangeable, and L2 writing teachers need to be aware of the differences among them. This does not mean that teachers should go into exquisite detail about gradations of meaning for all students. What it might mean, though, is that teachers should advise lower proficiency L2 writers of English to stick to all-purpose connectors such as *however*. As learners become more proficient and attempt to use more specialized connectors, teachers can provide explicit information on their use, as well as contextualized practice.

There is another distinction to be made in this small set of connectors: The sentences with *although* are slightly different from all the others. This is because *although* is also syntactically different from the rest of the connectors. This is a difference in structure rather than meaning. *Although* is used to connect a main clause and subordinate clause, whereas all the others connect two main clauses. This means there are additional differences—differences in distribution and punctuation. *Although* introduces a subordinate clause and thus requires a main clause as well. The other connectors can introduce a single (main) clause.

> **Although* there are many points of disagreement.

> *However*, there are many points of disagreement.

These examples are limited to the marking of contrast and are specific to English, but the concerns involved in the use of different words and phrases are not restricted to this semantic domain or to English. It can also be helpful to know something about learners' L1s. For example, in Chinese, contrast markers are generally found in both clauses, something like this:

> *Although* it was late, *but* he finished studying for the exam.

Writing teachers need to understand the grammar of writing in order to understand students' difficulties and explain to them what they are doing wrong. We discuss the role of grammar in teaching writing in greater detail in Chapter 7.

Reading to Discover Structure

We have explored direct ways of showing learners important features of written discourse. It is also useful to encourage learners to read to discover grammatical and discourse features. This is a very different process from reading for meaning. Reading for linguistic features can help learners to notice how structural elements operate in discourse and also provide authentic contextualized examples of their usage. Consider this short section of text in English:

> A new analysis of a major study of childhood nutrition shows that early maturing girls are more likely than other girls to be obese, whereas in boys, early developers are less likely to be obese than other males. Although previous studies have suggested that early maturity is associated with obesity in females, little was known about the relationship in boys until now. The finding of a reverse association between early maturity and obesity in boys sheds new light upon this issue, providing additional evidence for the influence of sexual maturity on fatness.[6]

At first glance, from the point of view of a native speaker, there seems to be little of note in this passage. However, a closer analysis shows that it can offer many insights to the inexperienced writer. For example, the following grammatical and syntactical features can be found in the first sentence:

- Article use: The new referents *new analysis* and *study* are introduced with *a*. The second clause contains examples of generic article use, with *girls, boys,* and *males* used with no article. These are points of confusion for many L2 learners.
- Complex nominals: This sentence has several examples of how nominals are formed in English. These "heavy" nouns are difficult for learners. Teachers can help learners consider the difference between the *nutrition of children* and *childhood nutrition*, as well as the many alternatives to *early maturing girls*, such as, *girls who reach maturity early*.
- Comparisons: This sentence contains a clausal marker of contrast, *whereas*, and a verbal marker of comparison, *are more likely than*. Though the former may have been covered in a previous ESL class, it is less likely that the latter has been taught.
- Cohesion: Still in the first sentence, cohesion is achieved in part through the repetition of *obese* and *girls* and the use of the synonyms *boys* and *males*.

Similarly, the following features are found in the second sentence:

- Contrast: This sentence also shows clausal contrast (*although*). Why has the author chosen to place the subordinate clause first?
- Extratextual reference: The author ties the text to information outside of it with the reference to *previous* studies, perhaps assuming some knowledge on the part of the reader.

- Article use: The use of the definite article in *the relationship* requires the reader to infer that the relationship is already known. Yet the word *relationship* has not been used; rather, the verb phrase *is associated with* is used to indicate relationship.
- Verb/preposition collocation: *Associate* requires the preposition *with*.
- Tense use: The choice of the present perfect implies that association has been suggested by many studies over a long period of time up until the present moment, setting up the context for the contrast presented by the current study. This is an extremely common device in reporting research.
- Quantifier use: The choice of the quantifier *little* leads the reader to infer a negative evaluation on the part of the writer: *too little*. Many L2 learners have difficulty distinguishing between this usage and *a little*.

This analysis illustrates some of the features of this short text. It is unlikely that a teacher would want to go into this level of detail for a long text; it would be too overwhelming. Yet unless this kind of activity is occasionally included in writing class, it is unlikely that learners will notice many of these features on their own. With extensive reading and exposure, of course, learners can gradually absorb these patterns, just as native speakers do. However, this process takes a very long time, and many L2 writers do not have that luxury.

So far, we have looked at a variety of activities that will help learners of different proficiency levels to improve their language proficiency and writing skills. One thing we have not yet considered is how technology can enhance both of these processes, a topic to which we now turn.

TECHNOLOGY IN SECOND LANGUAGE WRITING

Several references to the use of technology have been made in this chapter. The following section briefly reviews how computers can be used in teaching L2 writing. The field of technology in language learning is more generally referred to as **computer-assisted language learning (CALL),** and there are two major types: self-contained software packages and network-based activities. In addition, there are multimedia applications that include videos, music, and so on, which are not related directly to the teaching of writing. The field of CALL is large and growing all the time. Much of the work done in L2 writing and technology also references the even larger field of computers and composition, to which entire books and journals are devoted. It is beyond the scope of this book to discuss all the possibilities of technology either in language learning or in composition. This brief survey simply outlines the relevant issues and some future directions in the field.

Technology offers many exciting options in teaching L2 writing, but there are drawbacks as well. Many students and their teachers become frustrated with the barriers that computers sometimes present: hardware and software glitches, the complexity of tasks that are more immediately accessible with pencil and paper, and the occasionally misleading assistance computers can give. Teachers need to consider whether the potential headaches of the electronic classroom are offset by the advantages it offers. Finally, access is always an important issue. Not all L2 writers have access to computers, to appropriate software, or to the Internet.

Self-Contained CALL Activities

Word Processing

If learners have access to computers, they should be encouraged to start using them for their L2 writing. Although most of the texts they produce are relatively short and might be done more easily longhand, students will soon see how much easier it is to revise and edit when they have an electronic version of their text. Word processing is undoubtedly, the most common use of the computer in the writing classroom. Intuitively, we feel that composing on the computer should ease the writing process and consequently improve the written product. The entire notion of separate drafts may even be irrelevant because there is no clear point at which one electronic draft is finished and a revision begins. Revision, especially deep revisions that involve moving text around, is much easier on the computer than in longhand. Additionally, writers can try out revisions and reverse them if they don't work out.

However, this ease and flexibility may also mean that learners invest less time in planning. In fact, studies of the effect of word processing on writing have had somewhat mixed results, although most have been small scale and few have examined L2 writers. Some have looked at the effects on writing process, some on final product, and some on student attitudes. The most robust effect that has been found is that writing done on the computer appears to be longer than writing done with paper and pencil. Some studies have found more and a greater variety of revisions on computer-written papers. Finally, most studies have found improved student attitudes toward writing.

There can be some practical drawbacks to using the computer in class. Not all students have had keyboarding experience, and there are the inevitable password glitches, malfunctions, and lost documents. In spite of these problems, current reality demands that students use word processing for their papers, and they would do well to start using it in their L2 writing class. At the same time, these tools are only as good as their users. Students must be shown how to exploit the benefits of word processing programs. The fact that revision is easier on the computer does not by itself impart strategies for effective revision. Like all other aspects of the teaching of writing, word processing as a tool in the writing process needs to be modeled and explained so that new writers can become familiar with its features.

Spelling and Grammar Checkers and On-Line Dictionaries

Most word processors are now equipped with various tools for checking spelling and grammar. Some people argue that spelling checkers prevent learners from acquiring automaticity in their spelling knowledge. This may be true, and if so, it represents a trade-off. Most teachers prefer that their students spell-check all their writing before handing it in; indeed, there seems to be little excuse for turning in texts with misspelled words. Of course, spelling checkers cannot catch errors of the *form/from* variety, but they can go a long way toward improving formal accuracy. Although some writers may simply accept the corrections provided by the spelling checker without much thought, other learners benefit from the attention that the checker draws to their errors. For them, it may be all that is needed to raise their awareness and make changes in their explicit knowledge. With spelling checkers, there are no false negatives. If a word is incorrectly spelled (i.e., doesn't represent the spelling of *any* word), the checker will catch it. On the other hand, it will flag many words that are acceptable and miss others that are wrong choices.

Grammar checkers present a very different set of circumstances. First, grammar checkers often flag as questionable sentences that are perfectly acceptable and appropriate. Native speakers are in a position to reject the grammar checker's advice. This is less likely to be true with L2 writers. In addition, L2 writers may not know how to act on the advice that the checker gives. They may simply accept the suggestions of the checker without question and assume that there are no remaining errors. Thus, grammar checkers may promote dependence rather than useful, proactive monitoring strategies. As a result, many L2 writing instructors prefer to develop their own editing-strategy inventories. Some software is designed specifically to assist L2 writers, and it is generally easier for L2 writers to use than the standard tools in word processing packages. Software is available for foreign language learning as well, as part of writing-assistant packages, such as Didaktik for German, Atajo for Spanish, and Système-D for French. As with all other reference tools, the use of these programs needs to be modeled so that learners can see their utility.

Many L2 writers are also aware of on-line dictionaries and translators that are available on the Internet. However, both teachers and learners should be aware of the limitations of such resources. They often provide single-word translations for words that may have complex and multiple meanings. For example, a recent test for the English-to-Spanish translation of the word *take* yielded *tomar*. The translation is not wrong, of course, but such "definitions" can easily lead an L2 writer astray.

Concordances/Corpus-Based Tools

Concordances offer learners a chance to see how words are really used in the language they are learning. These tools are based on large corpora of millions of words of written and/or spoken text. They can show learners how words function in context and how they pattern with other words and with specific grammatical structures, such as tenses. Some concordances also offer information about discourse and about the social context in which words or structures are likely to be used: in speaking or writing, in different kinds of genres, more by women or by men, and so on. Clearly, these tools are for more proficient users, but they offer a wealth of information that is not readily available in textbooks or even dictionaries. L2 learners might discover, for example, that in speaking, Americans rarely use the modal *must* to express obligation (*I must go to the store*). It is limited almost exclusively to inferential meaning (*They must be stuck in traffic*). These are facts they may not have learned in their language classes; indeed, they may contradict what they have been taught. Commercial concordances are available for classrooms, and others are available on the Internet. Some of these services are free; others require subscription but allow free trial demonstrations. Because websites are subject to rapid change, URLs are not included here. However, they can be found readily by searching with the key words *corpus* and *concordance*.

Text Analyzers/Writing Assistants

The tools described thus far are designed to provide general assistance with language—with grammatical accuracy and word choice. Several other packages are available to help learners throughout the composing process. Most of these programs include assistance at the prewriting, drafting, revision, and editing stages. One such package, Daedalus Integrated Writing Environment (DIWE), is a suite of programs that helps students generate ideas and plan their writing. It can also be used to facilitate peer response activities (see Chapter 4). The programs offer interactive features that allow students to chat with the teacher about their developing text (see Responding Electronically later in this section). All on-line discussions and conferences can be recorded as transcripts and stored on the network server or saved to a disk. Students can review the session and use the ideas developed during interaction later in their writing. Teachers can use transcripts to document who is participating and to identify problems. They can also unobtrusively observe the small group interaction, intervening where appropriate.

Essentially, these programs deliver, by computer, much of the writing instruction that we explore in Chapter 4. They offer brainstorming tips and open-ended questions that can help learners expand, narrow, or develop the topic. Once a draft is completed, the software generates questions that can help students revise their text. Some L2 educators express concern that L2 writers will limit themselves to the somewhat generic questions and suggestions offered by these programs, such as, *What else do I know about this topic?* (*El tema: ¿cómo se define?*). Like grammar checkers, the programs were designed for native speakers, so they can be a challenge for L2 students. Teachers need to make sure that students have understood the questions and suggestions. Again, if the use of these programs is carefully modeled, they can offer students both assistance and autonomy in the writing process.

Network-Based Learning

Network-based language learning differs from other kinds of CALL in that it focuses on the communicative aspects of language. As such, it also offers a social rather than a solely cognitive perspective. Instead of just interacting with the packaged software, learners interact with other people when they use intelligent, network-based CALL.

Pause to consider...

the advantages of network-based CALL for L2 writing instruction over earlier, self-contained software-based CALL. How do the contexts of the two types of instruction differ? How do learning opportunities differ?

Email, Discussion Boards

The application that is most likely to be familiar to learners is email. Email seems to be ubiquitous; thus, many students may already use it regularly. There are many uses for email, from management issues (e.g., *Read Chapter 2 for next week*), to collaborative brainstorming, to the provision of feedback by the teacher or peers. For FL learners, email, in the form of keypals (an updated version of pen pals), can be an especially effective instructional tool, because it puts a human face on the language. There are international organizations that can assist in setting up keypal relationships or linking an entire classroom to one in another country. (The best known can be found at http://www. iecc.org/.) Email can also be used to link classrooms or students within the same country, city, or institution, as a way of helping learners to practice their new language in an informal setting. Email is an asynchronous application, that is, writers can compose their message at their own pace and then send it. The receiver picks up the message later. Of course, the instant messaging function available with some Internet service providers has allowed these exchanges to occur practically in real time. In spite of its asynchronous format, email is very message oriented, even for native speakers. Students will probably not use formal, targetlike forms or be terribly concerned about accuracy.

Discussion boards (also called message boards or newsgroups), another form of asynchronous communication, allow groups of learners to discuss topics, often several at once. The different topics are called *threads*. Threads can be set up by the teacher or initiated by students. All users can respond to initial prompts, and the discussion can continue as long as the board's moderator permits. Discussion boards use simple technology, so they are accessible and inexpensive. Discussion boards can be used in L2 writing classes to stimulate and extend class discussion on a topic prior to a formal writing assignment. Like journaling, it is an informal, ungraded space in which learners can write freely and focus on development of ideas. Again, the practice must be modeled for students who are unfamiliar with it, perhaps with posts to the discussion given initially as required assignments.

Chats/MOOS

Email relationships are two sided and asynchronous. For interaction in real time with many participants, students may want to try chat rooms that are available for L2 learners. Even more high tech than chat rooms are **MOOs,** in which entire environments are created and learners can take on new identities, or they can simply observe without participating. (The term MOO comes from Multi-User Domain [MUD], Object Oriented.) The advantage of these technologies is that, unlike email, they are synchronous, that is, the interaction takes place in real time and the feedback is instant. This real-time feature can be a double-edged sword, however, because interruptions and overlaps can often make these exchanges difficult to keep up with and follow, especially for low-proficiency learners. By the time a learner has composed a response, the conversation will probably have moved on.

Responding Electronically

Both teachers and fellow classmates can respond to a written text electronically using a variety of programs, simply with email or with specially designed software (e.g., DIWE). Doing so has the advantage of providing more immediate feedback than is possible with papers that are handed in for teacher response. This practice also obviates the need for physical proximity. Research on the use of networked classrooms suggests that the exchange among students may be more equitable than in face-to-face interaction, because less vocal students participate more in electronic exchanges. Writing-assistant programs and most electronic classroom software (e.g., Blackboard's Discussion) include a chat function. Some, such as DIWE's Interchange, are language neutral and have been widely used in FL classes. Students can be placed in peer feedback groups and exchange views on student texts that are viewed on a separate screen or, in the case of remote communication, sent as attachments. With writing-assistant programs, this kind of exchange generally has to be done on site, because the software typically resides on institutional servers rather than on personal computers. Programs designed for distance learning, such as Blackboard and Web CT, can accommodate this function from home. A final significant advantage of responding electronically is that the teacher (or classmate) can respond directly on the document; when responses are made on paper, the process can be cumbersome and sometimes confusing.

Internet-Based Research Activities

This topic of web-based research activities could be and is the topic of entire books, so clearly, it is beyond the scope of our discussion here. As we are all increasingly aware, a wealth of information is available on the Internet, covering a bewildering array of topics. For FL learners, it can bring resources to the classroom and home computer, such as FL newspapers and magazines, that were not previously available. As with print materials, students will not know how to exploit these resources unless they are shown how. Another consideration is that the content of websites is, for the most part, unregulated. Part of teaching students to use the Internet for research is to help them make judgments about which information is reliable and what is simply someone's personal opinion, or worse. There are many sites, most of them library sites, devoted to helping students learn how to evaluate web-based information. A final issue in having students use the Internet is plagiarism. Because the material is so readily accessible, web-based plagiarism can be an even bigger problem than print-based plagiarism.

In this chapter, we have concentrated on target tasks for L2 writers. However, these tasks cannot be accomplished in a single step. What we know about the writing process tells us that writers go through many steps in completing any piece of writing, often returning to earlier stages of the process to revise what they have written. In the next chapter, we focus on this process and on how teachers can most effectively help L2 learners become better writers.

SUMMARY

The following general guidelines are useful for designing a writing program for second language students:

- The program should include a lot of writing practice.
- Students should write in a variety of genres and for a variety of purposes. These should reflect authentic genres and writing purposes.
- Teachers must provide scaffolding for writing tasks. This scaffolding may take a variety of forms, such as beginning with a simpler version of the task, breaking it down into steps, modeling the process, and providing feedback.
- Content and activities should be recycled.
- Course and teacher expectations should be clear to the students.
- The course should reflect the twin goals of increasing language and writing proficiency. Where possible, tasks should speak to both purposes.

Writing can be used for language practice, though it is also important for the writing to have a communicative purpose. Writing can facilitate language learning through strengthening form-meaning connections, increasing monitoring, and creating communicative need. Writing activities for lower proficiency students include interviews, strip stories, writing advice and instruction, and journaling, as well as collaborative activities such dictoglosses and scripts.

For higher proficiency students, the activities should be oriented more toward academic writing, especially expository writing. A needs analysis can establish the actual writing needs of a specific set of students. Possibilities include reports, summaries, case studies, and bibliographies, in addition to the well-established five-paragraph essay. Learners may not be ready to tackle such tasks without assistance, and teachers may have to address the subtasks involved in doing so. Academic writing activities can be divided generally into those that involve gathering and generating information and those that involve analyzing and organizing information. For the first category, possible activities include surveys, observations, and oral histories. For the second category, activities may require students to analyze, synthesize, or evaluate information they have generated. Again, these tasks may need to be broken down further into subtasks such as defining, summarizing, and comparing and contrasting.

In addition to learning these skills, learners need to become active readers and work to increase their vocabulary. Small vocabularies can be a barrier to success in both academic reading and writing.

Finally, technology can greatly facilitate the teaching of L2 writing. There are also drawbacks to its use, however. Valuable uses of computers include word processing, electronic checkers and dictionaries, concordances and other corpus-based tools, writing-assistance programs, and networked communication for collaboration and feedback.

CHAPTER NOTES

1. A *classifier* is a grammatical word (or words) used to mark semantic classes of nouns in some languages, such as Japanese, Chinese, and Thai. For example, classifiers

may describe the shape or purpose of these nouns. Thus, instead of saying *pencil*, you might have to say something like *"long thing" pencil.*

2. The italicized words should offer some clues:

   Giselle is a high school student in Chicago. *She* always has a suntan, even in January. How does she do *this*? She doesn't go to the beach every weekend. *Instead*, she goes to *a tanning salon* once a week. *She* agreed to talk to us about her visits to *the salon. However, she* did not want to give her last name because she doesn't want *her mother* to find out about *them. Her mother* thinks Giselle's tan just comes from a bottle of *tanning lotion*. Using *lotion* is much *safer* for your skin than going to a tanning salon. Giselle knows tanning is *not healthy for her skin*. She does it *anyway* because all the other kids in her school do it.

3. For an example, consult "Body Rituals Among the Nacerima," by H. Miner, 1958, *American Anthropologist, 58*, pp. 503–507. Also available at http://www.stanford.edu/~davidf/nacirema.html.

4. *The Concise Oxford Dictionary of Linguistics* (p. 81), by P. Matthews, 1997, London: Oxford University Press. Reprinted by permission of Oxford University Press.

5. ACLU on-line archives. http://archive.aclu.org/profiling/. Retrieved October 24, 2002. Reprinted by permission of the American Civil Liberties Union.

6. News Bureau, University of Illinois at Chicago. (November 1, 2002). Available at http://tigger.uic.edu/htbin/cgiwrap/bin/newsbureau/cgibin/index.cgi?from=Releases&to=Release&id= 306&fromhome=1.

READ MORE ABOUT IT

General Reading on L2 Writing Pedagogy and Classroom Activities

Grabe, W., & Kaplan, R. (1996). *Theory and practice of writing*. London: Longman.

Johns, A. (1997). *Text, role and context*. Cambridge: Cambridge University Press.

*Reid, J. (1993). *Teaching ESL writing*. Englewood Cliffs, NJ: Regents-Prentice Hall.

Reid, J., & Kroll, B. (1995). Designing and assessing effective classroom writing assignments for NES and ESL students. *Journal of Second Language Writing, 4*, 17–41.

*White, R. (1995). *New ways in teaching writing*. Alexandria, VA: TESOL.

Needs Analysis

Carson, J. (2001). A task analysis of reading and writing in academic contexts. In D. Belcher & A. Hirvela (Eds.), *Linking literacies* (pp. 48–83). Ann Arbor, MI: University of Michigan Press.

Horowitz, D. (1986). What professors actually require: Academic tasks for the ESL classroom. *TESOL Quarterly, 20*, 445–462.

Reid, J. (2001). Advanced EAP writing and curriculum design: What do they need to know? In T. Silva & P. Matsuda (Eds.), *On second language writing* (pp. 143–169). Mahwah, NJ: Erlbaum.

Plagiarism

Currie, P. (1998). Staying out of trouble: Apparent plagiarism and academic survival. *Journal of Second Language Writing, 7*, 1–18.

*Accessible reading for beginning students

Foreign Language and Bilingual Contexts

*Olmedo, I. (1993). Junior historians: Doing oral history with ESL and bilingual students. *TESOL Journal, 2,* 7–10.

*Reichelt, M. (2001). Writing in a second-year German class. *Foreign Language Annals, 34,* 235–345.

Technology and Second/Foreign Language Writing

*Bicknell, J. (1999). Promoting writing and computer literacy skills through student-authored web pages. *TESOL Journal, 8,* 20–26.

*Bikowski, D., & Kessler, G. (2002). Making the most of discussion boards in the ESL classroom. *TESOL Journal, 11,* 27–30.

FLTEACH (Foreign Language Teaching Forum). http://www.cortland.edu/flteach/flteach-res.html. A site with multiple resources for FL teachers, including http://www.cortland.edu/www/flteach/methods/, a module that introduces FL teachers to the use of technology in the classroom.

Schetzer, H., & Warschauer, M. (2000). An electronic literacy approach to network-based language teaching. *Network-based language teaching: Concepts and practice* (pp. 171–185). Cambridge: Cambridge University Press.

Schultz, J. M. (2000). Computers and collaborative writing in the foreign language curriculum. In M. Warschuaer & R. Kern (Eds.), *Network-based language teaching: Concepts and practice* (pp. 121–150). Cambridge: Cambridge University Press.

Sengupta, S. (2001). Exchanging ideas with peers in network-based classrooms: An aid or a pain? *Language Learning & Technology, 5,* 103–134. http://llt.msu.edu/vol5num1/sengupta/default.pdf. Retrieved February 16, 2003.

CHAPTER 4

Teaching the Writing Process

Chapter 2 introduced the process approach to teaching writing and pointed out some differences between the process-oriented approach and those approaches that focus more on the writing *product*. We return to the writing process here. Remember that there is no single writing process; thus, how writers approach their task will vary from one individual to another and with task and context.

CONSIDERING AUDIENCE AND PURPOSE

As we have noted, the process approach to writing involves more than just dividing assignments into stages. The emphasis throughout is on the production and communication of ideas, which requires that learners focus from the outset on *purpose* and *audience*. For whom are they writing? What do their readers know about the topic they have chosen? In most product-oriented approaches, the writing is shaped and given purpose by the rhetorical form to be practiced. For example, students might be asked to practice writing about a process or to illustrate a chain of cause and effect. With these rhetorical patterns as starting points, students then have to think of a process (e.g., making a microscope slide for biology class) or a cause and effect (e.g., the causes and effects of premature birth) about which to write. It matters little whether these topics are of interest. With process writing, in contrast, writers begin with a purpose and only then consider what rhetorical forms and structure best fit their purpose.

In school, students usually write because their teacher tells them to, the assignment is due the next day, and they want to pass the course. In the world outside the classroom, people write for real purposes: They write grant applications, poems, memos, instructions, reports, and news articles. It can be a challenge to bring this sense of reality into the classroom; everyone in the class understands that part of the purpose of any task is to practice and display writing skills. To the extent that it is possible, however, L2 writers will be well served if their writing activities can be given a sense of purpose.

One way of bringing both purpose and a sense of audience into writing activities, even for lower proficiency learners, is to exchange personal information. This exchange can take a variety of forms, both structured and open ended. Students are usually interested in getting to know one another, and they may be even more interested in learning about people they don't know. The following are a few possibilities for this kind of writing; they are short pieces, not full-fledged essays that will go through the multiple-draft process.

- Interviewing classmates
  In L2 classes, students often come from many different countries; in contrast, in an FL class, it is likely that students' backgrounds and experiences will be more similar. Shared background simply means that the specific topic will have to be tailored to the group of students—perhaps musical tastes or high school experiences. In both FL and L2 classes, specifying the topic will help ensure that students stay on task and will make them more accountable. As we noted in Chapter 3, this kind of activity can also be expanded into a publishable project.
- Journal partners
  Sometimes exchanges work best with unfamiliar partners. Some teachers prefer "secret" journal friends; that is, they match students from different classes who don't know each other and have them exchange journals once a week, again usually assigning a specific topic. This activity can work between two sets of L2 writers or between L2 writers and native speakers. In college ESL programs, the activity can be done most easily in exchange with native-speaker composition classes.
- Keypals
  For students with access to the Internet, keypals are an attractive alternative, as mentioned in Chapter 3. Keypal exchanges usually involve two languages: English and another language. FL learners in North America can practice the language they are learning, and the keypal can practice English. Again, it usually works best if teachers give specific assignments rather than just letting students chat. One problem for FL learners in the United States is that the English of their keypals is usually far superior to their FL proficiency. Lower proficiency learners (and their keypals) are easily frustrated because they are often unable to express anything beyond the simplest thoughts. It is easy for the conversation to settle into mostly English.

In these activities, the purpose and audience are clear. Other writing genres have similarly explicit purposes, such as writing letters to the editor, which are staples of the writing classroom. In academic writing, however, the purpose of student writing is usually to display knowledge and writing facility, and the audience is usually the teacher, no matter how much she tries to convince her students otherwise.

APPROACHING WRITING AS A RECURSIVE DISCOVERY PROCESS

Writing is not just production of text; it is also a learning and thinking process in which writers may discover what they think as a result of composing. Writing is a naturally recursive process rather than a linear, predetermined set of activities. A process approach stresses the overlapping stages of writing, such as prewriting, drafting, revising, and editing. Many new writers think that they should sit down and write their assignment in one draft. Once they have written a text, it is finished. In contrast, in process writing classes, students are required to reconsider and revise most of what they write. As much time is spent in planning and revising as in writing.

Those who are skilled in L1 composing may tap into some of this ability when writing in their L2, naturally revising as they write. Yet clearly, emerging L2 proficiency also has a role, and all but the most proficient L2 writers will be unable to simply transfer their L1 skills to their L2 writing. It is generally not realistic to expect L2 writers to produce a sophisticated written product in a language they only partially control. Those with less developed L1 composing skills, such as the generation 1.5 or heritage learners we discussed in Chapter 1, face an even bigger challenge, because their academic literacy skills may be weak in their home language as well. Unskilled writers generally spend less time on planning and revising, which are crucial to effective writing, and they may get hung up on surface-level revision and grammatical errors. Unfortunately, this heightened concern with grammar is sometimes reinforced by teachers if there is primary stress on the linguistic accuracy of the final text. Finally, L2 writers need more time than native speakers for all phases of the writing process. They also need more discussion and more feedback in order to compensate for their lack of intuition and linguistic knowledge, a topic we explore in the next chapter. In short, all writers, and especially L2 writers, benefit from approaching writing as a multiple-stage, recursive process of discovery and learning. We turn now to a closer look at those stages.

Getting Started: Invention and Discovery Strategies

Some L2 writers have trouble generating and developing ideas for writing. To assist them, many textbooks present invention and discovery strategies for use in the early stages of composing, or *prewriting*. Some of these strategies are more appropriate than others for L2 writers. For example, those that depend on fluency may not work well with L2 writers, who may struggle with vocabulary and structure choices. In addition, strategies for getting started may vary considerably according to the assignment, or *prompt*. To explore this idea, let's consider four different examples of writing assignments from L2 textbooks:

1. Write about a special food from your country.
2. Write a short response to the following question: What is the value of foreign language education?
3. Write an essay describing an experience in which you were the object of a stereotype or prejudice. Did this experience change you in any way? How? Compare your experience to the one described in the story we read in class.
4. Write an essay (3–5 pages) explaining if and how you think views of the American Dream have changed in the last 50 years. Be sure to state your claim clearly and to support it, using the information in the class readings and the data from the surveys you conducted. Your grade will

depend on how clearly and persuasively you present your argument. You will also be evaluated on your essay's grammatical accuracy. The class will choose the best three essays to publish on our American Dream class website.

Pause to consider...

the differences among these prompts. Would some of them work better than others? Would some work better with specific students or in particular contexts?

These assignments vary considerably in length, specificity, and clarity. Clearly, they cannot all be approached in the same way. Prompt (1) is quite broad and offers almost no guidance about how the writer should proceed, yet such a prompt is not unusual. For these kinds of assignments, **invention techniques** are often a good way for writers to begin. Most writing textbooks have adopted the same invention techniques that are commonly used with native speakers. Two widely used techniques are *free writing* and *looping*. In free writing (or fast writing), learners write continuously on a topic without taking their pens off the paper for 5 to 10 minutes. If they can't think of something right away, they write, "I don't know what to write" repeatedly, until an idea emerges. They then go back over their writing to look for useful ideas that may have emerged. The idea is that if they don't think too hard and don't worry about form, something useful may come out, almost without their realizing it.

Looping is a recursive technique in which writers write for a few moments—perhaps a paragraph or two—then go back and summarize what they have written in one sentence, then repeat the process, each time creating a new "loop."

Pause to consider...

these invention techniques. Do you think they are appropriate for L2 writers? Why or why not?

Other techniques depend less on fluency. With an unguided prompt like (1), the main goal is to generate lots of ideas about the topic. Writers can choose from among these ideas later when they begin drafting, considering which ideas might be appropriate for different purposes or audiences. For example, copy for a tourist brochure describing an indigenous dish might be one outcome; a description of the role of food in a religious holiday might be another. One method for generating ideas is unstructured *brainstorming*, in which an individual or, better still, a class simply lists as many ideas about the topic as possible. Brainstorming can help learners develop the topic, narrow it, broaden it, or consider different audiences and ways of organizing information. Learners should understand that not all of the ideas generated in this process will be used when drafting begins. The idea is to begin with more than are needed and select among those relevant to the task and its purpose.

Simply jotting down notes can also be an effective way to begin. Consider topic (2), the importance of foreign language education. This prompt provides slightly more guidance, because it seems to suggest that a persuasive text is in order. Thus, notes would probably consist of a list of reasons. A writer might note down:

Importance of FL for me

- Economic opportunities
- Making friends
- Learning about other cultures
- Reading publications in another language

Importance for my country

- Economic need
- Globalization
- International relations

In this example, the writer has broken the topic into two main categories beforehand, almost like an *outline*. Some teachers suggest that writers make a formal outline before they write, and indeed, some writers find this useful. However, requiring an outline in advance assumes that writers know what they are going to write about, and this is not always the case. Categories are often only discovered later.

Some teachers and students prefer *mind maps,* or *brain diagrams,* as shown in Figure 4.1, a response to prompt (1) (*Write about a special food from your country).* Mind maps are useful because they do not require that students already have a fully developed and organized set of ideas and because they allow the relationship among subtopics to emerge more clearly than in unstructured brainstorming. Using the diagram in Figure 4.1, the writer might discover that he has three potential subtopics: how to prepare the dish, the memories it evokes, and the role food appreciation plays in Singapore. With this material, he will be well prepared to begin drafting.

Some teachers and writers prefer to get started on a topic by asking *questions.* For example, prompt (3), about experience with stereotypes, offers more guidance for the writer than the first two prompts. It asks for a narrative and for comparative reference to in-class readings, but it also seems to ask for more—what the story might mean in a broader context. Here are some questions that might get the writer started:

- What is a stereotype? How does it differ from prejudice? (definition, contrast)
- What happened to me? (description, narrative)
- Had anything like this ever happened to me before? To the character in the story we read in class? (comparison/contrast)

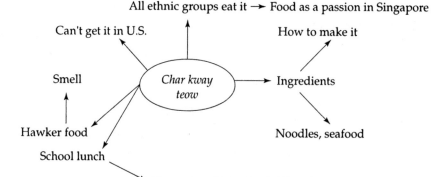

FIGURE 4.1 Example of a mind map

- What was the author's point? (analysis)
- Why did it happen? (determination of cause, evaluation)
- What was my response to the event? How did I feel? (reflection)
- What did I learn? How did it change the way I think or act? How do I feel now? (analysis of result)
- What advice can I give based on the experience? (application of experience)

Each of the questions suggests a subtask of the assignment and even the rhetorical form that it might take (given in parentheses).

The last prompt (4), on the American Dream, provides the most guidance on how the writer should approach the assignment, what the teacher's expectations are for the essay, and how it will be evaluated. For this assignment, invention strategies may not be as necessary. With this kind of writing task, the first and, for some, the most difficult step is the reading phase. Writers first need to examine the prompt carefully and decide what is being asked. It seems the writer will have to

- summarize, analyze, and incorporate material from the readings;
- summarize, analyze, and incorporate findings of the surveys;
- compare and contrast various views/definitions of the American Dream;
- provide reasons for differences/changes in these views;
- perhaps make predictions about future perspectives on the American Dream.

Learners need practice in this first step of analyzing the prompt. It would not be obvious to many of them from the short prompt that the assignment requires all of the preceding elements. Thus, although the prompt is more precise than the others and offers considerable guidance on how it should be answered, it is also in many ways the most difficult. For this reason, any L2 writing class aimed at academic writing should include practice in deconstructing prompts. We return to this issue later in this chapter in the section on essay test questions.

Creating the First Draft

Having used one or more of these techniques to get started, the writer can begin *drafting*. Although there is no clear division between prewriting and writing, at some point the writer will have to simply begin. At this stage the process is called drafting, because there is no expectation that this is its final form. Many textbooks on writing begin by telling students to draft an introductory paragraph, in which they state their central claim, or *thesis*, and their plans for developing it. The problem is that often learners are not quite sure what their thesis is (or even what a thesis is!) or what their plans are for supporting it. Instead, they discover it as they write. Thus, although starting at the beginning makes sense for some learners, for others, it works better to start in the middle. Learners should understand that they are not writing a final draft and that it is both normal and productive to return to earlier stages in the process. It is possible—and often useful—to do more prewriting even after drafting has begun.

Let's return to our earlier examples. In prompt (4), writers are asked to address the topic of the American Dream, using materials they have gathered and read. It is quite possible that they have not yet formulated a clear view of the changing perception of the Dream, even though they have read the articles and gathered survey data. Therefore, it may make sense for them to begin the drafting process there, that is, with what they already know. As they summarize the data they have collected, they may begin to discern generalizations, ones that they can compare to their summaries of the readings. Only then will they be able to discover what their thesis should be.

Eventually, though, they will have to write an introduction to their paper, and in most cases, it will have to include their thesis, or main point. This is sometimes the hardest part, especially for inexperienced writers. One way of assisting them is to reduce the use of pedagogical jargon and metalanguage. If the term *thesis statement* is daunting, the concept of main point may be more accessible. Whatever terms are used, writers must ask themselves:

- What is my paper about?
- What am I claiming?
- Can I support that claim with the rest of what I have written/will write?

Students may not know that, in fact, many good writers often go back and forth between the body of their paper and their introduction as they write. If we look back at our prewriting for prompt (1), our writer might have begun with a thesis such as

Char kway teow is a popular food from Singapore.

Then he could try to build an introduction around this statement. However, there is not a great deal that a writer can do with this thesis statement. It will not easily support a paragraph, let alone an essay. What could he possibly write to support such a claim? Statistics on the number of people who eat this dish per day? This does not seem like a promising avenue to pursue. But if we return to the mind map (See Figure 4.1), we can discern a richer set of ideas, something that could not necessarily have been predicted or developed if the writer had begun from a predetermined thesis statement. Closer examination of the mind map reveals that the invention technique resulted in the following subtopics:

- Preparation of the dish: ingredients, cooking method
- Memories: school lunches shared with classmates, evenings at the street markets with friends, the smells and sounds of the hawker stalls
- Singaporeans' love of food: Diverse members of ethnic groups appreciate one another's cuisines; all Singaporeans who go abroad pine for food from home; food is something all citizens can agree on

In reviewing this list of topics, the writer might see that the actual dish has receded in importance. Instead, another topic emerges, perhaps one about food as a theme of life in Singapore, one that both acts as a source of national unity and pride and reflects the rich diversity of the population. This topic is something that the writer could probably only discover by "writing from the middle." The piece is no longer about char kway teow; it is about a broader and much more interesting topic.

Whether writers choose to start writing from the middle or the beginning, they will need to write a clear introduction. Although the prose of experienced writers will vary from this format, in general, inexperienced writers will need to include the following in their introduction:

- The topic of the piece—what is the text about? In this example, the topic might be the role food plays in Singaporean life.
- A thesis statement—what am I claiming? In our example, the thesis statement could be, *Food illustrates both the diversity and unity of Singaporean society.*
- (A statement of a plan for development of the supporting arguments).

The last may be optional, depending on the length of the text. The rest of the text should support the point(s) that are proposed in that introduction. Of course, longer, more complex texts may contain several cycles of claims and support, but beginning writers will probably begin with this fairly straightforward pattern.

Even with good preparation, writers can get stuck when they draft, wondering how they should develop their idea further. Some writing experts suggest a variation on the questions we looked at in the prewriting stage.[1] These *planning cues* can help writers continue generating and developing ideas. Teachers can develop their own set of planning cues that are appropriate for their classes. Students can select among these cues, using them to think of new ideas and inspire further development. Here are some examples.

For developing new ideas:

- A point I have not addressed is . . .
- Another aspect of this argument is . . .
- The reason for this is . . .
- This reminds me of . . .

For elaborating a point:

- An example of this is . . .
- My opinion of this is . . .

- Another reason for this is . . .
- This is true, but . . .
- Another way to express this is . . .

For improving a text:

- Maybe this idea is not relevant . . .
- I am getting off topic so . . .
- My argument would be more convincing if . . .
- I could clarify my point by . . .
- I could make this more interesting by . . .

Revising

Writing is hard work, and it is difficult to be objective about our own writing. It is always a good idea for writers to put their draft aside for a while and let some time go by before returning to it. Tight academic schedules often do not permit students this luxury, but writers' ability to revise usually does improve when they are able to leave some time between drafts. In most composition classes, writers will get some kind of feedback between drafts, either from their teacher or from peers or both. We discuss feedback in detail in Chapter 5.

For many writers, a lot of rewriting may actually take place during the drafting process. Such rewriting is sometimes referred to as *internal* revision— an exploration and shaping of ideas—as writers discover what it is they want to say. *External* revision, which may be more familiar, is the shaping of a text for public consumption, including the accommodation of audience.

It is important to distinguish between editing, which is usually limited to addressing surface-level issues, and *revising*. Revising, as the Latin root implies, is to look at a piece of writing again, to reconsider the entire piece and rework it as needed. Most inexperienced writers, including many L2 writers, tend to focus more on editing than on revising, making small changes in short stretches of text rather than critically considering the text as a whole. FL learners are particularly likely to blur the distinction between editing and revising. Research suggests that they, even more than L2 writers, tend to limit their revision to surface features; in effect, they are editing rather than revising. FL learners may do this in part because they view writing as little more than a demonstration of their language skill. Thus, these learners may be more likely to require explicit instruction on strategies for the revision of content.

Pause to consider...

your own writing process: Do you know what you will write before you begin writing? How much do you backtrack and revise during the drafting process? Do you reread sections and rework them, or do you finish the whole text first? Do you edit grammatical structures and vocabulary as you write, or do you wait until you have finished the draft to do so?

Developing strategies for revision takes a long time, and frankly, writers often resist the process. They have worked hard to produce their text, and they don't want to tear it up and start again. And, in fact, when writers first attempt global revising, their texts sometimes do get worse instead of better! Taking risks and stretching as a writer sometimes involve backsliding. This is because the writers may be attempting something new and more difficult, something for which they do not quite have the resources. Both teachers and students have to be patient with this slow and sometimes painful process. Fortunately, ready access to word processing has made some aspects of this process a lot less painful than it used to be. Moving text around and experimenting with different formats and sequences no longer means hours of retyping.

Despite the advances of technology, revising is still not easy. One strategy that writers can use to facilitate revision is *outlining*. In our discussion of getting started, we touched on outlining as a way of organizing a text before drafting. We noted that it can be a useful strategy for some writers but not so helpful for others. Most writers, however, can benefit from outlining a text *after* drafting. An outline gives only the essential elements of a text. If a writer can see a clear central idea for every section or paragraph of the paper, it is likely that the text is coherent and well organized. The outline should begin with the thesis statement. Each major section of the outline corresponds to a *topic sentence* for a paragraph. The topic sentence tells what that section or paragraph will be about. As an example, consider the essay in Figure 4.2 on prejudice and stereotyping, written in response to prompt (3) (note that this draft still contains some errors).

An outline would show that the writer had done a good job of organizing her material, but some problems remain. An outline of the draft might look like this:

Thesis: Stereotyping is destructive to all parties

    I. Introduction
       A. Importance in society
       B. General consequences
   II. My experience as an object of stereotyping
       A. At the mall
  III. How stereotypes affect those who use them
       A. Science group
  IV. My own experience of believing a stereotype
       A. People said negative things about black people
       B. My own experience with a black friend
    V. ??
       ?Mexican students in my high school
  VI. Conclusion
       A. Stereotypes are unacceptable
       B. Individuals do not always reflect group behavior

As a result of outlining after the draft, this writer might discover that although most of her essay makes sense, the paragraph on Mexicans in her high school is not well integrated with the rest of the text.

The Effects of Stereotyping
and Prejudice

The issue of prejudice and stereotype is a fundamental issue in society today, and has been discussed for decades and even generations. Prejudice and stereotype can lead us to making assumption about people before we actually know that person. It can lead to serious misunderstanding, emotional suffering, and reduce our self-esteem.

I experienced the pressure of stereotyping as a Chinese immigrant. We did not speak much English. In fact, we were definitely overwhelmed by the incomprehensible barrier of the English language, just like the narrator of the story we read. For example, once when I went shopping with my mother, my mother and I walked in one of the stores in the shopping mall. The salesclerk started to follow us closely, acting as if we were going to steal something. Later my mother found one dress, but in a very big size, so she decided to ask the salesclerk for a smaller size. However, that salesclerk did not respond to her and pretended not to understand her. She treated us in such a disrespectful manner, solely because of her stereotype of people who did not speak English.

Stereotypes don't just hurt the people they are about. When I was in high school, one time we had to do a science project. One of my group's members asked an American girl to join our group to do the science project. That American girl thought that because our English were not good that we could not be very smart, and so she joined another group. In the end, our group got an A, but her group not.

In my first years in America, I had conflicting experiences about black people. I often heard that black people were lazy, cheap, criminal and dumb. One time, I noticed that a police officer kept a closer watch on a black teenager than a white teenager when they were hanging out in front of a store. On the other hand, I had a very good friend who was black. I met her during my first year in high school. We were in the same English class. She was always ready to help me if I did not understand the assignment or did not understand what the teacher was saying. Sometimes she went over my paper and helped me with vocabulary that I did not know. She was very friendly, kind, smart, and hardworking. Her parents were very educated people too.

In high school, there were a lot of Mexicans. I thought they did not like Chinese because they treated us very impolitely. When we were in gym, sitting on the side of the gym room, sometimes they suddenly threw the basketball very fast toward us. It felt to me that it was a sign to warn us. When we left our school bag in classroom, we often found put someone put some scraps of paper or gum in our bag. Even at lunch, sometimes they threw beans or corn at our backs to tease us. All their behavior made me feel they do not like us.

Prejudice and stereotypes are not acceptable. People should not treat someone unfairly because of their differences, and should be careful of jumping to conclusion based on generalizations or other's opinions. No one should oversimplify and make generalizations about a group of people, because all groups have both good and bad individuals.

FIGURE 4.2 Sample student essay for revision

Editing

Our perspective on errors has changed considerably in the last 30 years. Errors are now seen as evidence of risk taking and therefore of learning. We expect to see errors throughout the writing process. Nevertheless, writing inevitably ends as a product, and that product should be as accurate as possible. Because we encourage students to focus on meaning rather than error-free writing in the formative stages of writing, sometimes the importance of accuracy gets lost. At some point, learners will need to address the formal correctness of their texts. This occurs as part of the *editing* process. Editing focuses on the final shaping of the text: sharpening word choice, correcting grammatical errors, and making surface-level changes.

Editing is usually seen as the final stage in the writing process, for two major reasons. First, it makes little sense for writers to focus on sentence-level problems if they are going to undertake substantial revision of their drafts. Editing changes that writers make may well disappear in the next draft, which means they will have wasted their time. Second, if learners—especially L2 writers—focus too much energy and attention on surface features, it detracts from the attention that they could and should pay to the more important revisions of content and organization.

That said, there are also good reasons for L2 writers to maintain some awareness of grammatical and lexical accuracy, even as they draft and revise. First, most skillful writers do some of their editing as they write, and it's a good practice to encourage. Second, if no editing at all is done during the writing and revising stages, errors will accumulate and can become overwhelming at the final stage. Too many things to correct can be discouraging for inexperienced writers. In addition, when editing is left to the end, students often run out of time and never get a chance to do a proper job. Finally, learners should be encouraged to think of content and form as a unified whole rather than separate concerns. How can a piece of writing reveal worthwhile content when it is filled with errors? Part of the message that a piece of writing presents is its form. For these reasons, teachers should encourage writers to include the editing process to some degree in the earlier stages of writing.

The writing process is a long and complex one. For someone expecting to sit down and type a piece of writing in one sitting, all of these steps may seem unduly cumbersome. Teachers need to assure their students that the time spent on these activities is part of the process and is not wasted—that the effort expended in the "process" really does show in the final "product."

THE ROLES OF TEACHERS AND PEERS

Changes in our view of writing and the teaching of writing over the last 30 years have also altered how we view the teacher's role. Teachers are now expected to intervene at various points during the process rather than simply to evaluate the writing or correct errors at the final stage. They are expected to react as much to the ideas as to the form. In fact, initially, some teachers do not respond to formal errors at all. Changes have also occurred in criteria for evaluating writing. Students' writing assignments are no longer evaluated simply for accuracy or adherence to an expected format; rather, they are evaluated in terms of audience needs, writer purpose, and task fulfillment.

Thus, the teacher's tasks have become more complex, and she must take on a variety of roles: task setter, audience, assistant or facilitator, and evaluator. Balancing all of these roles takes time and practice. We discuss the role of the teacher as a provider of feedback at greater length in Chapter 5, but for now we return to the role of the teacher at the beginning of the process, as the person who assigns writing tasks in the first place.

Designing appropriate writing assignments can be harder than it looks. We looked at several sample prompts at the beginning of this chapter, many of which may be familiar. It may be tempting to assign tasks that require learners to practice the use of structures and vocabulary they have just learned. This is not necessarily a bad practice, but it can be problematic if language practice is the beginning and the end of it. It is important that assignments include a communicative goal as well. Specialists in the field advise that a good writing assignment should

- have a communicative purpose;
- provide a context so students understand the purpose of the assignment;
- fit into a sequence of writing tasks that build toward a clear goal;
- have content that is interesting and accessible to learners;
- be written in clear and unambiguous language so learners know how to tackle the task;
- be narrow enough so that students can complete the assignment in a reasonable amount of time but broad enough to further their knowledge of the content;
- provide direction about the expected format;
- provide direction about how the task should be completed (how detailed this direction is will depend on the background and current skills of the students);
- include some guidance about what would be considered a good job.[2]

Pause to consider...

a writing assignment you have given in the past or one you find in a published textbook. How closely does the assignment adhere to these guidelines? How could you improve it?

Teachers are not the only source of ideas and feedback in the process-oriented classroom. A collaborative, supportive environment for composing includes the participation of peers. All students are expected to take on an active role, participating in the development of the texts of classmates as well as their own. Many students wonder what their peers can possibly offer them, and indeed, there are many things that a teacher can do better. Nevertheless, a peer can offer ideas in a less threatening manner than a teacher can. In addition, learning to give helpful feedback to a peer can help writers become better judges of their own writing. We explore these benefits further in Chapter 5.

WRITING UNDER PRESSURE: RESPONDING TO ESSAY QUESTIONS

The majority of the writing tasks for higher proficiency learners that we have looked at assume that most of the writing occurs outside of class, at the writer's own pace and in multiple drafts. However, for many students, an important part of learning to write in an L2 is doing so under pressure and in a single draft, because they will often be judged on their ability to perform under these conditions. They will have to write, for example, in gate-keeping situations, such as entrance and exit exams, where they may have little opportunity to put into practice the lessons they have learned in composition class: There is little time for planning, much less for multiple drafts. They will also have to take tests in their classes that include essay questions. Needless to say, most L2 writers find these tasks challenging. Some instructors have argued that this is a reason to focus on written products rather than on the writing process. Yet responding to essay questions under pressure is simply a somewhat different writing process. Indeed, some of the steps involved in timed writings are similar to those involved in multidraft writing, although there are differences as well.

Analyzing the Prompt

Not only do essay-type tests vary a great deal across disciplines; they vary in the way instructors judge responses to these tests, with some valuing content more than organization, some penalizing language errors more heavily than others, and so on. One thing is certain and constant: Essay questions are a mainstay of assessment in academic settings. Many colleges and universities require essay writing on competency tests that determine where a student will be placed in composition courses or, more importantly, whether a student can pursue further study or even graduate. L2 writers are also likely to encounter many such tests in nonlanguage courses. Responding to essay exam questions is a skill that students need to learn and one that should be addressed in any L2 writing class.

The first thing learners need to do for an essay exam is read the question carefully. Researchers who have investigated essay exam responses have found that many students, both native speakers and L2 writers, get tripped up at this point. They don't analyze the question. Well-written prompts may offer guidance on how to answer. They usually have two parts: In the first part, the question is framed, often with a statement, a quote, or some data (e.g., *The immigration rate from Latin America has more than doubled in the last 10 years*, or *It is claimed that global warming has led to a variety of changes in the environment*). The second part includes the question and may also provide instructions on how it should be answered. However, not all prompts are well written. Compare these two examples on the topic of bilingualism:

Version 1:

Discuss the following statement:

A bilingual speech community will maintain its different languages, and not undergo language shift, as long as the functional differentiation of the varieties in its linguistic repertoire is systematically and widely maintained.

Version 2:

In writing about bilingual communities that have maintained both languages for many generations, one linguist wrote

"A bilingual speech community will maintain its different languages, and not undergo language shift, as long as the functional differentiation of the varieties in its linguistic repertoire is systematically and widely maintained."

Interpret and evaluate this statement in light of the readings we have done in this course. As you explain the statement, be sure to define such terms as "language shift," "functional differentiation," "varieties," and "linguistic repertoire."

Version 2 obviously provides considerably more guidance on how to answer. In version 1, L2 learners may be at a loss about the exact nature of the task.

Understanding Instructional Verbs

It is clear that instructional verbs play a crucial role in essay question prompts. Most essay questions ask writers to do something. The key to an appropriate answer is often in the instructional verbs, but L2 writers in particular may have difficulty figuring out exactly what those verbs mean. Thus, practice in answering essay questions should include a focus on analyzing the verbs used in the prompt. In version 2 of the essay question just given, four verbs specifically instruct writers on how the question should be answered. Version 1 offers only the verb *discuss*, providing learners with few clues about how they should proceed. The following is a list of action verbs in English often found in essay prompts. Analogous lists could be developed for other languages.

Analyze	Define	Identify
Characterize	Describe	Interpret
Comment (on)	Discuss	List
Compare	Evaluate	Outline
Contrast	Explain	Suggest
Critique	Explore	Summarize

Some of these verbs, such as *compare, contrast, define,* and *list* have specific meanings. Interpretation is probably not a problem because their meanings are clear. Others are not so transparent or may be unfamiliar to L2 learners.

What exactly do the instructional verbs *describe, discuss, explain,* and *explore* mean? In the sample question, a learner would have to infer that *discuss* actually implies several subtasks: *definition* of terms, *descriptions/examples* of bilingual communities, *comparisons/contrasts* among them, *application* of this concept to these examples, and *evaluation* of the thesis that is presented in this statement. Learners need practice in deconstructing and responding to these kinds of more ambiguous prompts. If instructional verbs are not provided, learners need to develop their own response strategies.

Understanding What Is Being Asked

Because instructional verbs are sometimes misleading or absent, another approach to essay questions, which has the additional advantage of being language neutral, is to analyze them in terms of knowledge or skill display that they require.[3] At the broadest level, most essay questions fall into one of the following categories:

- Display familiarity with a concept. This category may include providing definitions, examples, descriptions, or purpose.
- Display familiarity with the relation between/among concepts. This category may include comparison, contrast, or tracing of cause-and-effect relationships, including identifying the factors involved.
- Display familiarity with a process. This category usually involves a description of that process.
- Display familiarity with argumentation. This category may involve retracing an argument made elsewhere or an evaluation of the validity of that argument.

Learners do not always need to write out the response; it may be enough to read the prompt and decide what kind of response is required.

> ## *Pause to consider...*
>
> some timed essay questions that you have given or answered in your classes. What instructional verbs, if any, were provided? What were the questions really asking the writer to do? What kind of familiarity did they ask the writer to display?

Many composition courses focus exclusively on multidraft writing. However, because students will probably have to engage in both multidraft and impromptu writing, L2 writing classes should include both and have students write under a variety of authentic conditions. An exclusive focus on just one kind of writing process will place L2 writers at a considerable disadvantage.

As L2 writers become familiar with the many processes involved in composing, writing tasks will come more easily. In time, they may come to see that although writing well is often a laborious and time-consuming activity, it is one that usually rewards the time and effort put into it.

SUMMARY

Teaching the writing process is more than taking students through the stages of writing. It also asks the writer to consider audience and purpose. Just as important, it focuses on the discovery of meaning in one's writing. Many writers figure out what they want to say only after they have begun writing.

The stages of writing often form the backbone of writing instruction. Many writers begin the process by generating lots of ideas, only some of which they will pursue in their draft. Discovery and invention techniques used in the prewriting stage include free writing, looping, brainstorming, note taking, mind maps, and questioning activities. Sometimes, rather than generating ideas, writers are simply required to uncover what the task is—that is, deconstruct the prompt. This involves careful reading of the assignment. Drafting is the next stage. Writers do not need to start at the beginning and write to the end. Sometimes it may work best to start in the middle, with what the writer knows, and only later write an introduction. Whenever it is written, the introduction will need to include a statement of the writer's central claim, often called the thesis. Much of the rest of the essay will be devoted to providing support for this claim. Once the draft is complete, writers will undoubtedly need to revise, a stage that involves more than surface-level editing and may in fact require that the entire essay be rethought. Outlining can help writers see whether the essay is clearly organized. Editing, which focuses on linguistic accuracy, usually takes place at the end of the process. However, it is important for writers to do some editing throughout the writing process, lest the task at the end become too overwhelming.

One of the teacher's primary responsibilities is to design effective assignments. Prompts should provide a purpose, context, and adequate guidance for carrying out the task. Instructions and expectations for task completion should be clearly expressed. Peers also have a role in the process-oriented classroom, especially in providing feedback on classmates' writing.

Multidraft writing is the core of L2 writing instruction. However, it is equally important to give students practice in single-draft writing under pressure, such as they would experience in essay tests. Here again, deconstructing prompts in essay questions is an essential skill for L2 students to master.

CHAPTER NOTES

1. *The Psychology of Written Composition*, by C. Bereiter and M. Scarmadalia, 1987, Hillsdale, NJ: Erlbaum.
2. These ideas are based on "Designing and Assessing Effective Classroom Writing Assignments for NEW and ESL Students," by J. Reid and B. Kroll, 1995, *Journal of Second Language Writing, 4*, 17–41.
3. "Essay Examination Prompts and the Teaching of Academic Writing," by H. Horowitz, 1986, *English for Specific Purposes, 5*, 107–118.

READ MORE ABOUT IT

General Reading on L2 Writing Pedagogy—Focus on Teaching the Process (see also **Read More About It** in Chapters 1 and 2)

Hyland, K. (2002). *Teaching and researching writing*. Harlow, UK: Longman.

Spack, R. (1988). Initiating ESL students into the academic discourse community: How far should we go? *TESOL Quarterly*, 22:29–51.

*White, R., & Arndt, V. (1991). *Process writing*. London: Longman.

Writing Exam Responses

Horowitz, D. (1986). Essay examination prompts and the teaching of academic writing. *English for Specific Purposes, 5*, 107–120.

Johns, A. (1991). Interpreting an English competency examination: The frustrations of an ESL science student. *Written Communication, 8*, 379–401.

Weigle, S., & Nelson, G. (2001). Academic writing for university examinations. In I. Leki: (Ed.), *Academic writing programs* (pp. 121–135). Washington, DC TESOL.

*Accessible readings for beginning students

CHAPTER 5

Responding to Second Language Writing

Responding to L2 writing is a broad topic. In this chapter we address this topic in terms of a general distinction between peer response and teacher response. Beyond that, we consider such issues as when to respond—between drafts or on the final draft—how to respond—in writing, in face-to-face conferences, or in some other format—and what to respond to—content, form, or both. Our discussion begins with the assumption that at least some writing, in the form of a draft, has already been done.

PEER RESPONSE

All writers can benefit from having a real audience to write for, especially if the readers can provide helpful feedback. A readily available audience in the classroom is the writer's classmates, or *peers*. The **peer response** trend comes from studies of composition instruction with native speakers. In the collaborative spirit of process writing, peers have an important role to play. In fact, peer work can take place at many stages in the writing process: discovery, drafting, revising, editing, and so on. Collaborative composition activities find their origin in a social constructionist view of learning, which holds that knowledge develops through social interaction. In this view, learners are seen as participants in a community of writers rather than as solitary writers. For L2 writers, additional support for this approach comes from research underscoring the importance of interaction in second language acquisition (see Chapter 7). The hope is that learners will develop linguistic knowledge and writing skills in a mutually supportive environment.

Peer response is not a single or specific method; it can be approached in many ways. In some classes, it is a highly structured activity; in others, the tasks are relatively open ended, and students have considerable freedom and flexibility in how they may respond to their classmates' texts. Peer response is also just one kind of collaborative activity. Students can benefit from working together at various stages in the writing process, for example, as learners generate and develop their ideas for writing. The success of peer response is partly under the teacher's control, and in this chapter we explore ways to make it as productive as possible. However, success also depends on an array of student variables, such as L2 proficiency, prior experience in writing, cultural and educational background, and group dynamics. It does not always work out, and it does not work for everything. Although peer response is widely embraced in the field of composition, it is important to consider carefully the extent to which such a practice is appropriate for students who are still learning a new language. Some adaptations and restrictions may be advisable. Also note that peer response can never substitute for teacher feedback. However, with good preparation, peer response groups can be an important and effective tool in L2 writing instruction.

Pause to consider...

the benefits of peer response for L2 writers. Should peer work be handled in the same way with native writers and L2 writers? Should there be restrictions on peer work with L2 writers; that is, are some aspects of writing better left to the teacher? If so, which ones?

Benefits and Drawbacks of Peer Response in Teaching L2 Writing

Most of the research and practical experience with peer response in L2 writing comes from ESL classrooms; far less comes from FL classes. Thus, most of what is reported here is based on English learners in an L2 context and must be weighed carefully before being adopted for FL learners. That said, the following are benefits claimed for peer response:

- It provides writers with an authentic audience. Through interaction with peers, students may come to understand what works in their writing and what does not. If a fellow student does not understand what they are trying to express, chances are the text needs more work.
- It provides multiple audiences. Teacher response is limited to an audience of one. Peer response gives writers several perspectives on the developing text.
- It provides several levels of feedback. Peers may focus on issues that the teacher has not noticed or prefers not to address. For example, teachers tend to comment on global issues, whereas peers may point out more specific areas that need clarification or elaboration. Teachers simply do not have time to give detailed feedback to every student. The two forms of feedback can complement each other.
- It provides feedback in a collaborative, relatively low-risk environment. Writers can try things out without losing face in front of an authority figure. In reviewing the texts of their peers, they may come to realize that no one is a perfect writer and that drafts do not emerge fully formed. Their own experience and struggle are perfectly normal and to be expected.

- Learners take on a more active role in the writing process, rather than waiting passively for teacher guidance.
- The critical reading ability that writers acquire in reading and responding to the work of their peers may eventually transfer to their own texts.
- The interaction involved in peer response can push the development of all L2 skills, not just writing but listening, speaking, and reading, as well. This development is an additional benefit of peer work that is not mentioned in the L1 literature, for obvious reasons.
- Peer response can give the teacher an opportunity to work with individual students in brief mini-conferences while their classmates read and respond to one another's work.
- It helps learners get to know one another better. At big universities, students often move from one large class to another without becoming acquainted with their classmates. Collaborative activities provide a greater sense of community.

In spite of all these purported benefits, research on the effectiveness of peer response in the L2 classroom has yielded mixed results. Peer response may be less than successful for the following reasons:

- Students are not always very good at it:
  - Their L2 oral/aural proficiency may not be adequate for understanding their peers' text or successfully commenting on it.
  - They may not have the skills and experience to offer advice on the "big picture," which is what their peers really need. Instead, they may focus exclusively on surface features.
  - Their suggestions may be vague and unhelpful (e.g., *Can you make this paragraph clearer?*).
  - Their suggestions may be wrong.
  - They may base their suggestions on L1 rhetorical conventions that are not appropriate in an L2 context.
  - They may be tactless.
- Students sometimes resist peer response activities:
  - They may not believe they have anything valuable to contribute.
  - They may be unaccustomed to this kind of learning activity.
  - They may not believe that their peers can offer any valuable advice, and therefore they ignore their suggestions.
  - They may hesitate to offer any negative responses, resulting in empty praise that will not help the writer.
  - Group dynamics may make the process difficult or unproductive. For example, if one member of the pair or group becomes aggressive or domineering, it may cause others to withdraw from the process.
  - They may view it as a waste of time or a chance to chat and so end up paying attention only to the teacher's feedback.
  - They may think of it as a time-consuming activity that takes away from other learning activities.
  - The teacher may not have adequately prepared students for the activity.

Guidelines for Effective Use of Peer Response

Some of these problems can be addressed through careful preparation and selective use of peer response activities. One thing is certain: If the teacher is not committed to the practice, students will quickly catch on that it is not an integral or important part of the course. Many L2 writing teachers say they have tried peer response activities but have found that they don't work very well. Some of these reported failures may occur because the teachers have not shown their students how to do it or because they have tried using it in inappropriate ways. Of course, in some cases, even thoughtful preparation may not yield good results.

The following suggestions have been gathered from L2 writing teachers and researchers who have used peer response successfully. The key advice that seems to permeate all writing on this topic is that students have to be shown how to respond effectively. They also have to become familiar with many different aspects of the process. At the outset, students need to understand the purpose and the potential benefits of the process. The point is not obvious to most learners, and many may initially view it as a waste of time. They may not know what to look for when they read their classmates' work, or they may have little experience with the language of responding, that is, how to frame their suggestions in a cooperative and constructive manner. Studies of peer response uniformly demonstrate that students who have been trained in responding are more effective than those who have not.

So what does preparation for peer response involve? A first step for teachers is to model the process. In general, L2 writers are not familiar with the language of response. Some teachers role-play responding with another faculty member, teaching assistant, or perhaps someone from the university writing center. Other teachers prefer to use an anonymous draft, perhaps from a previous student (a practice that requires written permission from the student.) The best approach is to use an overhead projector so that everyone can see what is going on. The teacher can start the process with some comments and suggestions to point students in the right direction and then elicit more responses from them. It is a good idea to do this several times, using different drafts of varying quality and addressing a variety of issues. Some teachers provide written examples of helpful and less helpful responses or examples of ways in which vague or confrontational responses can be reframed. Students can also practice rewriting unhelpful responses so that they are more constructive. For example, consider the following introductory paragraph:

> People complain that the United States have too much freedom for kids, for them to play all kind of stuff, like heavy metal music, and let them drive with loud music, modify their cars which have a big sound. This kind of stuff makes people go crazy. All that prejudice ruins people's life. Well, this is true, but does that make this country not a good place to live? I don't think so.

Here are two responses that are not particularly helpful:

> Your paragraph is hard to understand. Can you make it clearer?

> Heavy metal music is not good. I don't think you should write about it.

The first might be rewritten to be more specific:

> It seems as if your introduction is all about freedom. I don't understand the sentence about prejudice. How does it relate to your topic?

The second might be rewritten in a less confrontational manner:

> I agree with the people who say that heavy metal and these other things are bad. I am not sure if you do. Do you mean that people are free to do both good and bad things in America? I think you should make it clear to the reader that these are bad things, but in a free country you are allowed to do them.

Once the practice has been modeled, students should practice on their own with sample texts before they start working on one another's drafts. Finally, students need to see how peer suggestions can lead to improvement in their writing. The class can follow the process from the initial draft, through peer response, to revised drafts based on the peer response. Only then will students really see the utility of this activity. The time spent up front will pay off with more productive responses throughout the course and better use of peer response in revision. That said, it should not be assumed that once students have gone through this preparation, peer response activities will proceed without a hitch. Just because they are interacting does not mean they are providing one another with helpful feedback. The teacher should circulate to the various peer groups to make sure they stay on task and maintain a cooperative and constructive tone in their responses. Although it is not always crucial for teachers to review the actual peer suggestions, from time to time they should look over the kind of advice that students are giving one another. If responses seem inappropriate in any way, the class can review the process again as a whole class activity, using examples from class papers.

Besides modeling the process, teachers can help students with peer response by providing them with materials to guide their response, usually a set of questions or features to check for in the draft. Some teachers argue that learners should be relatively free in how they respond and that a predetermined set of questions is just one more way of promoting the teacher's agenda rather than eliciting the students' real views. This may be a valid view, especially for native speakers. However, for most L2 writers, a certain amount of guidance and structure seems to be both welcome and needed. For more advanced learners, more critical or probing questions may be appropriate, such as, *What methods has the author used to persuade you of his/her argument?* For most learners, though, general questions on content and organization work well. A sample peer response sheet is shown in Figure 5.1.

A peer response activity should have the following characteristics:

- It should relate to specific elements of the text rather than ask for a subjective or emotional response. Questions such as *What did you like best about this text?* rarely yield useful suggestions.
- It should require that the respondents do something. For example, instead of asking if a paragraph was clear, it should require that the

Peer Response Sheet

Writer: _____   Responder: _____

Look at the first paragraph.

1. What does it say the essay will be about?

_____

_____

2. What is the writer's main point?

_____

_____

3. Does the essay answer the assigned question?

_____

_____

Now look at the rest of the paper.

4. What claims does the writer make about advertising strategies?

_____

_____

_____

5. What evidence does the writer give to support each of these claims?

_____

_____

6. Read the first paragraph again. Do the claims and evidence in the body
   paragraphs support the main point in the introduction? Explain.

_____

_____

7. How does the writer conclude?

_____

_____

8. Are there parts of the essay you don't understand? What are they?

_____

_____

9. What other suggestions do you have for the writer's next draft?

_____

_____

FIGURE 5.1 Sample peer response sheet

Note. From *Getting There* (pp. 131–132), by J. Williams and J. Evans, 2000, Boston: Heinle.
Reprinted with permission of Heinle, a division of Thomson Learning: www.thomsonrights.com.
Fax 800 730-2215.

respondents indicate where in the text the writing is not clear. If the question is about topic sentences, respondents should restate or underline what they see as the topic sentence. In this way, if the writer had a different intention, it will be immediately apparent.

- It should ask for suggestions as well as criticism; that is, if respondents feel that a claim has insufficient support, they should offer advice about how the writer might strengthen the argument.
- It should be specific and tied to work being done in class. Having the same predictable questions for each assignment will quickly stifle student interest. If the class has been working on conclusions, the peer response sheet should include a question on conclusions. It is also beneficial to connect it to course content rather than maintain a generic format. In the sample shown in Figure 5.1, for example, one question is related to the topic of the assignment, advertising.
- It should be linked to evaluation criteria. If students know what they are aiming for, giving helpful suggestions becomes easier.

Including these features in peer response will help learners see the value of the activity. Their investment in the activity is increased when both the responder and the recipient of the feedback are made accountable. Many teachers require that the peer response be handed in with the drafts, increasing the likelihood that the responses will be thoughtful. Although it would seem counterproductive to grade the peer response, perhaps a check or minus could be given or a specific number of points could be awarded as an incentive. To make sure writers take the peer responses seriously, teachers may want to refer to another student's suggestions in their own comments. Another strategy is to require that writers explicitly address the peer suggestions and say if they found them useful.

Just as writing tasks build in complexity as the writing course progresses, so, too, should peer response activities. As students become more comfortable with the process, they can handle more challenging tasks. They can also be steered back to their own writing. After they have worked on the texts of others a few times, they may be able to view their own drafts more objectively. Ideally, they should begin to sense where their drafts need work. Some teachers have their students submit their drafts with some commentary, requesting help in specific areas. This process can also be used in peer response. A student might ask his peer partner, *I am not sure if my example illustrates the point I am trying to make. Do you think it works? Can you think of an example that might work better?*

A final word of advice on peer response activities is that practices from native-speaker composition cannot necessarily be directly imported into L2 writing instruction. One example is the "author's chair" technique, in which writers read their drafts aloud and then ask for suggestions from their classmates. Reading aloud is thought to help writers "hear" the text differently, often allowing them to catch problems on their own. For L2 writers, however, reading aloud can be extremely challenging, often monopolizing their cognitive resources to the extent that they are unlikely to notice much of anything in the text. Second, as threatening to self-esteem as this activity is for native speakers, it is likely to be even more so for L2 writers, especially those from non-Western cultures. Smaller groups or pairs are generally a better idea for these students.

Learner Attitudes Toward Peer Response and the Use of Peer Suggestions

Clearly, some of the responsibility for student attitudes toward peer work rests with the teacher. How teachers prepare for the activity can make a big difference in how students feel about it. This is especially true of international ESL students, who may have had little experience with any kind of group work. Not all students will be convinced that it is a good use of their time. Studies of students' attitudes have found largely positive results, that is, students appreciated their peers' comments and found them helpful. However, there have also been less glowing views:

- Most students continue to find their teacher's feedback more helpful than peers'. This is to be expected. Peer response should be in addition to, not instead of, teacher feedback.
- Some students find peer response groups too confrontational. Several studies of Asian students in peer groups found that these students' main goal was often to maintain harmonious relations in the group rather than to provide constructive though sometimes painful criticism.
- Some complain that the feedback they receive is not useful. This suggests that they may not have been sufficiently prepared for the activity or they are not asking appropriate questions.

Studies of peer feedback in L2 writing classes have also yielded mixed findings regarding its effects on revision. Some studies have found peer feedback to be as effective as teacher feedback, as measured by the amount and nature of revisions; others have found that writers incorporate very little of what their peers suggest (as little as 5%), and still others have found that writers are selective in what suggestions they choose to follow. L2 writers may fail to take advantage of peer collaboration for a variety of reasons: They may experience cultural conflict, they may not like the limitations of the peer feedback format, they may not be sufficiently trained in the process, or they may think the teacher provides better guidance.

One fairly robust finding is that when peers enter into cooperative interaction about points in a text, revision is more likely. Conversely, revision is less likely if peers simply tell their classmates what to do or if the interaction becomes tense and the participants become defensive. Some research on the topic suggests that as many as 75% of the points discussed during peer sessions are revised. Other research found lower rates, but in these studies, suggestions that were not used were often explicitly rejected; in other words, the negotiations resulted in revisions that involved thoughtful and conscious choices about advice from their peers. Finally, these findings pertain to whether or not suggestions offered by peers are used. They say nothing about whether the resulting changes are positive. There is less research on this question, but again, what evidence exists points to general improvement in texts that have been revised based on feedback from peers.

A teacher has many choices in setting up peer work. The first question is, Should all L2 writing students be involved in peer response activities? More specifically, Is it an appropriate activity for students at every proficiency level? Researchers and experienced teachers would probably answer this question in a variety of ways. Some researchers have found that learners at the low-intermediate level are successful at addressing important issues in their classmates' drafts, often identifying the same problems as the teacher. The important thing to remember is that peers should be responding to issues of writing: clarity, organization, support, coherence, and so on, not necessarily issues of linguistic accuracy. If learners are still writing at the level of language practice, there will be little for their peers to respond to in their writing. Peer response should begin when students start to write for a communicative, rather than an exclusively pedagogical, purpose. This requirement may rule out many students in basic language programs.

Another question teachers have to ask is, What should peers be responding to in their classmates' writing? Learners often tend to respond initially to surface features of the texts, largely grammatical accuracy. There is nothing inherently wrong with one student pointing out a grammatical error to a classmate. Discussions about what word/tense/preposition fits best in a specific context can be helpful for both parties. However, that should not be the focus of the peer activity. One reason is that at lower levels of language proficiency, learners may well be wrong in their judgments. More importantly though, such a focus can take their attention away from the real job of peer response, that is, acting as an authentic audience and constructive critic of the text as a whole. Language use is a part of the whole, but it is not a good starting point.

Teachers also have to think about management issues. How should the groups be formed? Should the teacher choose them, or should students self-select? Should they be fixed, or should they change throughout the course? The answers to these questions vary, depending on the classroom situation. Sometimes it may be a good idea to let students choose partners and observe their performance. They may bond and work well together, complementing each others' strengths. On the other hand, they may not work well together, and the teacher will want to make changes. Sometimes it is helpful to pair a weaker student with a stronger one: The weaker student gets more help, and the stronger student gets to demonstrate her skill. However, it would be unfair to always place this burden on the better student or to keep the weaker student in a pair in which he will constantly be outdone. A perpetual question in L2 classes is whether students with the same L1 should be allowed to work together. (In FL situations, there is usually no choice.) Again, this pairing may be appropriate on some occasions. It is true that students who share an L1 will have a greater tendency to go off task and simply chat. On the other hand, there may be writing issues that can be discussed profitably in the L1. Of course, if the teacher has no knowledge of the L1, there is no way he can tell if the students are on task. One strategy is to ask students to try communicating first in the L2 and to switch to the L1 only if they are unsuccessful in the L2 but think they have important advice to offer.

A final logistical consideration for teachers is whether the peer feedback should be given orally or in writing. Oral responses are the quickest and easiest, although the peer needs to be sure that the writer takes in the suggestions (preferably writes them down) and doesn't just nod and forget everything later. Students should check that their partner understands the advice being offered. One way to do this is to have students reflect back the suggestions (e.g., *So, you think I should move this paragraph to the end?*). Oral feedback places more of the responsibility on the writer. Written feedback makes the respondent more accountable. It also provides the writer and the teacher with a tangible record of the exchange, ultimately making the writer accountable as well. On the downside, it is more time consuming and requires more advance planning. One other possibility is responding electronically. Electronic peer response can be done in class, in a networked classroom, or from a remote location, either in a synchronous or asynchronous environment. As discussed in Chapter 3, any of these variations will provide a written transcript of the interaction, which both the writer and the teacher may find useful.

TEACHER RESPONSE

Not all teachers use peer feedback in their classes, but it is safe to say that just about all L2 writing teachers respond to their students' writing at some point. We all do so in the hope and belief that it will be useful. Unfortunately, research on the topic has not always provided clear support for this belief.

The Changing Role of the Teacher

Teachers wear many hats in any classroom; this is especially true of the writing teacher. Once teachers receive a student text, the first role they take on is that of reader. Generally, we read because we want to learn something, be entertained, or a myriad of other reasons. The writer tells us something we don't know but would like to. In the classroom, however, the teachers are the experts and students are required to demonstrate their expertise and skill to them. These circumstances create quite a peculiar reading situation. Teachers tell the students what to write about and how to write it, and then they read and evaluate the students' performance. This sequence of events flies in the face of just about everything we teach our students about audience and purpose in writing. Yet all of this is part of the apprenticeship process. Teachers must first set the task, then act as audience and respond accordingly. Their role then changes to a more teacherly one, as they become coach or assistant, suggesting ways in which writers can make their texts more effective. Toward the end of the process, teachers evolve into judges or evaluators, often awarding a grade for performance. Ultimately, they may be called upon to judge a student's entire body of work to determine placement, assign a final grade, or recommend promotion. These roles are difficult to balance. It is hard to judge a text, for example, when one has participated in its creation.

Teachers new to the writing classroom usually have many questions about how to respond appropriately and effectively to their students' papers. One of their questions may be, Should response be to form, or content/organization, or both? I have stressed the centrality of communication in writing, so clearly there should be an emphasis on the message in the teacher's response. However, it is difficult to separate the message from the form in which it appears. In fact, it is probably far too simplistic to present form and content as a dichotomy. Most teachers and researchers stress that teachers should respond to all aspects of writing, though probably not all at once! Students appreciate advice on grammar as well as on content. And if a teacher does not comment on errors, there is a danger that students will think that everything in the draft that has no comments is just fine.

A second procedural question is, In the context of a multidraft assignment, when is the best time to respond, that is, on which draft? Should all aspects of writing be addressed on all drafts? The answer is that there is no single best procedure. For some time now, the received wisdom has been to respond to content and organization first, keeping grammatical corrections and suggestions to a minimum in the initial stages of writing. However, research has increasingly shown that the order in which feedback is given is not terribly important and the best practice may be to give a mix of feedback. It should be clear, though, that if a teacher comments on absolutely everything in a single draft, learners will quickly become overwhelmed.

The consensus among most teachers and researchers is that the teacher should intervene with feedback during the writing process rather than after. This is the perspective taken in this text. The argument behind this position is that the teacher, in her role as reader and coach, can help writers improve their next draft. If the teacher responds only on the final draft, comments will have little effect; it is possible or even likely that writers will not even read them. Some disagree with this approach, however, arguing that the authority that teachers carry is simply too strong to allow a writer to objectively consider and possibly reject their suggestions. Writers feel that they must revise according to their teachers' advice. Thus, the next draft may improve, but there may be little effect on long-term writing proficiency. Proponents of this position hold that the best time for a teacher to offer a response is on the final draft and that only peers should offer suggestions prior to that. The question then becomes, Why should a student pay attention to comments on a final draft? How will these comments help the student to improve as a writer, rather than just improve a specific paper? One solution is to ask the students to respond to the final comments by keeping a running log of what they plan to do to improve their writing on the next assignment, based on these comments. Before they turn in their next assignment, they can be asked to review their log to check that they have followed their own advice.

A third procedural concern is whether responses should be made in writing, on audiotape, electronically, or face-to-face (we discuss this last option in the section on teacher-student conferences). Teachers have experimented with all of these methods. To some extent, the choice is based on teacher and student preference and the availability of resources. Written comments are the most common and, arguably, the easiest to make. However, they can be time consuming and if handwritten, sometimes difficult to read. Another option is an audiotaped commentary keyed to the draft, combined with minimal written comments. Some teachers believe they offer more complete responses when they can comment verbally, often mentioning things they would not have bothered with in writing. However, this form of response depends on the student's having good listening comprehension skills or listening to the tape repeatedly.

If the draft is submitted electronically, the teacher can insert comments in the text. Some word processing programs (e.g., Microsoft Word) also have an Insert Comment or similar command that allows the teacher to make hidden queries or comments that do not appear in the written text. Instead, the relevant spot in the text is highlighted and the comment pops up as the writer passes the mouse over it. This method also provides students with a written record of the feedback they receive. Most word processing programs also have a change-tracking feature. The teacher can suggest changes directly on the electronic form of the text. The editing suggestions appear in a different color or font. The problem with using this feature for feedback is that it allows the writer to simply accept the teacher's suggestions with a keystroke without much thought. A solution to this problem is to print out the amended draft and return it to the student, who sees the changes but has to think about them and input them himself.

Teachers can also place more of the responsibility on the learner by asking students to submit their drafts with *annotations*. These notes point out places where they have experienced difficulty: *Is there enough evidence for my argument? Is this transition smooth? Is this the right word? Did I choose the right tense here?* In this way, the teacher can respond first and directly to students' concerns. This is a technique that requires some training for students and is probably one that that should come later in a course, when students already have some experience with teacher feedback.

A fourth question is, What form should the comments take? Should they be at the end? In the margins? Or both? Again, there is no single right way to make comments. Most teachers comment both in the margins and at the end of a draft. In general, they make marginal, or interlinear, comments when the problem can be addressed briefly. They use end comments to summarize the overall strengths and weaknesses of the writing. Research suggests that students will act on the suggestions in the margins, provided they are easy to achieve. They generally find the end comments more challenging, not because they are at the end but because they ask for changes that are more difficult to make. Several studies have looked at the form of comments (questions, statements, imperatives, with or without hedges) and their substance (requests for more information, offers of new information, instructions for change, praise). In general, the differences among these forms in terms of their effect on student revision are not large.

Teachers may also ask, How direct and explicit should feedback be? Once again, these are pros and cons to different approaches. Some studies have found that when feedback is indirect, for example, in the form of a question (e.g., *How do you think the author would respond?*) or a heavily hedged suggestion (e.g., *You might want to think about some other possible outcomes*), learners may not be aware that the feedback actually contains a suggestion that the teacher wants them to consider. On the other hand, simply telling the writer what to do in the next draft has its own pitfalls. Writers may simply follow the teacher's suggestion in the new draft with little critical consideration, or, worse, they may do so in spite of the fact that it does not match their communicative intent. Teachers do not always understand their students' intentions and as a result may make inappropriate suggestions. Decisions about what to do with a teachers' suggestions depend on the language and writing proficiency of the students, as well as their experience with teacher feedback. No comment or suggestion is useful if the writer does not know what to do with it.

A final procedural question is, Should a grade be attached to the response at all stages? This decision may depend as much on institutional policy as personal preference. There are reasons for and against assigning grades prior to the final draft. Many teachers feel that doing so puts too much emphasis on the grades and not enough on the learning process. On the other hand, offering a provisional grade has several potential benefits. It lets students know where they stand and how much work they must do to bring their grades up. If early drafts are graded, it is advisable to set up the grading so that all students, even strong ones, are motivated to make revisions. For example, students who write a reasonably good first draft might be penalized if they fail to revise and improve it, perhaps leading to a lower grade. Unfortunately, students who are accustomed to copious teacher feedback may shift some of the responsibility to the teacher and turn in very rough or sloppy first drafts that do not reflect their best efforts. In this case, less detailed feedback is advisable.

Pause to consider...

teacher response to a first draft. What form do you think teacher response should take? Where should comments be written? How extensive should they be?

An example of teacher feedback to a student's first draft—a text about TV commercials—is shown in Figure 5.2. How do you think this teacher has handled the issues just discussed?

Guidelines for Good Practice in Teacher Response and Student Revision

Teachers have to make many decisions when they are responding to student writing. Most teachers have developed their own response practices, and not all agree on the best procedures. Originally, advice on responding to students' writing, like so many things in L2 writing, was based on the experience of

Commercials

Commercial play a big part of our lifestyle [Do you mean a big part in our lives?]. In the time of watching television, commercials always play the major time. [I don't understand this sentence. Are you saying they are very frequent?] Why do we have to have **commercial** while we watching TV? While watching TV, **commercial** almost come up every fifteen minutes for three minutes. Even during the NBA or other sports, commercials always come up during the "time out". What is the meaning of the commercials that come up time to time ["from time to time" means sometimes, but you have just said they are very frequent. Maybe you mean "time after time."] and why do **company** pay a lot of money to do a 30 second commercial about their products?

One reason that **company** pay a lot of money for commercials is to get the viewer know what they are selling. The second reason is to let viewer know what they can get from that commercial. The last reason is to get the viewer to have a better feeling about their products. [If I understand what you are saying, these are three good reasons. Let me see if I understand.

1. The commercial <u>shows</u> the viewer the product.
2. I am not exactly sure about this one. Do you mean the commercial shows how viewers will <u>benefit</u> if they buy the product?
3. The commercial can get the viewer to have a <u>favorable opinion</u> of the product.]

To prove these reasons, I have been watching TV commercials [In this kind of writing, it is not important to tell what you have done. It is better to simply present the examples. For instance, you might say: <u>*We can see examples of this in many commercials.*</u>] One of the commercials is about the famous basketball player who selling Hanes underwear for men. In this commercial there is a group of men in a locker room wearing **a white underwear** and chatting. Then they saw Jordan come in wearing red Hanes underwear and the next day this group of men **change** their underwear to Hanes. However that day Jordan was wearing purple [polka] dot underwear. In this commercial the Hanes company **try** to use the famous Jordan to sell their product. The meaning of the commercial is, if you wear Hanes underwear you are one step closer to be the famous Jordan because you were wearing the same brand of underwear. [So, would this be an example of all of the reasons you gave in the last paragraph? Do you think the commercial is effective?]

Next commercial is about drinking Sprite. In this commercial they sell Mountain Dew Code Red. In the commercial there are two famous basketball player name Mac Grady and Webber. In the beginning two **player** showing off **there** moves at the basketball court and later they both drink Code Red at a store. The next thing they do is tell the owner to drink Code Red because they both drink and the people who drink it have a chance to win a trip to the NCAA final four, a final four cap, or a final four champion jersey. [So this also shows a benefit for the viewer, but it uses a very different strategy. In this case, the viewer might actually win something. The first commercial tries to convince viewers that they will become like Michael Jordan. Which strategy do you think is more effective?]

In conclusion, I think commercials are one of the good things to have on TV. The reason is that people can keep up with the outside world and know what is new. Companies use **commercial** to sell the product and get the viewer to have good first impression about the product and try to build up a good feeling with the viewer.

(continued)

You have written a strong first draft. You have offered reasons why companies use television commercials and provided two persuasive examples. In your next draft, you need to address some of the other information you gathered as you watched TV. When were the Hanes and Sprite commercials on TV? During what kinds of programs? Why do you think the companies chose to put the commercials on at those times? Do you think the strategies you saw in those two commercials would be used in other kinds of commercials?

Read over the comments I have made and come see me if you have any questions. Pay special attention to some of the words and phrases I have underlined. You may want to use some of them in your next draft. You also need to pay attention to some grammar points in your next draft. I have put a few of the problem words in boldface. Check each one for the following:

Should it be plural or singular?

Should it have a plural or singular verb?

Should it be in the present or past tense?

Underwear is a mass noun—likes clothes. Can you use "a" with a mass noun?

FIGURE 5.2 Teacher feedback on a first draft

teachers of native speakers. Recently, an increasing amount of research has been directed specifically at the experience of L2 writers. It points to the following suggestions for good practices in responding to students:

1. Explain your feedback practices to students. Learners will use your responses more effectively if they understand the system you are using. For example, you can tell them that just because you do not comment on a feature of their draft, it does not mean that feature cannot be improved. Let them know you expect them to be active partners in the revision process.

2. Model the feedback process. Learners are more likely to use teacher feedback if they see that it is useful. As described earlier, you can model the feedback process using anonymous drafts. Show the first draft on an overhead, and then show the comments that you made on it, explaining why you offered the comments. Also point out the features you chose not to comment on but could still be improved. Better still, begin by asking your students to offer suggestions for revision, much as they do in peer response activities.

3. Demonstrate the benefits of feedback on revision. Show the next step in the process—what students are expected to do with teacher feedback. With a handout or an overhead transparency, show students the next draft, which should include the student's revision. The best kind of text for this activity would be a draft that includes revisions that are traceable to the teacher's comments as well as revisions that are not.

4. When reading a student text, read the whole text through before making any comments. You may find that your understanding of the text changes as you read. Reading it completely first may help you avoid writing misleading or unnecessary comments.

5. Be clear in your suggestions. One recurring finding of research in this area is that learners often misunderstand or simply don't understand what the teacher is suggesting. Being clear may include the following:
   - Be careful when you respond in question form. What is the nature of your questions, and how do you expect students to respond to them? Are your questions ones that students are to answer by making changes in their text, or are they designed to help the writer think more critically about the topic? Learners may not recognize the difference.
   - Don't be too indirect in an effort to be polite (e.g., *Would it be possible to develop this idea a little?*).
   - Be sure your handwriting is legible.
   - Model good writing. Don't write your comments in fragments or other ungrammatical form.

6. Offer advice that students can act on. Comments should
   - Suggest a strategy for improvement.
   - Suggest that students do something they know how to do.
   - Offer suggestions that are text specific (e.g., *This point needs an example to illustrate it*) as well as suggestions that may help them in subsequent assignments (e.g., *Be sure you always define your terms when you introduce them. For example, in this essay, the reader cannot be sure what you mean by "declining values." How you understand this idea may be different from how others understand it, so you need to explain what you mean from the beginning*).

7. Be consistent. Try to carry your focus on elements in students' work across drafts and across assignments. In this way, they will know these points are important. Be sure that the practices you advocate in class are the same ones that you reward in your feedback. Don't give mixed messages.

8. Be positive. Students appreciate praise. One study showed that although learners also wanted constructive criticism, they remembered the words of praise best, often word for word. Learners need to know what they are doing well as well as what they are doing wrong. You might want to make it a practice to begin all feedback with some words of encouragement. Try to mention something completely positive; don't end your compliment with *however* or *but*. At the same time, make sure that students don't interpret such comments to mean that no further work is necessary, as this is usually not the case.

9. Focus on the communication of the writer's intent.
   - Respond to content and organization.
   - Respond to grammatical errors throughout the writing process, but in the initial stages, keep these comments somewhat general, rather than focusing on specific words or structures (e.g., *Your narrative takes place in the past, yet most of your verbs are in the present tense. Make sure you edit for these errors in your next draft*).

10. Tie your comments to work done in class. If you have been focusing on improving introductions, for example, make sure that some of your comments address how the student has handled the introduction.

11. Make comments that take into account students' increasing autonomy. As students become better writers, they need different kinds of feed-

back and/or perhaps less of it. Your commenting strategies should not remain the same throughout an entire course.

12. Respond to changes in task and genre. Your responses may also differ depending on the kind of assignment students have written. You are likely to offer different suggestions for a personal narrative and for a survey report.

13. Reflect your understanding of the draft back to the student. Sometimes it is helpful if you rephrase what you think the writer is trying to say or what you understand that she has said (e.g., *In this paragraph, you seem to be saying that there is no solution to this problem. Is this what you mean?*). This can limit misunderstandings.

14. Develop a system of accountability for the use of teacher feedback. After working so hard to provide thoughtful and helpful feedback, you certainly do not want your students to ignore it. Sometimes students may have good reason for doing so, but they should be ready to provide those reasons. Some teachers suggest that writers turn in a letter with the next draft, stating how they have processed feedback (teacher and peer comments, suggestions from conferences). Other teachers suggest a more structured approach, in which learners are guided in their choices. An example of this kind of approach is shown in Figure 5.3. The form shown has been filled out by a student who received a peer's comments on his essay about computer use. Using such a form not only gives students guidance in using feedback but also increases their accountability for attending to it.

If you would like to practice giving feedback using these guidelines, you will find sample essays provided for this purpose in Appendix 1. Essays are included in English, French, German, and Spanish.

Some teachers require that writers submit their final draft as a "packet": a set of all the drafts along with the intervening feedback and plans for revision. In this way, teachers can see the progress that the writer has made. Such packets may be included in a portfolio and may be required for portfolio evaluation (see Chapter 6).

Pause to consider...

the feedback offered by the teacher in Figure 5.2.

- To what extent do the teacher's comments conform to the guidelines given in the text?
- What is the balance between the teacher's comments on content and on grammatical errors?
- What is the difference between the comments within the text and at the end?
- Are there any comments the writer might find hard to understand or to act on?
- How has the teacher handled formal feedback? What kind of grammatical errors has he focused on?
- Are there other issues the teacher should have commented on but did not?

Name _____

What to Do When the Draft Comes Back

1. Read through your teacher's comments and the Peer Response Sheet(s).
2. Find some of the suggestions they have made.
3. Write the most important ones below. Then write what you think of each suggestion. How will you respond to it? If you do not plan to follow it, why not?

   A. <u>I need to make my main point clearer in the introduction. My main point should be about age.</u>

     i. I plan to ignore the suggestion because

     ii. I plan to change my draft in the following way:
     <u>I will add some sentences to the first paragraph to show the main point and also tell what the body paragraphs will be about: (1) age and how people feel about computers, (2) age and how much people use computers and (3) age and the Internet</u>

   B. <u>I need to make claims in the first two body paragraphs.</u>

     i. I plan to ignore the suggestion because

     ii. I plan to change my draft in the following way:
     <u>I will make one for each.</u>

   C. <u>It seems like my response partner thinks I shouldn't write about equipment.</u>

     i. I plan to ignore the suggestion because
     <u>I think equipment is very important, so I want to keep it but I will try to relate it to my main point about age better.</u>

     ii. I plan to change my draft in the following way:

4. Perhaps you have thought of some other changes you would like to make. List them below:
<u>I will divide the first body paragraph into two separate ones.</u>
<u>I think I will also write about why different age groups act differently.</u>

5. Are there any comments or suggestions on your paper that you did not understand? You may want to discuss them with your peer response partner or arrange a conference with your instructor. List them below and bring this sheet with you to help guide your conference.

FIGURE 5.3 Sample form showing student use of feedback

Note. From *Getting There* (pp. 91-92), by J. Williams and J. Evans, 2000, Boston: Heinle.
Reprinted with permission of Heinle, a division of Thomson Learning: www.thomsonrights.com.
Fax 800 730-2215.

Do Students Use Teacher Feedback in Their Revisions?

Early research suggested that teacher comments on students' writing were largely ignored. More recent research, however, points in the other direction and indicates that students at least try to act on most of the comments that their teachers offer. In addition, most revisions based on teacher feedback represent an improvement in the text.

Not all feedback, of course, is revision oriented. Teachers often offer praise to let students know what should not be changed. Nevertheless, most feedback is aimed at revision, and students do use a considerable amount of this teacher feedback in subsequent drafts. Studies have shown little difference between students' revisions whether comments are positive or critical, polite or very direct. Longer and more text-specific comments appear to lead to more revision. Suggestions for changes, whatever form they take (question, statement, imperative) also seem to be effective in fostering revision. One type of comment that does not seem to lead to change is the reflective question that does not suggest specific changes (e.g., *Do you think this will happen?*). Students may not perceive these kinds of comments as ones on which they should be acting.

In short, there seem to be many ways to provide effective feedback, but none of them is guaranteed to produce the desired response. Students appear to ignore some advice offered in teacher feedback and follow other advice. Perhaps the clearest finding on student revision based on feedback is that whatever form the feedback takes, students are most likely to revise problems in their texts that are easily resolved. These instances involve straightforward editing changes as well as easily followed instructions such as *You need one more example here.* In contrast, students tend to ignore advice that is more general and contains suggestions that are more difficult to follow, such as *You have not presented a convincing argument to support your point*, or *How are these two thoughts connected? I don't understand their relationship.*

It should not be inferred that revision is completely dependent on a teacher's ability to provide effective feedback. The picture is far more complicated, and many other factors play a role in the extent and quality of student revision. These factors include language proficiency, type of assignment, previous educational and writing experience, time constraints, and age. It is also worth pointing out that not all student revision is based on teacher feedback. In fact, some studies have shown that most revision is not in response to teacher feedback, although other studies show a larger influence for teacher suggestion. Students get suggestions from other students and friends, they consult reference materials, and sometimes they simply rethink their texts and make changes on their own. There is some evidence that simply building in time for revision will lead to changes—usually improvements—in the next draft.

Finally, some teachers, perhaps influenced by the literature in native-speaker composition, worry that providing extensive and explicit feedback means they are "appropriating" their students' texts, imposing their own ideas and agenda, and exerting undue authority, thus stifling their students' voices and creativity. These concerns may have been justified in the past, when teachers saw their primary job as correcting rather than reading and responding. As they reconsidered their role, many teachers retreated from providing explicit feedback and began to offer more global, nonspecific feedback instead, pushing learners to figure out many things on their own. L2 writers are often looking for explicit guidance, however, and they may see this retreat as an abdication of the teacher's responsibility. ESL expert Joy Reid argues persuasively for an active role for the L2 writing teacher. Her comments pertain to ESL students, but the same claims can be made for FL teachers.

> Do ESL students expect and need directive teacher response? Because academic writing is a social endeavor, and because, as a teacher, I know more about the parameters and constraints of academic writing, I believe that it is my responsibility to intervene in my students' writing. The teacher is a resource and an authority as well as a facilitator and member of the classroom community—which, like all communities, comprises a hierarchy.[1]

One final issue is perhaps the most important one of all—the long-term effects of teacher feedback on student revision strategies and writing ability in general. There is almost no research on this issue. Although students' progress in draft-to-draft revision is important, unless they internalize the suggestions that teachers offer and use them in future writing tasks, we cannot really consider the feedback to have been effective. We know very little about what kinds of responses are likely to carry over into subsequent assignments. In spite of the lack of empirical evidence, it makes intuitive sense that long-term change is unlikely in the absence of short-term change. One implication of this conclusion is that it is a good idea to include suggestions that are generalizable to other assignments and other contexts.

An example of a student revision following teacher feedback—the second draft of the text about TV commercials—is shown in Figure 5.4.

Pause to consider...

the first draft shown in Figure 5.2 and the second draft shown in Figure 5.4.

- How did the writer respond to the teacher's feedback?
- Did she use all the suggestions he made?
- Did she make changes independent of teacher feedback?
- Did she correct errors that the teacher pointed out?
- Is the second draft an improvement over the first?

Learner Attitudes Toward Teacher Feedback

As in many other areas of L2 writing research, research on student attitudes toward teacher comments has produced mixed results. Results probably vary with the type of students who are asked to evaluate teacher response. In general, students want and expect teacher feedback, and they want it on both content and sentence-level errors of grammar and word choice. They appreciate positive comments, but they often say that critical feedback is the most helpful. This is not to imply that they follow every suggestion made by their

Commercials

Commercials play a big part of our lives. When you watch television, you see commercials very often. They almost come up every fifteen minutes for three minutes. Why do we have to have commercials while we are watching TV? Even during the NBA or other sports, commercials always come up during the "time out". What is the meaning of the commercials that come up all the time and why do companies pay a lot of money to do a 30 second commercial about their products? One reason that companies pay a lot of money for commercials is to show the viewer what they are selling. The second reason is to let viewer know that they can benefit from that product. The last reason is to get the viewer to have a favorable about their products.

We can see these reasons in many commercials. One example of these commercials is about the famous basketball player Michael Jordan who is selling Hanes underwear for men. In this commercial there is a group of men in a locker room wearing white underwear and chatting. Then they saw Jordan come in wearing red Hanes underwear and the next day this group of men change their underwear to Hanes. However that day Jordan was wearing purple polka dot underwear. In this commercial the Hanes company tried to use the famous Jordan to sell their product. The meaning of the commercial is, if you wear Hanes underwear you are one step closer to be the famous Jordan because you were wearing the same brand of underwear. This commercial will does the three things, it shows the product, the benefit and will make people want to buy it.

Another commercial is about drinking Sprite. In this commercial they sell Mountain Dew Code Red. In the commercial there are two famous basketball players name Mac Grady and Webber. In the beginning the players showing off their moves at the basketball court and later they both drink Code Red at a store. The next thing they do is tell the owner to drink Code Red because they both drink and the people who drink it have a chance to win a trip to the NCAA final four, a final four cap, or a final four champion jersey. So this commercial is like the Jordan commercial but tells the viewer about an extra benefit, the chance to win a trip. Everyone will want to go to the NCAA tournament.

These two commercials are on sports programs at night so the commercials also have sports start. People who watch sports maybe pay attention what sports star say. Many people watch sports but I think it is a lot of men watching. So I think the company put the commercial on the sports show because they want men to listen and buy the product. Maybe these men have more money to spend.

In conclusion, I think commercials are one of the good things to have on TV. The reason is that people can keep up with the outside world and know what is new. Companies can choose the show to tell the right people about the product because they can guess who is watching the show. Companies use commercials to get these viewer to have good first impression about the product and try to build up a good feeling with the viewer. Then the people will buy the product. I think I sometimes buy the product I see on TV and I think other people do this too.

FIGURE 5.4 Second draft following teacher feedback

teachers. Sometimes they disagree with comments, and sometimes they ignore them. Their preference for specific types of feedback often seems to reflect instructional practices. If linguistic correctness is stressed and rewarded, students tend to prefer feedback that focuses on these concerns. Such may be the case more frequently in FL than in ESL classrooms. Most writers express a preference for comments that are explicit and directive, claiming to make the most use of these kinds of comments. This finding does not necessarily mean that all teacher comments should be explicit and directive, of course. Students may prefer such comments because most of the work is done for them. Students' responses to teacher feedback are not necessarily easy to predict or explain. Ultimately, the decision to revise a text rests with its author.

TEACHER-STUDENT CONFERENCES

Sometimes there is simply no substitute for sitting down and talking to a student face-to-face. Most teachers who can afford the luxury of time with individual students like to have periodic individual conferences. If time is not available outside of class, teachers can have mini-conferences with individual students when the rest of the class is engaged in collaborative activities. It can take considerable classroom management skills to orchestrate such arrangements. Logistical obstacles notwithstanding, this one-on-one interaction can personalize and tailor feedback in a way that is not possible in general classroom instruction. It can also clear up misunderstandings, such as when the teacher cannot untangle what a student has written or when a student cannot understand the teacher's feedback. One-on-one interaction allows students who are too shy to speak up in class to ask questions and express opinions. For some students, however, this kind of interaction with the teacher can actually be more intimidating than speaking up in class. Their speaking and listening comprehension skills may be so taxed that they have difficulty using the feedback they receive. Further complicating the situation is the fact that the rules of speaking suddenly change in a teacher-student conference. The interaction begins to resemble a conversation, yet the teacher is still very much the authority figure. Some students may be unsure of what the rules for interaction are. There may also be cross-cultural issues of which the teacher is unaware. For all these reasons, teachers need to take time at the beginning of the conference to make students comfortable, perhaps by finding out a little more about them and what they do outside of class.

Teachers should also tell students what to expect from a conference and make clear what their role is. Conferencing is time consuming, so both the teacher and the student should prepare well and use the time wisely. The roles and responsibilities of the participants should be clear ahead of time. One consistent research finding is that students who come prepared with questions and ideas and who actively negotiate in the conference session derive the most benefit in terms of improvement on subsequent drafts. Of course, it's easier and faster to tell students what to do than it is to get them to take the initiative, so teachers have to find ways to make students active participants. The following are some ways in which teachers can encourage active student participation in conferences:

- Read and make notes about the draft before coming to the conference.
- Schedule the conference after the student has received written feedback from you. You can vary this format later, but it's a good idea to start this way.
- Encourage students to take the initiative by beginning the conference with questions and concerns of their own. Make preparation for the conference a homework assignment.
- Begin your part of the interaction with general and leading questions, such as, *What is the main point of your paper?* or *What was the hardest thing about writing this paper?* rather than starting at the beginning and reviewing your feedback sentence by sentence.
- When you do begin looking at specific parts of the draft, ask questions such as, *What do you mean here?* Don't assume you know what students mean. You might launch into a long explanation only to find out that the writer intended something quite different.
- During the conference, periodically check for comprehension by asking students to review what has been discussed.
- At the end of the conference, ask students to summarize what has been addressed and outline what they plan to do.
- Consider developing a revision sheet to give students at the conference, so they can take down notes and plans in an organized way.
- If students have grammar questions, don't deflect them, but don't let them dominate the whole session either. You want most of the conference to be about the writing, but grammar questions are legitimate too.
- Be positive and encouraging, but be clear about where students stand in the course and what work remains to be done.

Students can also make a conference more effective in the following ways:

- Don't come to the conference expecting simply to be told what to do.
- Come with a set of questions and notes on your draft regarding issues you would like to discuss or things you do not understand.
- Make a recording of the conference if you think you will forget, or take notes, or both.
- Jot down what you plan to do in your next draft right after the conference, before you forget what you have discussed.

These guidelines may help to make conferences more productive, but they are no guarantee. Although sessions are more productive when students come with their own agenda and actively pursue it by negotiating with the teacher, such an interaction is not always easy to achieve. Some students do not really know how to take the lead. They may also find the notion of questioning the teacher—which is, after all, what negotiation is about—a taboo that they find difficult to break. Some students may find it difficult to process advice in this setting, especially if their comprehension skills are weak. For these students, it is important that some record of the conference be made, preferably a written one. Audiotapes are another option because students can replay them and process them at their leisure. Whatever the method, students should in some way be held accountable for what happens in the conference. Accountability does *not* mean that they must take every piece of advice that is offered; it does mean that they thoughtfully consider the suggestions.

TUTORING

Many universities and colleges, and even some high schools, have tutoring or writing centers where students can go for extra help on their papers. Tutoring is available primarily for writers of English, but FL departments may have tutoring programs as well. These centers do not provide editing or proofreading services, as some writers hope. Rather, they provide one-on-one assistance in a nonthreatening atmosphere. Tutors collaborate with writers to help them understand a writing assignment or to improve a specific text; their overall goal is to help the student to become a better and more confident writer.

Most tutors are native speakers or highly proficient L2 speakers, so they are often more knowledgeable than the writer's classmates but less intimidating than the teacher. However, they are not substitutes for the teacher. They are often fellow students, and they typically see themselves as the peers of those who come to the center for assistance. Most writing centers espouse a collaborative, nondirective philosophy in which writers are encouraged to discover what they mean and to solve their problems in expressing it on their own. Final decisions about what and how they will write are always left up to the writers.

It has been suggested that a writing center is the perfect place to address the challenges of L2 writing. The advantages of writing centers are that they offer L2 writers the extra time and attention that may not be available in class, and they focus on the individual. In addition, tutors may be perceived as more approachable than teachers. A disadvantage is that not all the tutors may be trained for work with L2 writers. What tutors are prepared to do is collaborate, which can be frustrating for L2 writers who are looking for clear and direct answers. In addition, many writing center tutors tend to deflect questions about grammar, either because such a focus is not in accordance with the center's philosophy or because they do not feel capable of giving adequate answers. This, too, can be frustrating for L2 writers. Thus, teachers may want to find out what the center's philosophy is and how much preparation tutors have had for working with L2 writers before sending their students to the center. Some centers do have tutors who are specifically trained to work with L2 writers and are more attuned to their needs.

SUMMARY

There are two major audiences for student writers: their peers and their teachers. Peer interaction offers an authentic audience in a nonthreatening environment. The process of responding to classmates may also make writers better readers of their own work. Another advantage is that the interaction can have benefits for the development of L2 language proficiency. Peer response is not always successful, however, either because learners are not very good at it or because they resist it, for a variety of reasons.

Many of these problems can be overcome with careful preparation. It is important for the teacher to model the process for students unaccustomed to the practice. Once the practice has been modeled, students can practice with sample texts before they move on to classmates' writing. The teacher should monitor students' performance. Students often benefit from guidelines for how to respond appropriately. Especially for students new to the process, it is essential to provide some sort of written peer response sheets. Questions on these sheets should be tailored to the writing assignment, rather than vague and subjective. They should also require that the responder do something active, such as find claims or the thesis, rather than simply answer yes or no.

Studies of peer response suggest that although most learners prefer teacher feedback, they also appreciate the advice they get from peers. They are most likely to use this advice in their revision if it is given as part of collaborative interaction. Teachers need to consider several variables in setting up peer work, ranging from questions of appropriateness for their students to issues of classroom management and logistics.

Teachers are often the most important responders to a writer's text. It is just one of many roles that a teacher has to balance in L2 writing instruction. Teachers have numerous procedural issues they have to address in responding to student writing, including whether to respond to form or content or both, when to respond, what format or medium to use for response, where to write comments, how direct to be, and whether to grade drafts. However teachers choose to respond, they can follow a set of guidelines for good practice. It is important that they explain their feedback practices and expectations. Equally important, they should model how they expect writers to respond to feedback and demonstrate its benefits. Feedback should be clear and contain advice that writers can act on. It should include at least some positive comments. Perhaps most importantly, feedback should focus on the communicative intent of the writing.

Studies of the effect of teacher feedback vary widely in their results, some showing little student use of feedback, others showing much more. Research suggests that learners can cope with mixed response (on both content and form) as long as the feedback is limited and clear. One clear result is that writers are most likely to act on teacher feedback if the advice is easy to follow.

Student-teacher conferences are another valuable avenue for teacher response. Writers who take an active part in conferences are likely to get the most benefit from them. Students can also benefit from the use of tutoring or writing centers, as long as teachers have made sure the tutors are trained to work with L2 writers.

CHAPTER NOTE

1. "Responding to ESL Students' Texts: The Myths of Appropriation," by J. Reid, 1994, *TESOL Quarterly*, *28*, p. 285.

READ MORE ABOUT IT

Peer Response

*Berg, C. (1999). Preparing ESL students for peer response. *TESOL Journal, 8,* 20–25.

*Ferris, D. (2003). *Response to student writing.* Mahwah, NJ: Erlbaum.

Hedgcock, J., & Lefkowitz, N. (1992). Collaborative oral/aural revision in foreign language writing instruction. *Journal of Second Language Writing, 4,* 51–70.

*Liu, J., & Hansen, J. (2002). *Peer response in second language writing classrooms.* Mahwah, NJ: Erlbaum.

Mendonça, C., & Johnson, K. (1994). Peer review negotiations: Revision activities in ESL writing instruction. *TESOL Quarterly, 28,* 745–769.

Mittan, R. (1989). The peer review process: Harnessing students' communicative power. In D. Johnson & D. Roen (Eds.), *Richness in writing: Empowering ESL students* (pp. 207–219). New York: Longman.

Paulus, T. (1999). The effect of peer and teacher feedback on student writing. *Journal of Second Language Writing, 8,* 265–289.

Villamil, O., & De Guerrero, M. (1998). Assessing the impact of peer revision on L2 writing. *Applied Linguistics, 19,* 491–514.

Teacher Feedback

Ashwell, T. (2000). Patterns of teacher response to student writing in a mulitple-draft composition classroom. *Journal of Second Language Writing, 9,* 227–240.

*Boswood, T., & Dwyer, R. (1995/6). From marking to feedback: Audiotaped response to student writing. *TESOL Journal, 5,* 20–23.

Ferris, D. (1995). Student reactions to teacher response in multiple draft composition classrooms. *TESOL Quarterly, 29,* 33–53.

Ferris, D. (1997). The effect of teacher commentary on student revision. *TESOL Quarterly, 31,* 315–399.

Hedgcock, J., & Lefkowitz, N. (1996). Some input on input. *Modern Language Journal, 80,* 287–308.

Hyland, F. (1998). The impact of teacher-written feedback on individual writers. *Journal of Second Language Writing, 7,* 255–286.

Reid, J. (1994). Responding to ESL students' texts: The myths of appropriation. *TESOL Quarterly, 28,* 273–292.

Teacher-Student Conferences

Goldstein, L., & Conrad, S. (1990). Student input and negotiation of meaning in the ESL writing conference. *TESOL Quarterly, 24,* 443–460.

Tutoring and Tutorials

*Reid, J., & Powers, J. (1993). Extending the benefits of small-group collaboration to the ESL writer. *TESOL Journal, 2,* 25–32.

*Williams, J. (2002). Undergraduate second language writers in the writing center. *Journal of Basic Writing, 21,* 16–34.

*Accessible readings for beginning students

CHAPTER 6

Assessing Second Language Writing

Teachers are usually more interested in teaching and responding than evaluating, but most will eventually have to engage in some form of assessment, if only in their own classrooms. We have already looked at the changing role of the teacher in the classroom, until this point focusing primarily on the teacher's roles as audience and coach. For good or for bad, most teachers at some point must also be evaluators. Thus, it is important for writing teachers to become familiar with the process of assessment.

Given that assessment is such a broad topic, we focus here on the types of assessment that most teachers will have to use and only briefly address standardized testing. References at the end of the chapter are provided for those who would like to read more on that topic. In this chapter we explore three areas of assessment: (1) summative feedback on individual papers, (2) summative feedback on a writer's overall progress (in a course), and (3) institutional assessment: placement and exit exams. We begin by considering a number of terms, concepts, and issues teachers are likely to encounter in the area of assessment.

Pause to consider...

the kind of assessment measures you have used in the past. How well have they served their purpose? What problems have they presented?

TERMS, CONCEPTS, AND ISSUES IN TESTING

In order to understand the literature on testing and to participate in testing programs, teachers need to understand the different kinds of tests and their purposes and assumptions. The first major distinction is between *indirect* and *direct* tests of writing. Indirect tests of writing require that we make inferences about a student's writing ability based on other types of information. For example, multiple-choice tests of grammar and usage may tell us something about writing proficiency. Some institutions use these kinds of tests as a rough indication of writing ability, mostly because they are relatively cheap and easy to administer and score. Direct tests of writing actually sample students' writing; they are considered a better way to find out about students' writing ability. Most institutions and even most standardized tests, such as the SAT, the Test of English as a Foreign Language (TOEFL), and the Advanced Placement language exams, now include a direct writing assessment measure. We limit our discussion here to direct tests.

The next aspect is the purpose of the assessment. For example, if students are evaluated at the end of the semester, a test is likely to focus on *achievement*— did the students learn what they were taught? Many exit examinations are actually achievement tests. For example, high-proficiency students might be asked to summarize and respond to an argument presented in a reading, as in the following prompt, which asks for a response to an article about the social isolation of those who spend all their time on-line:

> Why is Internet usage worth studying? In what ways are the statistics presented in this article supportive of the author's argument? In what ways do they actually support the opposite position from the one the author is taking? How?

Lower level students might be asked to narrate a story presented in a picture sequence or write about information of a more personal nature, as in this prompt:

> Write about a piece of technology that has changed your life significantly. What does it do? How did you make it part of your life? What have you learned from making use of it?

Other tests do not try to measure a specific body of knowledge or a skill that has been taught; instead, they seek to measure more general *proficiency*. The results of a proficiency test may indicate a learner's readiness to take on certain academic tasks or enter an academic institution, so they are often given for *placement*. Examples include the TOEFL and tests based on the guidelines of the American Council on the Teaching of Foreign Languages (ACTFL). These kinds of tests usually extend beyond a single skill such as writing.

One other type of test that may be useful is the *diagnostic* test. This kind of test attempts to determine the specific strengths and weaknesses in a learner's language ability or skill. In fact, the tasks in a diagnostic test may be similar to those in an achievement test (for example, the prompts given earlier), but their purpose is different. These have particular pedagogic value because they can tell teachers what areas need to be addressed in class. Some institutions use diagnostic tests, such as the Michigan English Language Assessment Battery (MELAB), in the placement process. There are other kinds of tests, but the ones mentioned here are the most common.

Although most teachers are unlikely to be involved in constructing tests outside of their own classrooms, understanding some testing terms can help you judge assessment measures. These terms are used to describe tests that have a scope beyond individual classrooms. The two terms most frequently used in evaluating tests—and arguably the most important—are *reliability* and *validity*. For tests of writing, *reliability* refers to the extent to which a given response will always be judged in the same way and with the same result. For example, if a student writes a paragraph in response to a prompt, would two readers give it (approximately) the same rating? Would one reader give it the same rating today as well as next Tuesday? If different prompts are used for this test (say, in different testing sessions), are they similar in terms of the demands they place on the writer?

Validity is a more complex concept, but for our purposes, we can understand it to mean that the test measures what it is intended to measure. For example, one might ask if an indirect test, such as a multiple-choice test in which students must find grammatical errors, is a valid test of writing ability. Does it measure writing skill or something else? We address validity when we discuss the assessment of writing in the next section.

Another important concern in testing writing is *authenticity*. We try to create tests that mirror as closely as possible the kinds of writing tasks that will be required of students outside of the testing situation. It is easier to create authentic tests in ESL classes than, say, intermediate FL classes. What kind of authentic situation could we create that would require students of Japanese to write? Probably none, so in these situations, perhaps the authenticity requirement would have to be relaxed. For most institutions, *practicality* is also an important issue. A test that meets all of the criteria mentioned so far may simply be impractical because it is too expensive or time consuming, either for the students taking the test or for those rating the responses.

Finally, decisions about test construction and implementation must take into account how the results will be used. Some assessments have extremely high *stakes;* they may determine admission or graduation from an academic program. Some results have less dramatic impact, such as a placement test to determine the level at which a student should begin study in an FL sequence. In addition, the type of test that an institution chooses will inevitably have a **washback effect** on instruction. At its most negative, *washback* means "teaching to the test." At its most positive, it reflects an integration of teaching and assessment philosophies, such that students are tested on what they have been or will be taught.

Pause to consider...

how to balance the many facets of testing in a context that you know well. Which of those facets—reliability, validity, authenticity, practicality, washback—would be most important?

Direct writing tests usually consist of several parts. At the most general level, the term **task** is used to describe what the writer is expected to do (e.g., write a phone message, write a set of directions based on a map, read two passages and respond to them in terms of a personal experience, and so on). The **prompt** is the question or instructions that the writer must respond to, such as

TABLE 6.1 Aspects of Writing Assessment

Task fulfillment	Does the response address the prompt? Does it use the stimulus material if required? Does it demonstrate audience awareness?
Textual knowledge	Is rhetorical framing appropriate? For instance, if the prompt indicates that a comparison is needed, does the writer follow this specification? Is the text coherent? Does it orient the reader? Is paragraph organization logical and unified? Is the text developed? Is the main idea elaborated in sufficient detail? Is the text cohesive? Do discourse cues indicate links across and between sentences?
Linguistic knowledge	Is the text linguistically accurate? Does the text contain varied and appropriate vocabulary? Does the text display varied and complex syntax?
Sociolinguistic knowledge	Is the register appropriate; that is, does it take the appropriate tone and level of formality with the reader?

Write a short essay describing the ways in which your educational experiences in high school and college have been different. There may also be a *stimulus.* A verbal stimulus might be a reading or a quote to which the writer must respond; a graphic stimulus could be a chart or a set of numerical data. Once the writer has finished, the test material passes into the hands of the reader(s). Readers usually have a *rating scale* with a **rubric** (set of rules or guidelines) on which to base their evaluations. We discuss rating later in this chapter.

One final issue in L2 writing assessment is the question of exactly what is being tested. Although it may seem obvious, we need to be explicit about what we are testing when we assess L2 writing. The answer will probably vary from group to group. A teacher devising an end-of-semester assessment for L2 writing students might want to know how well they have learned to revise and edit their work, summarize and incorporate readings, or use reference materials. He would be unlikely to discover anything about these aspects of their writing ability if he were to ask them to write for 30 minutes in response to a prompt such as, *Describe someone you admire very much and explain why.* However, if all he wanted to find out was whether a group of writers could write in an organized and coherent fashion and with linguistic accuracy, such a prompt might be adequate. It has the advantage of being neutral in terms of culture, gender, prior experience, and possibly even L2 proficiency. It can be administered and scored quickly for a large number of students. Thus, the decision about what should be tested is not a simple one. Aspects of writing that may be assessed include task fulfillment, textual knowledge, linguistic knowledge, and sociolinguistic knowledge, as shown in more detail in Table 6.1. Once the decisions have been made about what is being tested and for what purpose, the next step is to choose the most effective approach to assessment.

SUMMATIVE ASSESSMENT: INDIVIDUAL PAPERS AND FINAL COURSE GRADES

The most basic assessment task is *grading*. When an assignment is completed, teachers are typically required to award some sort of final grade, or *summative* evaluation. This differs from any *formative* evaluation the teacher provides as feedback during the writing process, which we addressed in Chapter 5. Summative evaluation tells students how they have done on the assigned task, not how they should improve it. This in no way means that the evaluation on the final draft precludes suggestions for improvement in writing more generally; it just means that this particular assignment is over.

The first decision a teacher must make in giving a summative evaluation is whether to break down the grade to identify the paper's strengths and weaknesses or simply to award an overall grade. The former is referred to as *analytic evaluation* and the latter as *holistic evaluation*. We discuss these two types of evaluation in more detail in the section on scoring large-scale assessment tests. Each approach has advantages and drawbacks. The most widely used analytic scheme for evaluating the elements of an English paper is shown in Figure 6.1. A version of this is also available in Spanish.[1] It was developed specifically for classroom use but is used for large-scale evaluation as well. It is a *weighted* instrument, with content as the most heavily weighted element. In spite of its focus on content, this instrument is not without drawbacks. In particular, there is little room to evaluate the extent to which the writer has incorporated source material, so it may be less appropriate for higher proficiency learners.

In spite of its shortcomings, this type of assessment allows students to see where they have done well and where they need to improve. With this type of assessment instrument, it is important to explain why the student received the points in each section and not just give a summation of points. The model shown in Figure 6.1 does more than simply provide separate grades on "content" and "form." Emphasizing the content-form dichotomy tends to give students the impression that the two are somehow separate when, in fact, they are intertwined. It is impossible to convey content effectively without attention to form.

The alternative approach, giving a single grade, reinforces the notion that all aspects of writing are integrated. If students receive a single grade for the final product, they should understand what the grading criteria are. What constitutes an A paper? B paper? In other words, even teachers who favor a holistic system and do not want to award a point value to separate aspects of writing may still wish to provide an analytic framework so that students can see, for example, why their paper received a B. An example of a detailed description of grading criteria for an advanced academic writing course is shown in Figure 6.2. It is designed for assignments that incorporate outside sources. For less advanced students, a simpler set of descriptions would be preferable. Another approach is to use a cover sheet that is returned to the student with the draft. An example of a cover sheet for a good but less than perfect paper, perhaps a B paper, is given in Figure 6.3.

In addition to deciding how they are going to evaluate the final written product, teachers also have to decide how they are going to evaluate the

ESL Composition Profile

STUDENT   DATE   TOPIC

	SCORE	LEVEL	CRITERIA	COMMENTS
CONTENT		30-27	EXCELLENT TO VERY GOOD: knowledgeable • substantive • thorough development of thesis • relevant to assigned topic	
		26-22	GOOD TO AVERAGE: some knowledge of subject • adequate range • limited development of thesis • mostly relevant to topic, but lacks detail	
		21-17	FAIR TO POOR: limited knowledge of subject • little substance • inadequate development of topic	
		16-13	VERY POOR: does not show knowledge of subject • nonsubstantive • not pertinent • OR not enough to evaluate	
ORGANIZATION		20-18	EXCELLENT TO VERY GOOD: fluent expression • ideas clearly stated/supported • succinct • well-organized • logical sequencing • cohesive	
		17-14	GOOD TO AVERAGE: somewhat choppy • loosely organized but main ideas stand out • limited support • logical but incomplete sequencing	
		13-10	FAIR TO POOR: non-fluent • ideas confused or disconnected • lacks logical sequencing and development	
		9-7	VERY POOR: does not communicate • no organization • OR not enough to evaluate	
VOCABULARY		20-18	EXCELLENT TO VERY GOOD: sophisticated range • effective word/idiom choice and usage • word form mastery • appropriate register	
		17-14	GOOD TO AVERAGE: adequate range • occasional errors of word/idiom form, choice, usage *but meaning not obscured*	
		13-10	FAIR TO POOR: limited range • frequent errors of word/idiom form, choice, usage • *meaning confused or obscured*	
		9-7	VERY POOR: essentially translation • little knowledge of English vocabulary, idioms, word form • OR not enough to evaluate	

(continued)

overall writing process. If students have invested time in developing their writing strategies, responding to feedback, and improving their drafts, it makes sense that they be rewarded with credit toward their final grade. What kind of evaluation, if any, should be given for intermediate drafts? Some argue that no grade should be given on drafts, lest students avoid the risks that could help them develop as writers but that might adversely affect their grade.

LANGUAGE USE	25-22	EXCELLENT TO VERY GOOD: effective complex constructions • few errors of agreement, tense, number, word order/function, articles, pronouns, prepositions
	21-18	GOOD TO AVERAGE: effective but simple constructions • minor problems in complex constructions • several errors of agreement, tense, number, word order/function, articles, pronouns, prepositions *but meaning seldom obscured*
	17-11	FAIR TO POOR: major problems in simple/complex constructions • frequent errors of negation, agreement, tense, number, word order/function, articles, pronouns, prepositions and/or fragments, run-ons, deletions • *meaning confused or obscured*
	10-5	VERY POOR: virtually no mastery of sentence construction rules • dominated by errors • does not communicate • OR not enough to evaluate
MECHANICS	5	EXCELLENT TO VERY GOOD: demonstrates mastery of conventions • few errors of spelling, punctuation, capitalization, paragraphing
	4	GOOD TO AVERAGE: occasional errors of spelling, punctuation, capitalization, paragraphing *but meaning not obscured*
	3	FAIR TO POOR: frequent errors of spelling, punctuation, capitalization, paragraphing • poor handwriting • *meaning confused or obscured*
	2	VERY POOR: no mastery of conventions • dominated by errors of spelling, punctuation, capitalization, paragraphing • handwriting illegible • OR not enough to evaluate

TOTAL SCORE   READER   COMMENTS

FIGURE 6.1 Analytic evaluation: Scoring guidelines for ESL composition

Note: From *Teaching ESL Composition: Principles and Techniques* (English Composition Program), by J. Hughey. Copyright 1992. Reprinted with permission of Global Rights Group, a division of Thomson Learning: www.thomsonrights.com. Fax 800 730-2215.

Others argue against grades on early drafts because those who do well will have little incentive to improve. Both arguments are valid, but it is possible to balance grading in ways that encourage students to revise, edit, and give and use peer feedback. Most teachers take drafts into account but weight the grade toward the final product, because this realistically reflects what students will encounter in other classes. For example, the teacher might give 20% of

An A paper exhibits most of the following features:
- Demonstrates full understanding of concepts in task/readings
- Gives an accurate and thorough treatment of issues
- Takes a clearly supported position
- Provides examples and illustrations
- Shows clear and unified paragraph development
- Shows logical sequence and organization
- Connects ideas smoothly
- Uses complex and varied syntax and academic vocabulary
- Contains few errors in grammar and vocabulary use
- Contains few errors in mechanics

A B paper exhibits most of the following features:
- Demonstrates good understanding of concepts in task/readings
- Gives a substantial treatment of issues
- Takes an adequately supported position
- Provides some examples and illustrations
- Shows adequate paragraph development, but may contain some irrelevant material or may contain some underdeveloped ideas
- Shows generally logical sequence and organization
- Has some missing or abrupt transitions
- Uses a mix of complex and simple syntax and some academic vocabulary
- Contains some errors in grammar and vocabulary use
- Contains some errors in mechanics

A C paper exhibits most of the following features:
- Demonstrates incomplete understanding of concepts in task/readings
- Treats issues incompletely and may contain inaccuracies
- Takes a position, but it is not well supported
- Provides few examples or illustrations, or these are not clearly linked to main ideas
- Shows lack of development
- Shows lack of clear organization or illogical sequence
- Does not connect ideas
- Uses simple syntax and vocabulary
- Contains a considerable number of errors in grammar and vocabulary use
- Contains a considerable number of errors in mechanics

A D paper exhibits most of the following features:
- Demonstrates little understanding of concepts in task/readings
- Treats issues incompletely and contains inaccuracies
- May not take a position or make any claim
- Provides few examples or illustrations
- Shows little development or connection of ideas
- Contains syntax and word choice errors that often obscure meaning

An F paper exhibits most of the following features:
- Demonstrates little or no understanding of concepts in task/readings
- Is off-topic
- Contains too little text to evaluate
- Contains formal errors that obscure meaning, making content difficult to evaluate

FIGURE 6.2 Sample of grading criteria for individual assignments

Task fulfillment	You have addressed the question in the assignment well. You have made a good argument for your position, with adequate support. However, you do not take into account possible other points of view, as directed by the assignment.
Rhetorical structure and organization	Your paper is well structured and organized, with each paragraph developed separately and sequenced in a logical order.
Cohesion	Most of the connections are smooth and clear, especially between paragraphs. Sometimes the relationship of the ideas in sentences within the paragraph is unclear. Check the use of *despite*.
Grammatical form	The final draft of your essay has very few grammatical errors. You did a great editing job!
Vocabulary use	There are still some problems with word form. Make sure that you use the right form, for example, a noun or an adjective. I have made a few notations on your final draft. I can see you are using your dictionary and trying out some new words. Good work!

FIGURE 6.3 Sample cover sheet for teacher response to the final draft of an individual paper

the grade on each of the initial drafts and 60% on the final draft. This 60% could include the understanding that the best papers will show consideration of feedback and evidence of editing. Alternatively, these aspects of the process could be given explicit point values. Not every paper needs to be weighted in the same way. Grading of papers written early in the term might be weighted more heavily toward the beginning of the writing process in comparison to those written later. Whatever the final decision, make these criteria clear to students.

Summative evaluations are given not just on individual papers but on the whole body of writing students produce during a course. The summative evaluation that is required at the end of the term at most institutions is usually done in one of two ways. In one approach, the evaluation is done by the teacher, who decides what the final grade should be based on the body of work the student has done in the course. In the other approach, the evaluation is done by the institution, usually by a group of trained readers who evaluate the work of all students, either in the form of an exit exam or in the form of a portfolio. We address the institutional alternatives in the next section; here we briefly consider the first approach, evaluation by the classroom teacher. This kind of evaluation is usually a matter of how to weight the various components of the course and the writing that the student has done. A final grade should take into account class participation, especially contributions in the form of feedback to fellow students. Not everything has to be graded, however. For example, teachers who assign journals usually give a small percentage of the grade for simply writing in the journal, but they don't evaluate its quality. Furthermore, not everything has to be graded equally. Short in-class writing assignments can be done to ensure that take-home writing reflects students' own abilities, not the work of someone else, but these writings should not count as much as major multidraft assignments. Individual papers can also be weighted differently, for example, with those written later in the term weighted more heavily.

INSTITUTIONAL AND LARGE-SCALE ASSESSMENT

When writing achievement or proficiency is assessed on an institutional level, its purpose is usually to determine either placement or completion of a writing requirement. Institutions may want to determine whether a student needs to take a composition course and if so, at what level. Such placement testing is almost universal for English composition at North American colleges and universities. Placement tests are also common in FLs, but they tend to measure overall proficiency rather than just writing ability. Institutions also use writing tests as exit exams, for instance, to determine completion of a writing proficiency requirement or eligibility for graduation. As mentioned earlier, end-of-term grading may be done not by classroom teachers but by a group of trained readers.

Institutional placement and exit tests are of two basic types. The first and by far more common is the one-shot, impromptu, timed test, in which learners sit down for a specified period of time and respond to a prompt. There are variations on this type; for instance, students may do readings before the test, or there may be several prompts or a choice of prompts. Obviously, when teaching has focused on the multidraft process of composing in which students are encouraged to reflect and revise, this kind of testing can present a serious mismatch between instruction and assessment. The second type of assessment involves the writing portfolio, a topic we address at the end of the chapter.

We turn now to several concerns in institutional and large-scale assessment—creating the task and prompt, scoring, training raters, and special issues in placement.

Creating the Writing Task and Prompt

The most important concern in creating writing assessment tasks and prompts for institutional or large-scale assessment tests is that they be clear to the students who take them. They should also be piloted to ensure that they are reliable and that they measure what they are intended to—that is, that they are valid. Authenticity may be a concern, but it may also be a luxury. When large numbers of students have to be tested, it may not be possible to create a task that closely reflects writing pedagogy. What are the specific attributes of a suitable assessment task and/or prompt? The following are some guidelines:

1. The task should be appropriate for the population being tested. For example, an intermediate FL class might be asked to read some stimulus material—perhaps tourist brochures or train schedules—and then write a note to a friend planning a holiday. Advanced academic learners of English, on the other hand, might more appropriately be asked to read and respond to a brief article on current events or to summarize and comment on information provided in graphic or tabular form. Choosing a topic can be tricky because a particular group may be advantaged if, say, the topic is technical or discipline specific.

2. The task should reflect a communicative purpose. The tasks just described require students to write for a purpose rather than simply to demonstrate their proficiency with a specific grammatical structure or range of structures. Although the linguistic accuracy and sophistication of the texts produced in response will inevitably form part of the overall assessment, sentence-level accuracy should not be the exclusive goal of writing assessment.

3. The task should be accessible to most test takers, with consideration for the time allotted. It should be neither too broad nor too narrow. If the topic is huge and/or unfamiliar, students may be overwhelmed by the task, (e.g., *What steps should we take to improve the environment?*). If it is too narrow or specific, some test takers may find themselves with little to say (e.g., *What steps should we take to control climate change?*).

4. The language of the prompt and instructions should be brief and clear but should provide enough detail to guide learners in their response. How much detail is included in the prompt and general instructions can vary but may include the following:
   - Audience and purpose. An example of this would be the holiday planning prompt.
   - Expected length of the response.
   - Rhetorical specifications. This feature is similar to the specifications of timed essay tests, discussed in Chapter 4. Prompts may direct writers explicitly to compare, evaluate, describe, and so on.
   - Possible procedures. Some instructions may tell writers how to approach the task, for example, that they should spend the first 10 minutes planning or that they may or may not use a dictionary.
   - Evaluation criteria. Writers may be reminded of what the readers value in a response: task fulfillment, complete development, accuracy, and so on, or what they don't value, such as neatness.

In an effort to develop prompts that any student could answer, institutions may end up with very bare prompts, such as this:

Write about a holiday in your country.

Such a prompt might be rewritten to conform to our guidelines as follows:

> Write some suggestions for an ethnic students' association that wants to host a festival marking a holiday in your country. Describe to them how it is celebrated and how they can adapt it to a school setting.

Pause to consider...

how a generic prompt might be rewritten to conform with some of the guidelines listed. Choose one of the following topics and change it to a more appropriate prompt.

- Write about what you like to do in your spare time.
- Write an essay about whether the children of illegal immigrants should receive government services.
- Discuss the advantages and disadvantages of second language study.
- Describe the controversy surrounding the construction of a new airport in Mexico City.

Procedures for Scoring

Once students have finished writing, the rating process begins. Once again, there are several choices; the two most widely used schemes are *holistic* and *analytical* scoring. Both have advantages and disadvantages. In **holistic scoring,** raters assign a single score to a piece of writing, based on a predetermined scale. The number of levels in a scale varies, usually from about 5 to as many as 10, depending on how the evaluations will be used. The scale is accompanied by a rubric that describes the characteristics of writing at each level. The rubric necessarily combines many aspects of writing, including focus, topic development, task fulfillment, thesis support, organization, coherence, grammatical accuracy, vocabulary use, and mechanics. We have already seen examples of such rubrics in Figures 6.2 and 6.3. The best known example of holistic scoring for English is included in the TOEFL (formerly the separately administered Test of Written English, or TWE). The scoring guide for the TOEFL is shown in Figure 6.4. There are similar guidelines for the evaluation of compositions in FL Advanced Placement examinations. An example of the German version is included in Appendix 2.

Another set of guidelines based on holistic assessment are those developed by ACTFL. The guidelines have been used primarily to test oral/aural ability, as in the widely used Oral Proficiency Interview. In fact, there is some debate over whether the original scale is an adequate instrument for evaluating the academic writing proficiency of FL learners, many of whom may have well-developed literacy skills in their L1.[2] The ACTFL guidelines for writing were originally issued in 1986; preliminary revisions were issued in 2001 (summary highlights are included in Appendix 2). The guidelines include consideration of writing functions (e.g., formal correspondence, research papers), writing skills (e.g., *can provide details, smooth transitions*), style, audience aware-

Writing Scoring Guide

6 An essay at this level
— effectively addresses the writing task
— is well organized and well developed
— uses clearly appropriate details to support a thesis or illustrate ideas
— displays consistent facility in the use of language
— demonstrates syntactic variety and appropriate word choice

5 An essay at this level
— may address some parts of the task more effectively than others
— is generally well organized and developed
— uses details to support a thesis or illustrate an idea
— displays facility in the use of the language
— demonstrates some syntactic variety and range of vocabulary

4 An essay at this level
— addresses the writing topic adequately but may slight parts of the task
— is adequately organized and developed
— uses some details to support a thesis or illustrate an idea
— demonstrates adequate but possibly inconsistent facility with syntax and usage
— may contain some errors that occasionally obscure meaning

3 An essay at this level may reveal one or more of the following weaknesses:
— inadequate organization or development
— inappropriate or insufficient details to support or illustrate generalizations
— a noticeably inappropriate choice of words or word forms
— an accumulation of errors in sentence structure and/or usage

2 An essay at this level is seriously flawed by one or more of the following weaknesses:
— serious disorganization or underdevelopment
— little or no detail, or irrelevant specifics
— serious and frequent errors in sentence structure or usage
— serious problems with focus

1 An essay at this level
— may be incoherent
— may be undeveloped
— may contain severe and persistent writing errors

0 An essay will be rated 0 if it
— contains no response
— merely copies the topic
— is off-topic, is written in a foreign language or consists only of keystroke characters

FIGURE 6.4 TOEFL scoring guide

Note: TOEFL Materials selected from TOEFL 2002–2003 Information Bulletin, Educational Testing Service, 2002. Reprinted by permission of Educational Testing Service, the copyright owner. However, the test questions and any other testing information are provided in their entirety by McGraw-Hill. No endorsement of this publication by Educational Testing Service should be inferred.

ness, comprehensibility, and grammaticality. Assessment measures based on these revised guidelines are in the early stages of development.

Another source of assessment information for FLs is the Center for Advanced Research on Language Acquisition (CARLA) at the University of Minnesota, which has developed an FL proficiency assessment measure for the intermediate-low level of the ACTFL guidelines. The Contextualized Writing Assessment (CoWA) is aimed at postsecondary learners and is designed as a placement or place-out test. It is graded holistically as pass or fail rather than by level. It is available for Spanish, French, and German at the CARLA web site.

Holistic grading is widely used because it is quick, efficient, inexpensive, and, with good rater training, quite reliable. Some educators also maintain that holistic grading is authentic because it parallels the evaluation procedures likely to be used by teachers outside language and writing courses. However, because the writing is scored as a whole, the rating gives few details about learners' writing. The procedure rests on the assumption that all aspects of writing proficiency develop at a relatively even rate, and as a result, the scoring procedure equates texts that can be very different. For example, two texts may be rated as a 3 on the TOEFL for different reasons. One may lack development, whereas the other may be well developed but rife with errors. Thus, scores are difficult to interpret and may mask rather than identify writers' weaknesses.

Analytic scoring, on the other hand, breaks down different aspects of a piece of writing and awards them separate scores. We have already seen this approach to evaluation in the guidelines for classroom assessment of individual assignments shown in Figure 6.2. Which components are rated and how points are awarded may vary. Other examples of analytically scored tests are found primarily in large-scale instruments, such as the Test of English for Educational Purposes (TEEP) and the Michigan English Language Assessment Battery (MELAB). Analytic scoring is far more laborious than holistic scoring and consequently is more expensive. However, because each aspect of writing is evaluated separately, scores are useful as a diagnostic tool. Both students and their teachers can use the detailed feedback that an analytic score provides. Such scoring is also highly reliable. A summary of the advantages and disadvantages of holistic and analytic scoring is given in Table 6.2.

Procedures for Training Raters

Rater training is crucial for all assessment programs, whether they use holistic or analytic scoring. The following procedure is typical for training raters:

- New raters study and discuss the rubrics with trained raters.
- Each level has at least one *benchmark* essay. New raters discuss why these essays exemplify a specific level. A benchmark essay typifies writing at a given level in holistic scoring or an aspect of writing proficiency in analytic scoring. In holistic rating, it is probably best to have

TABLE 6.2 Advantages and Disadvantages of Holistic and Analytic Scoring

Type of Scoring	Advantages	Drawbacks
Holistic	Easy and fast to administer Relatively inexpensive Appropriate for large groups	No diagnostic function Equates uneven writing Difficult to interpret Scales may be difficult for raters to understand and use; may require more extensive training
Analytic	Can provide diagnostic information Appropriate for writers with uneven skills Scales are easy for raters to understand Highly reliable	Time consuming Expensive

more than one example, because texts with the same score can be quite different.

- New raters are given a series of sample sets of essays to rate. In the first batch, it is helpful to provide one example text at each level. This makes the initial task much easier because raters know they must find one example of each rating level among the samples. In the second round, the sets of texts should be randomly distributed. The process continues until the new raters can use the rating scales with ease and rate essays with relative agreement. This process is called *norming*. It is not expected that all of the raters will agree all the time.
- Raters recalibrate before each session. If time has elapsed between the training and rating session or between the last and current rating session, raters should refresh their memories with a return to benchmark essays.
- Each essay should be read by two raters.
- Discrepant scores should be read by another experienced rater. In most cases, a two-level difference is considered a discrepancy in holistic scoring.

Pause to consider...

the kind of scoring approach—holistic or analytic—you have used in the past and why. Does it fit your students' needs? Consider the impact of changing to the other approach.

Computerized Scoring

The vast majority of essays are read by human raters, but increasingly, computers are offering another option. Recent advances in natural language processing have led to the development of automated essay analysis. Today, a program called e-rater, developed by the Educational Testing Service (ETS), is being piloted on the essay portion of the Graduate Management Admissions Test (GMAT). It is not yet being used on the TOEFL but someday may be used on that test as well. The program is based on a holistic rating system. It is "trained" on several hundred essays that represent the entire range of proficiency levels. It assesses 50 features of the writing samples, including vocabulary frequency and choice, syntax, length, and discourse cues, and then it uses a complex statistical procedure to weight the features. This weighting is used to evaluate the features of real test essays. Each time a new prompt is used, the program is retrained on a new set of essays. The program's results correlate well with external criteria, such as students' course grades, suggesting that the measure is valid. Results have also been found to be as reliable as human ratings. Currently, e-rater is not used by itself; tests are always rated by one human rater in addition.

Special Issues in Placement Testing

In FL and L2 programs, placement testing usually involves large and often diverse populations. Two populations that deserve special attention are heritage learners in FL testing and ESL learners who are tested together with native speakers in composition placement tests. In Chapter 1, I stressed the unique challenge of teaching and learning L2 writing because simultaneous linguistic development and writing skill development are required. However, in the case of heritage learners, the balance is quite different. These learners have varying degrees of competence in their home language, but many lack academic literacy skills, often in either the home or the school language or both. Thus, their placement essays may display very different characteristics from those of FL learners, who may have more firmly developed literacy skills in their L1 (usually English). On the other hand, heritage learners will usually have a better command of vocabulary and many grammatical structures than their English-speaking classmates, although certainly not without errors and interference from English. For example, Spanish heritage learners often have difficulty with mechanics, such as spelling (e.g., *echo* for *hecho*) and accent marks in their writing. This kind of profile may present particular difficulties for programs that use holistic rating. Programs that expect a significant number of heritage learners should account for this issue in their rater training and include benchmark essays with these characteristics. It may be necessary to modify the scale to flag essays that show the characteristics of heritage learners' writing.

In most college composition programs, all entering students are tested together, resulting in a combined population of native speaker and ESL students. Typical timed impromptu writing tests usually put ESL students at a disadvantage. If a significant number of ESL students are expected in the testing population, it is especially important to ensure that the stimulus is appropriate and accessible to ESL students and that prompts are clearly written. Time is also an issue for ESL writers. Most simply cannot read, analyze, and write fast enough to show their best work under these circumstances. Many may be capable of producing better work, but the raters never see it. One solution to this dilemma is the use of portfolios (discussed in the next section). In addition, rater training should include significant exposure to L2 writing. There is ample evidence that L2 writing teachers rate L2 essays differently than do composition teachers who work primarily with native speakers. If placement is to be both consistent and fair, raters must become familiar with the strengths and weaknesses of L2 writers.

PORTFOLIOS

Because of the weaknesses and lack of authenticity of one-shot timed essays, many educators in composition have sought alternative forms of assessment. Of these, the most widely used is the **portfolio.** Although not technically a test, a portfolio can give a broader and more complex picture of a writer's ability than a single piece of writing. A portfolio is a collection of a student's work, in this case, writing, that shows both progress and proficiency. Many consider portfolios to be an ideal way to assess L2 writers' work because they do not limit evaluation to a single piece of writing produced under difficult conditions, which often mask the writer's true abilities. In institutions that give a timed test as an exit exam with an option of subsequent portfolio submission by those who fail, L2 writers who do poorly on the exam often end up passing based on their portfolio. When raters have a chance to read the portfolio writing, produced under different circumstances, they can come to a different conclusion about a student's writing proficiency. A far higher proportion of L2 writers pass under these conditions. L2 writing professionals have shown particular interest in portfolio assessment.

A portfolio is a purposeful collection of writing that documents the writer's progress during the course. Portfolios typically include the following:

- samples of the writer's best work;
- samples from more than one point in the term;
- samples of in-class as well as at-home writing;
- several drafts of one paper to demonstrate the process the learner went through in arriving at the final draft, including revisions and editing;
- a reflective piece in which writers discuss either a specific text or their writing process more generally;
- a reader's guide to the contents of the portfolio.

In most portfolio-based assessment schemes, the writer decides what to include in the portfolio, perhaps in consultation with the teacher. In some instances, the decision rests wholly with the writer. In this way, the instruction and assessment processes are integrated and the student becomes an active participant in both.

Portfolios are generally rated holistically. Of course, this introduces all of the drawbacks of holistic rating several times over, because raters must now evaluate several different pieces of writing instead of just one. In most programs, portfolios are submitted to a panel of trained raters rather than to the classroom teacher. The intention of this practice is to increase reliability and objectivity. It also relieves teachers of the burden of evaluating their own students. As with the holistic rating procedures discussed earlier, the panel must establish a rubric for judging and go through training before doing any evaluation. Most portfolios are assessed on a pass/fail basis, but they can be used for grading and providing feedback to the learners if levels are established in the rubric.

The use of portfolios as an alternative assessment method offers many benefits but also has some drawbacks. It has the following advantages:

- It is congruent with the writing process approach and therefore a more authentic form of assessment.
- It provides a broader and richer picture of students' writing.
- It allows students to take more responsibility for the evaluation process and for improving their writing.
- It provides a sense of accomplishment for writers when they see the body of work they have produced.
- It takes the pressure off the classroom teacher to give final, high-stakes grades to students with whom they have worked closely.
- It is fairer to L2 students who can show their best work.

The use of portfolios also has the following disadvantages:

- Evaluating multiple pieces is a complex, time-consuming, and labor-intensive process.
- There may be a difference between evaluative feedback by the classroom teacher and the grade awarded to the portfolio by the outside panel, leading to student disappointment.
- This form of evaluation may be misleading to students because they are not likely to have this flexibility in other classes.
- Reliability may suffer.
- It is difficult to guarantee that writers submit only their own work.

Some programs have developed hybrid systems, with a one-shot timed test as a first tier and an appeal process that allows writers to submit a portfolio for evaluation. This approach allows large populations to be tested with efficiency and fairness.

Pause to consider...

the benefits and drawbacks of portfolio evaluation. Could it be effective in a program with which you are familiar? What would be the impact of such a change?

SUMMARY

Assessing student writing is an essential part of teaching. Teachers will encounter several kinds of assessment: summative evaluation of single assignments, summative evaluation of a student's work in a course, and large-scale or institutional testing.

Writing tests may be indirect or direct. This text considers the latter. Assessment may be done for different purposes. Test results may show achievement in a specific skill area or general proficiency. Tests may be given for placement or diagnostic purposes. The tests themselves can be evaluated in terms of their validity, reliability, authenticity, and practicality. They can also be described in terms of how their results will be used and the extent to which they create a washback effect.

Direct writing tests have a prompt, which tells students what they must do (the task). Many also have some sort of stimulus, such as a reading, to which students must respond. The test responses then pass to the hands of evaluators, or raters, who assess them based on a rating scale with rubrics describing various levels of expertise. In any test, it is important to understand what aspects of writing are being evaluated. These include task fulfillment, as well as textual, linguistic, and sociolinguistic knowledge. In classroom assessment, teachers will need to decide how much weight to give each aspect of writing. They may make this weighting explicit in an analytic evaluation, or they may grade holistically. In holistic grading, all aspects of writing are evaluated at once and given a single score. A final course grade should take all aspects of writing and class participation into account, but they can be weighted differently.

Institutional and large-scale tests are usually given to place students in different class levels or to determine whether they have reached a certain level of proficiency. Prompts need to be written carefully and clearly. They can be scored using either analytic or holistic scales. Holistic scoring is quick and efficient, although it requires careful training of raters. Analytic scoring is more laborious but very reliable and can also provide diagnostic details that are not always obvious from holistic scores. Computerized scoring of large-scale writing tests may be developed in the future. Two issues in placement testing are the special situation of heritage learners and the importance of evaluating L2 writers on terms different from those used to evaluate native speakers.

Many institutions have turned to portfolio assessment instead of or in addition to timed tests. A portfolio is a collection of a student's writing, usually including the writer's best work, documentation of progress through multiple drafts, an in-class writing sample, and a reflective piece. A portfolio gives a richer picture of a student's writing ability than an impromptu writing sample. It also focuses more on the writing process and gives the student an active role in evaluation.

CHAPTER NOTES

1. *Composición: Proceso y Síntesis,* by G. Valdés, T. Dvorak, and T. Hannum, New York: McGraw-Hill (2003).

2. See "The Development of Writing Abilities in a Foreign Language: Contributions Toward a General Theory of L2 Writing," by G. Valdés, P. Haro, and M. Echevarriarza, 1992, *Modern Language Journal, 76,* 333–352 and "Early L2 Writing Development: A Study of Autobiographical Essays by University Level Students of Russian," by K. Henry, 1996, *Modern Language Journal, 80,* 309–326.

READ MORE ABOUT IT

L2 Assessment

Braine, G. (2001). When an exit test fails. *System, 29,* 221–234.

Hamp-Lyons, L. (Ed.) (1991). *Assessing Second Language Writing.* Norwood, NJ: Ablex.

Hamp-Lyons, L. (2002). The scope of writing assessment. *Assessing Writing, 8,* 5–16.

*Hamp-Lyons, L., & Kroll, B. (1996). Issues in ESL writing assessment. *College ESL, 6,* 52–72.

Jacobs, H., Zingraf, S., Wormuth, D., Harefiel V., & Hughey, J. (1981). *Testing ESL: A practical approach.* Rowley, MA: Newbury House.

Johns, A. (1991). Interpreting an English competency examination: The frustrations of an ESL science student. *Written Communication, 8,* 379–401.

Reutten, M. (1994). Evaluating ESL students' performance on proficiency exams. *Journal of Second Language Writing, 3,* 85–96.

Song, B., & August, B. (2002). Using portfolios to assess the writing of ESL students. *Journal of Second Language Writing, 11,* 49–72.

Weigle, S. C. (2002). *Assessing writing.* Cambridge: Cambridge University Press.

FL-Specific Writing Assessment

Breiner-Sanders, K., Swender, E., & Terry, R. (2002). Preliminary proficiency guidelines—Writing, revised 2001. *Foreign Language Annals, 35,* 9–15. Available: http://www.actfl.org/public/articles/writingguidelines.pdf.

Valdés, G., Haro, P., & Echevarriarza, M. (1992). The development of writing abilities in a foreign language: Contributions toward a general theory of L2 writing. *Modern Language Journal, 76,* 333–352.

Center for Advanced Research on Language Acquisition (CARLA): http://carla.acad.umn.edu/CoWA.html. (CARLA's web site, devoted to testing writing proficiency in Spanish, French, and German. Samples available.)

The College Board: http://www.collegeboard.com/student/testing/ap/about.html. (Web site for the Advanced Placement examinations.)

*Accessible readings for beginning students

The Effects of Production, Instruction, and Feedback on L2 Writing

In this chapter, we return to some of the issues introduced in Chapter 1, particularly the relationship between L2 acquisition and L2 writing proficiency. Writing is a skill that not everyone learns and even fewer master. In contrast, nearly every human being acquires a language. In Chapter 2, I claimed that language has a major role in writing but that language proficiency—L1 or L2—does not guarantee writing proficiency. Language and writing are clearly intertwined, but how? How does one influence the other? This issue is made more complex when we examine what is meant by language competence. Do we mean just the ability to use grammar correctly? Do we mean having a large vocabulary? Or do we mean something more? Written communication may also require areas of competence outside of traditionally defined linguistic competence. For example, an academic writer will need to develop knowledge such as when it is acceptable to use the passive voice or how cohesion and coherence are established *across* sentences with the use of articles, repetition, pronouns, and logical connectors. Is this knowledge of the language or writing ability?

Wherever the dividing line is drawn, if at all, linguistic accuracy is an important issue in L2 writing. Learners are concerned about accuracy, and most wish to improve it. There are clear consequences for not doing so. Numerous studies attest to teachers' impatience with L2 errors in their students' writing and to learners' desire to increase their linguistic accuracy. Some L2 writing experts suggest that teachers who have both native speakers and L2 writers in their classes judge L2 errors more harshly than those made by native speakers. Most teachers report that such errors negatively impact their overall evaluation of the text. Thus, both L2 teachers and L2 writers can benefit by devoting time and attention to the promotion of linguistic accuracy.

In this chapter, we explore three major questions as they relate to these issues:

- Does output—language production—facilitate L2 acquisition?
  This is a broad question, one that is hotly debated in the field of L2 acquisition, and we can only begin to explore it here. Another way of

140

CHAPTER 7
*The Effects of
Production,
Instruction, and
Feedback on
L2 Writing*

looking at this question is, Might L2 writing play a role in L2 learning? Or is L2 writing simply an outcome made possible by L2 learning?

- Does any form of direct L2 instruction, including various kinds of **form-focused instruction,** have any impact on L2 production, in our case, writing?

The careful reader will notice that the question is framed in terms of L2 *production*. Production is necessarily related to acquisition, but they are not the same. This distinction is particularly important in writing. Most speaking is a real-time, spontaneous activity; writing, in contrast, can be produced "off-line," that is, with time and planning. Learners can draw on knowledge sources other than their linguistic competence. If we define linguistic knowledge as that which has been integrated into the internal system, it is possible for learners to produce forms that they have not actually acquired. They may draw on their explicit knowledge of the L2. Can instruction be helpful in this area? Although our ultimate goal as teachers is to encourage this kind of integration, it may also be possible and useful for learners to use parts of the target language that have not yet been fully incorporated into the developing system.

- If form-focused instruction is useful for improving L2 production, what is the best approach to instruction and feedback?

Should we rely exclusively on implicit learning? For example, should we expect exposure to the L2 through extensive reading and listening to result in successful acquisition and/or production? Or do learners just need a little extra nudge to draw their attention to problematic forms in the input, forms that they might not notice on their own? Some researchers believe this is the case and point to interactive and self-discovery activities as more beneficial than simply telling learners what they need to know. If this is the case, does the provision of rules and explanations even help? For L2 writers, does form-based feedback on their writing help them to change their behavior and improve their linguistic accuracy? Do they pay attention to it or know what to do with it? Can we give blanket advice about feedback and teaching that is valid for all aspects of the language, for example, would advice on teaching preposition use necessarily be valid for teaching tense use?

We certainly do not have the answers to all of these questions, and many are beyond the scope of this book. They extend beyond writing pedagogy to the central question of instructed L2 acquisition: Can instruction make a difference? For L2 writing instruction, this is a complicated issue. The practical question before us is, Can instruction improve L2 writers' linguistic accuracy? There is more than one avenue to linguistic accuracy, as we have noted. Among those avenues are the following: (1) Encouraging learners to use their explicit knowledge is one way to improve linguistic accuracy in production, even if doing so has little impact on their developing IL system. (2) Improvement can also occur through the process of L2 acquisition, that is, through gradual change in the implicit IL system in the direction of the L2. (3) Learners may become more fluent users of language they have already acquired by increasing their control over their knowledge. In this chapter we explore what is known about these avenues and try to develop effective strategies for helping L2 writers improve their linguistic accuracy. As noted earlier, we address the effect of production on acquisition and accuracy, the effect of form-focused instruction on linguistic accuracy, and the effect of feedback on linguistic accuracy.

> *Pause to consider...*
>
> output activities in a class you have taught, observed, or visited. Are these activities beneficial? What effect do they have on students' language acquisition or accuracy?

L2 PRODUCTION AND L2 ACQUISITION

We begin with a general, though necessarily brief, look at the claims that have been made for production as it affects L2 acquisition, and we consider how these research findings may be relevant to L2 writing instruction. Throughout this discussion, I use the term *output* to mean producing language to express meaning; I do not consider production activities that are simply language practice to be output. Most applied linguists agree that mechanical grammar drills are not useful for language acquisition.

Because writing instruction is more than just writing, we look at two bodies of research regarding the effects of production. The two relevant areas of research are (1) the impact of interactive/collaborative activities on acquisition and (2) the impact of language production on acquisition. We begin by looking at activities as learners begin to write, and then we consider the effects of writing itself.

Claims for the Effect of Collaborative Activities on L2 Acquisition

In Chapter 5 we discussed the benefits of peer interaction for writing, especially peer response activities between drafts. Other kinds of collaborative activities may take place as learners prepare to write. Such activities are often used in both L2 and native-speaker classes. What does L2 acquisition research have to say about the benefits of such activities? The findings can be divided into two basic categories. The first category addresses how interaction in general can facilitate L2 learning, and the second addresses how dialogic activities may actually help create new knowledge.

When L2 writers interact, in brainstorming sessions, peer response, and so on, there will often be points at which they have difficulty understanding one another. It may be that a speaker's IL is too far from the target: Perhaps his pronunciation is different, the utterance is ungrammatical, or he uses a word inappropriately. On the other hand, it may be that the listener's comprehension is limited. Whatever the reasons, the participant(s) will have to make changes in their output; they will have to request clarification or

142

CHAPTER 7
*The Effects of
Production,
Instruction, and
Feedback on
L2 Writing*

repetition. In short, they will have to negotiate toward understanding. This **negotiation** can bring about three important conditions that facilitate language acquisition.

- The changes made during negotiation can *tailor the input* to the listener's needs, increasing her comprehension of input. Most scholars in the field agree that for a listener to acquire an aspect of language, she must first understand the message that contains it. Thus, increasing comprehension is a crucial step toward learning.
- Negotiation can increase opportunities for *modification of a speaker's output* toward the target. If the listener signals incomprehension, the speaker will have to make a change in his production in order to make it easier to understand. The hope is that the change will be in the direction of the target language and that the change will "stick," that is, that the modified, more targetlike form will begin to replace the older form in the speaker's IL.
- Finally, the feedback that the speaker receives during negotiation may *draw his attention to features of the L2 forms* in the input that he may not have noticed before and/or to the gap between them and his own production. This increased attention may be the first step in the incorporation of the target form into the developing IL.

The following two excerpts are taken from prewriting activities. Excerpt (1) shows how one student modifies his output, tailoring it to create **comprehensible input** for his classmate, who is having problems with understanding. By the end of the exchange, S may be on his way to acquiring the new vocabulary word *kidney*. In (2), it is the speaker (K) who has some difficulty. She offers the word *twice*, but the response suggests she has not been understood. She tries it again and briefly searches for the right word. The listener then understands that she means *twins*. She offers this correction, which is then picked up by the original speaker. This **modified output** may eventually be integrated or consolidated in K's IL.

(1) C: I think so. We could . . . there were a lot of organs. I'm sure about two: heart and kidney.
   S: Kidney?
   C: Here. I don't know how. Kidney. Like ren—clean it the toxins
   S: I don't—
   C: Yes, you have two of these here (points to back). Kidneys. This organ that they—ren and clean the toxin. Do you know?
   S: I don't know.
   C: How explain kidneys? It's two organs and here and ren? and clean the blood?
   C: The blood. OK. I know.
(2) F: Yes. Gold ring 24 is perfect gold and the baby wear all gold. On finger all rings.
   K: This is good business. And after that, the mother make a beautiful ring with that!

F: Nooo! Some people usually buy the bracelet, but usually one year old buy the gold ring 24.

K: So if you have twice what?

F: Next?—you know, next child, when child get one year old, same thing. Then they buy some gold ring—

K: But twice? Tw. Two. They born at same time.

F: You mean twins?

K: Twins, yes.

F: Then you need to buy two.

In summary, the negotiated interaction that takes place during collaborative activities may have an indirect effect on acquisition by creating opportunities for modified input and output and by calling attention to important features in the input.

The perspective described here is essentially a cognitive one: Aspects of the negotiation trigger cognitive processes. A somewhat different perspective comes from the *sociocultural* theory of the mind. In this view, all cognitive functions are rooted in social activity. What a learner first experiences in social interaction is later transformed into internal mental processes. Thus, dialogue between peers takes on particular importance because acquisition occurs *in* interaction rather than as a result of it, as was claimed in the interactional perspective just presented. The proposal is that new knowledge is actually created and old knowledge is consolidated during interaction. Often this is knowledge that was not part of any participant's individual competence; rather, it emerges dialogically. Put more simply: Two heads turn out to be better than one. Scholars who take a sociocultural approach to language learning place special emphasis on the role of talk, and specifically **metatalk** (talk about language), in learning. Concept and knowledge construction is mediated by language; talking makes the new knowledge available for inspection and discussion. This discussion is a precursor to the internalization of knowledge.

An example of this can be seen in the next excerpt, in which the participants are trying to sort out words that some of them have heard (or think they have heard) that they wish to use in their writing. The teacher instructs the group to attempt to figure out the meaning of *mugging*. They go on to compare its meaning to *smuggling* and *strangling*, in the process rejecting the proposed nontarget forms, *muggling* and *smiggling*.

(3) L: And muggings? I don't know what is mugging.

T: Muggings. Do you know what a mugging is? See if you can find out.

L: A kind of robber?

S: I think it's a kind of a robbery. What kind is it?

L: Asking?

M: Yeah . . . maybe asking for money and hurting the person.

S: Is it like carjack?

L: That's different.

U: What about the muggling? Muggling?

144

CHAPTER 7
The Effects of
Production,
Instruction, and
Feedback on
L2 Writing

L: Muggling? No. Smuggling?

U: No. Smiggling? I am confused.

L: Mugging or smuggling. OK.

S: Do you know what smuggling?

M: Maybe like trade . . . illegally.

S: Drug smuggling.

U: Yeah, something like that. Not muggling.

L: OK, mugging is asking for money. Smuggling like illegal trade or illegal trade between country. That's smuggling.

S: Strangling?

U: Strangling? No . . . Choking. No?

S: I don't know.

U: Choking to murder somebody.

S: With the hand?

L: Or with a rope.

It is worth noting that this example, and many others in the literature, does not actually represent the moment of new knowledge creation. Indeed, it is not possible for output to result directly in new knowledge; new knowledge can result only when the learner's internal mechanism processes the input. Instead, this process is more likely to be a sorting out and consolidation of linguistic knowledge that was already on its way to acquisition.

Claims for the Effect of Language Production on L2 Acquisition

Beyond the claims for the effects of output in the context of interaction that we just noted—providing opportunities for modification of output, usually as a result of negative feedback; directing learners' attention to differences between their own output and L2 input; and generating (new) knowledge through dialogue—does producing the L2 facilitate acquisition in any other ways? The following are some claims that have been made for output or production:

- It allows hypothesis testing.
- It encourages feedback.
- It forces syntactic processing.
- It facilitates the noticing of features and forms in the input.
- It pushes the limits of IL knowledge.
- When planned, it may reveal the leading edge of IL.
- It consolidates/deepens IL lexical knowledge.
- It promotes fluency.

Output Allows Hypothesis Testing

One widely held view of L2 acquisition is that it entails hypothesis formation and testing. Learners can try out their hypotheses and see if they are successful. If they receive negative feedback (when talking about writing, negative feedback is usually in the form of teacher response), they may have to reconsider the hypothesis. On the other hand, if they are successful in their communication, this may provide positive feedback and support for their hypotheses. This is perhaps even more likely in writing, where learners are not under time pressure and can thoughtfully consider how they wish to express their ideas. In other words, they can be quite explicit in their hypothesis testing. The problem with this equation, of course, is that a learner may be communicatively successful with nontarget production. In natural communication, we are loath to correct one another, lest we cause embarrassment or discomfort. Correction is far more likely in the classroom, but even there, feedback on error is inconsistent. Thus, though it is possible to disconfirm hypotheses based on negative feedback, it is difficult to unequivocally confirm them based on the lack of it.

Output Encourages Feedback

It should be obvious that if we consider feedback to be helpful (and not everyone does; see discussion later in this chapter), then output is beneficial. Without output, there is no feedback.

Output Forces Syntactic Processing

When learners are exposed to input, either as they listen or as they read, they process it first for meaning. It is unlikely that they will begin any conscious or unconscious analysis of the forms (that is, syntactic processing) contained in a message until they have understood it. Ironically, some researchers believe that *because* the message is understood, there is little incentive for learners to engage in any syntactic analysis (though surely, some degree of unconscious syntactic analysis is often necessary for message comprehension; see the examples that follow). Some even maintain that it is incomprehensible—or, more precisely, partially comprehensible—input that forces learners to consider structural aspects of the utterances they hear. They consider structure in order to comprehend the message. Thus, message comprehension and syntactic analysis are often hard to tease apart. One well-known example involves the passive voice in English, shown in (4).

(4) The *actress* was *kissed* by the *diplomat*.

Upon hearing such an utterance, a learner is likely to process the content words (in italics), ignoring the inflections and key grammatical words. This interpretation is reinforced by our natural tendency to comprehend the first noun in a sentence as the agent (doer of the action) and the noun following a transitive verb as its object, resulting in the following interpretation:

(5) The actress kiss(ed) the diplomat.

However, some passive sentences would not allow such an interpretation:

(6) The *letter* was *sent* by the *diplomat*.

Because an interpretation similar to the one in (5) would result in nonsense, the listener might be forced to pay closer attention to the structural features of the utterance. Although this is quite possible, word knowledge and the animateness of the two nouns would encourage the correct interpretation anyway, without recourse to syntactic analysis. Instead, it is the need to actually produce such sentences that may draw learner attention to these features

146

CHAPTER 7
*The Effects of
Production,
Instruction, and
Feedback on
L2 Writing*

and jump-start the process of full syntactic processing. In contrast, processing that is primarily semantic (that is, involving meaning) is often sufficient for comprehension. Production then, especially writing, demands a level of precision that is not required when a listener is processing input solely for meaning.

Output Facilitates the Noticing of Features and Forms in the Input

Another important claim that has been made for output is that it may help learners to focus on aspects of subsequent input. This may be especially true in writing. During the writing process, learners may come to the realization that they are unsure of how to express their thoughts or that they simply do not know the form they need—that is, that there is a "hole" in their IL. This awareness may cause them to be on the lookout for the form when they hear and read L2 input in the future, a first step in L2 acquisition. Output can also help learners add to explicit knowledge. Studies that include *think-aloud protocols*, the research technique in which writers verbalize what they are thinking, have demonstrated that writing encourages learners to notice problems they are experiencing in their output. This may lead to analysis of their own knowledge, which, in turn, results in increased accuracy in production. For example, an L2 writer of French might attempt to write a sentence such as the following:

> (7) Pour l'examen, il faut qu'on ___?___ toutes les dates et les faits de la Révolution française. (For the exam, it is necessary (for one) to _____ all the dates and facts of the French Revolution.)

He knows that *il faut que* requires that the following verb be in the subjunctive but is unsure of what the subjunctive form for *savoir* (to know) might be. Whether he looks it up in his verb book, asks a classmate, or simply guesses and then scans future input, the important thing is that writing has created a need for the form. The need to produce directs learners' attention to what they do not know or only partially know. This is sometimes referred to as *gap salience*. The learner who wrote (7) appears to be ready to acquire this knowledge because he knows that the subjunctive is required.

Output Pushes the Limits of IL Knowledge

Most adult L2 learners have a lot more to say or write than their IL competence allows. They are cognitively mature individuals with ideas, opinions, and needs, most of which must be expressed through language. Output, and especially writing, may push learners to the limits of their IL. Some researchers argue that it is in contexts where the learner is pushed and the IL is stretched that IL development is the most likely to take place. In short, output places demands on the learner that may stimulate IL growth.

When Planned, Output May Reveal the Leading Edge of IL

I have proposed that "pushed" output can stimulate IL development. How does this happen? One suggestion is that when output is planned—and this would include most writing—learners have an opportunity to try out new forms in their IL and perhaps to include items not normally available for spontaneous use because they are part of the learner's explicit knowledge. Studies of planned oral language show that such output tends to be more complex and contain more advanced IL forms than unplanned language. There are fewer studies of the planning effects on L2 writing, but there is a modest amount of evidence that points to the possibility of new IL forms appearing in written production before they appear in spontaneous spoken production.

Output Consolidates/Deepens IL Lexical Knowledge

Another proposed advantage of production over comprehension alone is that using incipient IL forms may deepen the level of processing of those forms. This claim has been particularly strong in regard to the acquisition of new words (as opposed to grammatical structures). The contention is not that output leads to initial acquisition but rather that once words become part of **intake** (that part of input taken in for further processing), then actually doing something with them promotes long-term retention and integration into the developing system. "Doing something" includes using them in writing, associating them with other words or structures, answering questions about them, and so on. This process is known as *generation*. Generative use of new forms is thought to consolidate IL knowledge.

Output Promotes Fluency

Some of the claims outlined here are controversial. Some scholars maintain that input is the only source for IL development. Indeed, most of the proposed benefits of output outlined here are indirect; that is, there is no claim for direct acquisition of new forms as a result of producing them. In contrast, most scholars will agree that output activities promote **fluency**. The more a learner accesses and produces a form or a word, the stronger and quicker that retrieval pathway becomes. This perspective sees language production as a skill, much like skills outside of language. The more you practice, the better and quicker your performance will be.

Thus, although there is no absolute consensus on the extent to which output activities such as writing contribute to L2 acquisition and accuracy, there are many intriguing proposals currently being investigated. We now turn our attention to another controversial question: whether instruction makes a difference.

LANGUAGE INSTRUCTION AND L2 WRITING

Throughout this book I have emphasized the idea that there are two knowledge stores on which learners may draw as they write: implicit knowledge and explicit knowledge. How separate they are and whether they interact are subjects of much debate. It is thought that in spontaneous communication, learners draw primarily on their implicit knowledge, because quick and automatic processing is required. When more time is available, as in writing activities, learners may rely less on these automatic processes. Thus, when we consider

148

CHAPTER 7
The Effects of
Production,
Instruction, and
Feedback on
L2 Writing

the question of the effectiveness of form-focused instruction and feedback, we can sidestep much of the debate on this topic. As far as instruction is concerned, much of the debate is centered on whether rule-based instruction and feedback, or the development of **metalinguistic knowledge** (knowledge about language, such as "i before e, except after *c*"), can contribute, either directly or indirectly, to acquisition, where *acquisition* is defined as the development of an implicit linguistic system. L2 writing teachers are naturally concerned with language acquisition and wish to facilitate the process in their classrooms. However, they also must teach their students to exploit all possible resources as they write, including explicit knowledge. Therefore, L2 writing teachers must also be concerned with the development of this knowledge source. Thus, as we consider the efficacy of various instructional interventions, we consider their impact on the development of explicit knowledge as well as implicit knowledge.

Full consideration of the effect of grammar instruction in all of its variants is far beyond the reach of this book, and the reader is referred to other sources on the topic. We limit our discussion here to a brief consideration and then address its implications for the teaching of L2 writing.

Undoubtedly, much of L2 acquisition occurs incidentally, that is, without intention, as learners are exposed to and interact with L2 input. However, it is equally clear that L2 writers continue to experience difficulty with sentence-level grammar and that their output is often far from targetlike in accuracy. L2 writing instructors may need to focus on some areas of grammar that seem to pose a special challenge to L2 writers. Five kinds of structures have been identified as requiring focused attention. The first category includes structures that are somewhat different in the learner's L1 but not so different that the differences are immediately obvious to the learner. For example, the distinction between the *pretérito* and the *imperfecto* in Spanish or between the *passé composé* and the *imparfait* in French are notoriously difficult for L1 English learners to master. On the surface, it may seem to these learners that the distinction should mirror that of the simple past and past continuous in English. Indeed, sometimes this is the case, but often it is not. In contrast, marking of past events in a language like Chinese is so vastly different from the system in English that the same sort of confusion is unlikely to occur (though other types of confusion surely will).

The second category includes structures involving L1-L2 contrasts that appear unlearnable from input alone. The best known example of this phenomenon is adverb placement in English. English allows adverbs of manner and frequency to occur in many places in an utterance (though some places may sound more natural than others):

(8) a. *Often* she has eaten dinner at 10:00 P.M.
    b. She has eaten dinner at 10:00 P.M. *often*.
    c. She has *often* eaten dinner at 10:00 P.M.
    d. She has eaten dinner *often* at 10:00 P.M.

The one place where it seems wrong is between the verb and its object.

(9) *She has eaten *often* dinner at 10:00 P.M.

French, in contrast, freely permits this position for adverb placement:

(10) Elle mange *souvent* le dîner à 10:00. (She often eats dinner at 10:00.)

French L2 learners of English, exposed to the many permissible L2 adverb placements, might be justified in thinking that (9) is perfectly fine. What is more, there is nothing in the input that would dislodge this hypothesis. In order for learners to discard this hypothesis, they would need to notice its absence in the L2 input. It is a lot harder to notice what is absent than what is present. Thus, many L2 acquisition scholars maintain that the only way to change learners' IL is to provide **negative evidence,** that is, information about what is not possible in the L2. This might be in the form of instruction or feedback on error.

In the third category are structures that are not salient. There are many reasons for a structure's lack of salience. Perhaps the structure is rarely used. For example, the input may contain very few examples of the so-called "urgent" subjunctive in English:

(11) It is essential that he report to the police immediately.

The learning difficulty associated with this rather rare form is probably exacerbated by the fact that the learner would have to notice that the expected *s* on the verb is not there. Another reason for lack of salience may be that the structure's meaning is carried by more readily apparent elements in an utterance, making it redundant. An example of this is inflectional tense marking. Often, the time frame of an utterance is made clear by sentence adverbials or simply by context, reducing the need for learners to notice the less obvious inflectional verb endings (*I finishe*d *it* last week). Some forms may also lack phonological salience in oral input, either because they are reduced (e.g., *He passed the test*) or silent (*ils faisai*ent). Lack of phonological salience can also make spelling a particular challenge for L2 writers.

A fourth type of structure that teachers may want to focus on is structures that are not important for communication of meaning. Some structures are simply formal; they carry no meaning at all. Gender agreement on adjectives, common in many Indo-European languages, is an example of this. It makes absolutely no difference in referential meaning if a learner writes *la pierna rota* or *el pierna roto* (broken leg). However, such an error does make a difference in a real-world context. Writers who make such basic errors will not go far using their L2 in the professional or academic world.

Finally, structures that have complex rules in the L2, such as article use in English, negation in Arabic, or the distribution of *wa* and *ga* in Japanese, are tied to both semantic and discoursal concerns that are too numerous for learners to grasp easily. With extensive exposure to input in L2 contexts, acquisition is possible, but in FL contexts, more direct instruction may offer an attractive shortcut.

Pause to consider...

your own language learning and teaching experience. How much of your learning was incidental, that is, unintentional? How much was the result of focus on formal features of language? What sort of learning do you encourage in your classroom? How do you choose formal features for instructional focus?

150

CHAPTER 7
*The Effects of
Production,
Instruction, and
Feedback on
L2 Writing*

Grammar Instruction in the Writing Classroom

So how can teachers help L2 writers move toward linguistic accuracy in their production? Three basic approaches have been used:

- Instruction, in a variety of forms
- Feedback on errors in learners' texts
- Editing training

Instruction is a huge topic that extends far beyond the writing classroom. Traditional approaches follow the *present and practice* model; that is, new forms are presented in context, often with rules for their use; then learners engage in controlled practice, followed by freer use of the form in communicative situations. This approach is based largely on the view that, first, knowing the rule is helpful and, second, using the new form can promote acquisition. Both these assumptions are controversial. Possible advantages of the second assumption, production practice, have already been discussed earlier in this chapter. On the first, research results are divided and lead to three very different conclusions: (1) Knowing the rules is completely dissociated from acquisition, where *acquisition* is considered to be development of implicit linguistic knowledge; (2) knowing the rules can lead to acquisition (the development of implicit knowledge); or (3) knowing the rules may indirectly facilitate acquisition by calling learner attention to relevant aspects of the input. Ironically, for the L2 writing teacher, the choice of conclusions is not terribly important, because none of them rules out a role for instruction. In view (1), even if instruction has no impact on the development of implicit knowledge, its impact on explicit knowledge is recognized. In view (2), the benefit of instruction is manifest because explicit knowledge can eventually become implicit. In view (3), instruction has a direct effect on explicit knowledge, which can in turn facilitate the development of implicit knowledge. Because learners need both kinds of knowledge in L2 writing instruction, it makes sense to include direct instruction on language as well as on composition, whatever one's view of the course of L2 acquisition.

Most recent work in this area has turned to three different kinds of techniques. One kind attempts to direct learner attention to the L2 forms to be acquired less obtrusively. A second kind of technique attempts to alter learners' faulty processing of L2 forms. A third kind of technique seeks to provide learners with natural opportunities to use L2 forms. Most of these techniques are *proactive*; that is, the teacher decides beforehand what the focus of grammatical instruction will be, whatever the form of delivery. Proactive techniques contrast with *reactive* techniques, in which the teacher simply responds to whatever issues emerge in the course of communicative activities. We very briefly review some of these techniques as they might be used in L2 writing instruction. As we do so, keep in mind that any blanket suggestions on how to improve linguistic accuracy should be approached with caution. Language is a complex and diverse system, consisting of many different elements that are not all learned in the same way. It would be foolish to assume that one pedagogical technique would be effective for all of them.

The first kind of technique—directing learner attention to L2 forms—includes many variations, ranging from the implicit and unobtrusive to the explicit and obtrusive. Some variations focus primarily on tailoring input to learners' needs. At the implicit end of the continuum are various forms of **input enhancement,** including flooding the input with the form in focus and using typographic enhancements, in which the forms are highlighted, for example, with bolding or font changes. In the writing classroom, input materials (readings) could be enhanced to highlight new or problematic forms. However, research findings on typographic enhancement have been mixed, with some reporting increases on measures of noticing but no firm evidence of greater acquisition of the enhanced forms. Other techniques in this category focus on learner production, specifically on non-targetlike production. These include various forms of feedback, such as response to written error, which we consider a little later in the chapter.

The second kind of technique involves trying to alter learners' faulty processing of L2 forms. **Structured input** is used primarily in teaching spoken language and targets the development of implicit knowledge. The goal is to counteract learners' natural inclination, often based on L1 strategies, to process L2 input in ways that can lead to non-targetlike IL development and resulting problems in comprehension and production. The best known example is the acquisition of clitic pronouns in Spanish by L1 English learners. The tendency of L1 English speakers is to interpret the first noun in any sentence as the subject, in part because English has rigid subject-verb-object word order. In Spanish, this strategy can lead a learner astray. Spanish is flexible in its word order (a) and does not require the use of subject pronouns (b):

(12) a. *La* sigue el perro por todas partes. (The dog follows *her* everywhere.)
b. *Me* levantó a las siete. (He woke *me* at 7:00.)

L1 English learners tend to interpret (a) as *She follows the dog everywhere* and (b) as *I woke up at 7:00.* Structured input is designed to call learners' attention to the fact that Spanish operates differently and that they need to change how they process incoming input. One problem for learners is that the signals for how to process the input correctly are not very salient. For example, in (b), the learner must realize that the first (pro)noun is *me,* an object pronoun, not *yo,* and that, in fact, the subject pronoun, *él,* is absent. The other clue is in the inflectional ending, *ó,* which signals that the subject is third person, not first person, and that the action is in the past. Yet when relatively low-proficiency learners process this sentence, they are likely to focus on *levant-* and *siete* because these words carry the message content. An effective pedagogical technique will force learners to pay attention to these reduced cues in the input. For example, presented with a choice of two pictures, one of a little girl waking up on her own and the second of her father waking her, the learner would have to process the less salient grammatical cues in (b) in order to make a decision. The hope is that this kind of input will begin to establish or to strengthen appropriate processing strategies. Because this pedagogical technique targets linguistic competence, its relevance to teaching L2 writing is indirect.

152

CHAPTER 7
The Effects of
Production,
Instruction, and
Feedback on
L2 Writing

The previous two approaches address learner attention to and processing of input. Most L2 instruction, and certainly all L2 writing instruction, includes output activities as well. The third type of technique for teaching L2 forms involves giving learners natural opportunities to use them. Many teachers and researchers believe that using new forms in an appropriate and meaningful context helps anchor acquisition. For this reason, many L2/FL texts abound in focused communication activities. Such tasks are designed to elicit the use of specific forms, although their use can never be guaranteed. For example, to elicit the use of the conditional, a text might ask learners to write a sort of "what if" response to various questions: What would you do if you were principal of the school? The president of the country? and so on. In writing tasks, the productive use of grammatical forms and discourse markers is also often linked to content and rhetorical structure. For example, one textbook links a unit on the effect of technology with instruction on adverbial clauses of result, such as *X is so fast/advanced/etc. that . . .* or *Y has so much/many . . . that . . .* Learners are exposed to the forms in related readings and are expected to use these forms in their writing.[1] In this way, the use of grammatical forms is integrated with communicative intent.

Issues of Integration and Coverage

The received wisdom on the establishment of form-meaning connections is that it is best achieved in the context of communicating or comprehending meaningful messages. This philosophy is apparent in L2 writing instruction, in which the teaching and/or reviewing of grammatical structure is integrated with the writing process, as in the example of adverb clauses (8) and in the examples presented in Chapter 3 on logical connectors of contrast. The strongest arguments that have been made for pursuing this approach have focused on the development of the implicit linguistic system. It is not clear that the mandate for integration of form and meaning is as vital for the development of explicit linguistic knowledge. Indeed, the goal of formal instruction is not limited to the development of the implicit system. Quite apart from any role in promoting the integration of these features into the developing system, formal instruction can improve accuracy in production by adding to explicit knowledge.

It is also worth noting that, at least in ESL instruction, after years of emphasis on the centrality of meaning and communication in language teaching and on process approaches to writing, there is a lingering reluctance to deal with grammar in any formal way in many programs. In FL pedagogy, this trend is less apparent, but many ESL writing textbooks include little, if any, attention to grammar. This trend has had demonstrably negative consequences for many L2 writers, particularly minority learners in the United States, such as those in generation 1.5. Yet there is evidence that the development of metalinguistic knowledge is linked to superior performance on tasks that exploit this resource. Writing is potentially such a task. It is therefore possible to endorse a program that includes both formal instruction on grammatical rules, enhanced input, *and* contextualized production as an appropriate component of L2 writing pedagogy. Such a mixed approach may also work well with different kinds of learning styles and with learning different aspects of language.

An additional advantage to going beyond a strict grammar-in-context approach concerns coverage of the linguistic system. In proactive techniques, the teacher can decide ahead of time what the grammatical focus of instruction and student activities should be. Of course, the decision to do so may be and should be based on the teacher's knowledge or experience of what has caused learners difficulty in the past and on learners' readiness to acquire. Nevertheless, hewing to the edict to link grammar instruction to content and communicative purpose may unnecessarily limit the scope of instruction. Although some links, such as past tense with narration and causal connectors with cause-and-effect essays, are obvious, the list of such special cases is a relatively short one. What about improving learner accuracy in case endings in Greek or gender marking in Italian? There are no "special" contexts for these forms; on the contrary, they will be present in every sentence a learner writes. Yet these kinds of structures continue to cause problems for L2 writers. L2 writers may need a more systematic treatment of grammar than is provided when instruction must be linked to content and communication.

FEEDBACK ON ERROR

Teachers spend a great deal of time responding to sentence-level errors in L2 writing. Studies of faculty across disciplines show that many professors and teachers are not very tolerant of grammatical errors; they may judge a piece of writing with grammatical errors quite harshly, even if it contains excellent content. Numerous studies attest to learners' desire for such feedback. Yet there is relatively little hard evidence for the effect of feedback on L2 writing or on L2 acquisition more generally. The role of feedback on error in L2 acquisition is the subject of some controversy.

> *Pause to consider...*
>
> your own views on feedback on error. What sorts of errors do you think require feedback, if any? Does your answer differ for speaking and writing? Has your experience, either as a provider or recipient of feedback, been positive?

As already mentioned, some believe that certain parts of L2 grammar may be unlearnable without negative evidence. However, it is difficult to isolate the specific effects of feedback on form. How do we know that any development in the IL system is due exclusively or even partially to error correction? How long does it take for feedback to have an effect? Does it have to occur once, twice, ten times? And even if we do observe an effect—perhaps learner repetition of a correction in a subsequent draft—are we justified in saying that this represents acquisition?

154

CHAPTER 7
*The Effects of
Production,
Instruction, and
Feedback on
L2 Writing*

In the classroom, the practical problems of measurement become quite complex. Teachers do not respond consistently to error, either in spoken language or in writing. The same error may pass without comment one time and be corrected the next. Obviously, not all errors can or should be corrected; otherwise, communication would stop dead in its tracks. At the same time, how are learners to know if lack of correction means that the production is acceptable? Indeed, how are learners to know that the feedback they are receiving is a correction or confirmation of form at all and not simply a response to content?

In the following excerpt of spoken interaction, the teacher demonstrates diverse responses to students' errors. In line 3, he reformulates and expands *to communicate* to the more suitable *language.* In line 5, he overtly corrects the student's misuse of *make* by fronting the substituted verb, *take,* and recasting the learner's utterance with the correct word. Learner S shows no sign of processing the feedback as she moves on to the next suggestion. In line 7, the teacher repeats the content word in the learner's utterance and expands on the content, offering a good target model. In line 9, he simply responds "OK," despite the non-targetlike nature of the student's prior utterance. The last line, 13, is just good-natured participation in the exchange; it ignores the lack of accuracy in the student's contribution in line 11.

> (13) 1 T: OK, what are some things that make life difficult? Being in a foreign country?
>   2 C: To *communicate.*
>   3 T: Language is probably number one . . . right.
>   4 X: Transportation. You have to make many kind.
>   5 T: *Take.* You have to *take* many kinds of transportation.
>   6 S: About post office.
>   7 T: OK. Post office. *Learning how to use the mail.*
>   8 S: How use toilets . . . quite different each country.
>   9 T: OK.
>   10 S: I confused.
>   11 X: In China have no door.
>   12 C: No door?!
>   13 T: Everybody comes to watch.

What is a student to make of such feedback? Some researchers argue that feedback like this is just too chaotic to be useful.

Does Feedback on Error Work?

Feedback on error in the writing classroom is different from this more general kind of feedback on error in (13). First, in most cases, writers receive feedback long after they have finished writing. Second, feedback does not always provide targetlike models of learner output that allow comparison. There are exceptions to both of these statements, however. Computer programs can often provide immediate feedback on error as the student writes (much like a spelling checker that underlines misspelled words as they appear). Some teachers also choose to write corrections with target models directly on students' papers. (However, it is not clear that this is always the best route, because many writers, particularly younger ones, may be tempted to simply copy models without processing them.)

A second major difference between feedback in the writing classroom and feedback in the general language classroom, also related to the issue of timing, is that most writing—and rewriting—is not produced extemporaneously. Rather, it is a planned activity, which allows writers to draw on explicit knowledge sources. Feedback on error may encourage writers to draw on their explicit knowledge in ways that may be difficult for speakers, who must react to feedback in real time.

One major similarity in the two settings is that feedback on writing errors, as on spoken errors, is contextualized; that is, it is provided in the context of the writer's making meaning. This is thought to be an important element of effective focus on form in teaching. Contextualized feedback stands in contrast to decontextualized grammar instruction in which individual sentences are studied and corrected.

There is considerable controversy regarding the efficacy of feedback on errors in writing. Some educators and scholars believe that it is a waste of time and that it has a negative impact on learning because it takes valuable time away from writing instruction. Yet L2 writing teachers around the world continue to provide such feedback, presumably because they think it is helpful to their students. In addition, one finding is clear: Students want this type of feedback and believe that it is beneficial. Of course, what learners believe and what can be proven with empirical evidence are not always the same thing. That doesn't mean we should ignore students' beliefs and wishes, even if we cannot always provide firm evidence to back them up. Failure to provide feedback can make many students extremely uncomfortable and even angry. In addition, some teachers feel that if they do not respond to learners' errors, the learners will come away with the impression that what they have produced is linguistically accurate, and they will not attempt to make any changes.

As we look at the effects of sentence-level error correction in the writing classroom, we may ask these questions:

- Do learners notice and respond to teacher feedback on error?
- Are certain kinds of feedback more likely than others to elicit a beneficial response?

Note that these questions address whether writers make draft-to-draft changes when some aspect of it is flagged by the teacher. However, this is not really the most basic issue. The questions we really want answered are these:

- Does feedback on error have any long-term effect on linguistic accuracy in writing?
- Are certain types of feedback or accompanying learner activities more likely than others to have a long-term effect on linguistic accuracy in writing?

Certainly, when teachers offer feedback on formal features, their hope is not just to improve a specific piece of writing; rather, their goal is to improve their students' linguistic accuracy in general. If a writer responds to all of the

156

CHAPTER 7
The Effects of
Production,
Instruction, and
Feedback on
L2 Writing

feedback and makes corrections in the next draft, yet makes similar errors in the next assignment, has the teacher wasted his time in providing the feedback, or is it possible that the feedback will have a delayed or cumulative effect? Learners may need repeated feedback on some linguistic features, and we should not expect them to make immediate changes based on a single correction. Another way to view this issue is this: It seems unlikely that long-term changes in accuracy will take place in the absence of short-term improvement, so perhaps we can view draft-to-draft increases in accuracy as part of this development process.

Although we do have some information about the first two questions regarding the immediate positive impact of feedback, we have less empirical information regarding the second two questions about long-term effects. However, data are beginning to accumulate that feedback on errors in writing can also have a more lasting impact. More longitudinal studies are needed before we can be sure.

Pause to consider...

the use of codes to indicate error type, such as vf = verb form, frag = fragment, agr = agreement. Do you use these kinds of codes with your students? Do you think they are effective? More effective than just underlining or circling errors?

How and When Should Feedback Be Given, and on Which Errors?

Most studies of draft-to-draft performance have found that students who receive feedback pointing out their errors are better able to correct them in the next draft, in general, than are those who receive no feedback. This statement requires some caveats, however. First, there is some evidence that if students are simply given more time specifically for editing, they can often do almost as well. This suggests that teachers should build in time for editing, at least in the beginning, to help learners understand that it is an important and often time-consuming part of the writing process, not just an optional activity tacked on at the last minute if time permits.

Second, there is debate about how direct feedback should be. Should teachers tell learners what the error is (e.g., tense error) or perhaps even provide the correct form (e.g., wait*ed*), or should they simply indicate that an error is present and allow learners to figure out what is wrong and make the correction themselves? For example, the teacher might circle all the cases of a specific type of error; or, even less directly, count the number of certain types of errors (e.g., agreement errors) and tell learners to find them on their own; or less directly still, simply instruct writers to look for agreement errors in the text.

Although there is no single correct answer to this question, L2 acquisition theory suggests that indirect methods are preferable. It is thought that when learners register the gap between their own production and the target form by themselves, they process the information more deeply, perhaps transferring the correct form to long-term memory, than if the teacher leads them to it. If, instead, the correct form is provided, the learner may simply transcribe the new form, never processing it beyond the surface level. It is likely that the learner will make the same mistake again.

Yet there are numerous cases in the literature of learners either failing to correct or miscorrecting errors even when their locations are pointed out by their teachers. Research on this question is conflicting. Most recent work suggests that there may be little difference between direct feedback, such as the use of codes, and less direct feedback, such as underlining. However, these findings are quite preliminary, and more research is needed before we have any definitive answers.

Two separate assumptions may contribute to the direct-versus-indirect controversy. First, there is an assumption in the indirect strategy that learners can recognize errors and have the requisite knowledge to correct them. Second, there is an assumption that all errors—and therefore all grammatical knowledge—are alike. They are not. Let's examine both of these assumptions.

Considerable evidence from L2 acquisition research shows that learners will acquire only what they are ready to acquire. Any instruction or correction of forms that is far beyond learners' current level of proficiency will have little effect. One example of this is the acquisition of the English past perfect (e.g., *I had studied Spanish before I got to college*). A study of how learners acquire this form suggests that there are two prerequisites.[2] First, learners must demonstrate stable use of the simple past tense, and second, they must attempt to produce contexts that require the use of this form. In other words, they must attempt narratives that express events out of chronological order: *We left early for the camping trip. We* had *already packed our bags.* When instruction and feedback were provided to learners before the emergence of these two developments, it had little effect.

Next, even if we assume that learners are ready to acquire the form, we really do not know whether one correction of the current IL form will be sufficient to move the learner toward the target form. It is likely to be a far more gradual process. Thus, it may be more realistic to expect feedback on error to be effective on forms that are already part of learners' knowledge, or at least on structures for which learners have made initial form-meaning connections. This knowledge may be explicit, that is, learners can actively apply rule knowledge (e.g., "this expresses purpose, so I should use *para*"); or it may be implicit, which means learners may operate by "feel" (e.g., "It sounds better like this"). The bottom line is that learners can benefit from feedback only if they know what to do with it, a fact that is both demonstrable empirically and intuitively appealing. This should not be taken to mean that feedback that is not acted upon has no effect. It simply means it may have no effect that we can discern. Its impact may be more gradual and cumulative.

The second assumption is that all errors are equal. Again, it seems intuitively obvious that this is not the case, but we often tend to assume that all errors can be addressed using a single type of feedback. Errors differ in many ways; not all language learning occurs in the same way. We often think of language as a grammatical system. This makes sense; learning something as a system is an efficient way to learn. For example, once a learner figures out

158

CHAPTER 7
*The Effects of
Production,
Instruction, and
Feedback on
L2 Writing*

that nouns generally mark plural with *-s* (English, Spanish, French), then forming plurals is simply a matter of applying this rule to new data. As mentioned in Chapter 1, this is called *system learning*. In providing feedback on a particular error, a teacher might be justified in expecting students to apply the rule to all similar instances in their writing. An error that can be explained through recourse to a rule is sometimes called a **treatable error.**

Compare this to preposition choice. Prepositions are more likely to be learned one by one, much like individual words, in a process we referred to as *item learning* in Chapter 1.

(14) a. I think I left my sweater *on* the bus.
      b. ?I think I left my sweater *on* the car.

In providing feedback on this error, the teacher might have very different expectations about what the student will learn than when providing feedback on an error covered by a general rule. There is no clear rule that the writer might be expected to apply in this case.

Errors differ in other ways as well. The following student text is a good example:

(15) In the last two decade, many people from all over the world started rushing to America. In recent years, people from other countries came to the United States has increased. Among of them, I think that almost who were immigrants and refugees came from poor country and different languages.

This paragraph contains several kinds of errors. Two obvious ones involve the pluralization of nouns and the formation of relative clauses. This learner seems to know the rule for pluralization: *other countries* and *different languages* are both formed correctly, yet *two decade* and *poor country* are not. It is probably safe to assume that this learner is capable of self-correcting these errors. Instruction to check for plural errors might be sufficient to get the learner to make corrections in the next draft. Of course, she may continue to make these errors in future writings in spite of the fact that she "knows" the correct form. This may occur for several reasons. First, writing is hard work that consumes considerable cognitive resources. Sometimes it is hard for L2 writers to juggle all of the tasks that are involved in writing, and as a result, some less important ones (like pluralization) don't get much attention. It is also quite possible that the writer was careless, didn't take time to proofread, wrote the assignment on the bus, spent all night on her chemistry homework, or any of a myriad of other possibilities.

Another kind of error in this text, relative clause formation, is a different kind of problem. Although we don't know much about this writer's linguistic development, she does seem to have some awareness of this structure (e.g., *almost who were immigrants*). There are two places in this text where a relative clause might or should be used and one place where the writer attempts it but probably shouldn't:

(16) People from other countries *who* came to the United States has increased. Almost *all of them* were immigrants and refugees *who* came from poor country and different languages.

Of course, there are other problems with these sentences, but the biggest problem seems to be with relative clause choice and formation. It is unlikely that the learner really has the proficiency to make these corrections based on her own knowledge. Thus, using a code such as RC or underlining the error would probably not do much good. To help this learner, the teacher will probably have to speak to her face-to-face, make sure that the corrections suggested in (16) are faithful to her meaning, and demonstrate how and why the changes must be made. If a specific structure appears to be problematic for many students in the class, a grammar *mini-lesson* may be called for in response. This would include (1) an explanation of the form, meaning, and use of the structure in question, (2) discussion of problems that L2 writers commonly experience using the form, and (3) practice in identifying and correcting errors, both in prepared exercises and in authentic writing samples.

We have looked at several examples, but teachers often wonder more generally about which errors they should bring to learners' attention. By now, it should be clear that the answer to this is never simple. As we saw in example (15), a teacher should give feedback on both types of errors, but the kind of feedback required is very different. Thus, we can answer this question in two parts: (1) Which errors should get feedback? (2) Which errors can we expect learners to self-correct if they do receive feedback?

Teachers can't give feedback on all errors (except perhaps in the case of very advanced learners with few errors in their writing). It would take up all of a teacher's time, and it would most likely have a negative impact on the writer anyway. No one wants to see all that red (or green or purple) ink; it's too demoralizing. Furthermore, no learner can process all that information. Consequently, teachers have to make choices. Some educators advise that teachers should provide feedback on errors that are *systematic*, that is, ones that recur throughout the text. This might be good advice for some texts, but it could also be the case, if the errors are consistent, that the learner does not know the form and/or perhaps is not even ready to learn it. Perhaps a better rule of thumb is to look for errors that are *inconsistent*, such as in the plural example given earlier. Inconsistency suggests that the learner has partial control of the form and may well be ready to self-correct, given the time and opportunity to do so.

One other often-repeated guideline is that teachers should respond to errors that *impede communication*. In fact, this is probably easier said than done. Sections of text that are difficult to understand because of lack of linguistic proficiency probably involve precisely those errors—or combination of errors—that will not respond to simple feedback. For example, in the text that follows, communication is clearly impeded. It is difficult to understand exactly what the writer is trying to say beyond a general idea, though he is clearly reaching for sophisticated vocabulary. This kind of problem will require attention, but probably not simple or isolated feedback.

(17) Big kids were afflicting for little kids, on the other hand big kids were enjoying it. That is why I am think for all big kids were bullies when I came here. In my school, couple big kids were harrass little friends and ignore other people.

160

CHAPTER 7
The Effects of
Production,
Instruction, and
Feedback on
L2 Writing

Another piece of advice that is often given regarding which errors to correct is that learners should be held responsible for what they have *recently been taught*. Again, this advice makes intuitive sense, but the caveat discussed earlier applies here as well. The fact that the teacher has recently provided instruction on a particular structure does not mean that learners have learned it or perhaps are even ready to learn it. If they haven't learned the form, it is not likely that they will be able to profit from feedback on it. That said, if the teacher has reason to believe that students have at least partial mastery of this structure, then such advice makes sense. Learners' developing knowledge needs to be reinforced with relevant feedback. If new structures are taught for a day or a week but then quickly dropped from focus, there is little chance that new knowledge will be retained.

The timing of feedback is also important. Many books counsel students not to worry too much about grammar in the beginning stages of their writing. Instead, they encourage students just to get their ideas down on paper and worry about attending to grammatical problems in later stages. This makes sense if the L2 writers are so concerned with grammatical accuracy that they hesitate to put any idea on paper unless it is grammatically correct. Clearly, this attitude will impede their writing process. But if initial feedback and revisions focus only on content and organization, to the exclusion of linguistic accuracy, both the writer and the teacher may regret it later. One reason is that, in some cases, it is no simple matter to separate content from form. In example (17), it would not be possible to avoid the issue of language use in revising the content of this passage; the content makes little sense as is. Another reason is that if errors are allowed to pile up from draft to draft, they may be overwhelming at the end of the writing process, as mentioned in Chapter 5. For every L2 writer who is obsessed with linguistic accuracy, there is one who has little interest in it and finds the whole topic quite tedious. Saving all editing until the end will just exacerbate the situation. If the teacher and the writer pay some attention to accuracy throughout the process, the editing task at the end will be more manageable, and the writer will be able to devote more attention to the errors that remain.

In Chapter 5, we discussed the importance of showing learners what to do with the feedback they receive on the content of their writing. For feedback on form, the desired response may seem obvious, but teachers are often frustrated when learners pay little or no attention to the often extensive feedback they provide. Two actions may help in this situation, at least in the beginning of a course. First, as always, it is essential to model the process. A sample draft from a previous year that includes feedback on form can be used to demonstrate what a writer might do with the feedback. Any codes, symbols, or shorthand comments should be clearly explained, perhaps more than once. Students also need to know how they are expected to respond to them. Second, teachers must build in time during class for learners to go through this process the first time so that they can ask questions. This will also help them to understand that responding to feedback takes time, time that they have to build into their own writing processes. A summary of information on teacher feedback on error is provided in Table 7.1.

- We have little definite information on the long-term effects of feedback on error.
- It is not clear whether direct or indirect feedback is more beneficial.
- L2 writers want teachers to provide feedback on their errors.
- Feedback should be contextualized.
- Not all errors are the same; therefore, not all feedback should be the same.
- Feedback on error will not have a long-term impact if the learner is not developmentally ready to process it.
- Feedback on error will only result in immediate change if the writer knows what to do with it.
- Feedback on error may work best with structures that learners partially control.
- Some form-based feedback should be provided throughout the writing process.
- Teachers should model a writer's response to feedback on form and provide time for students to practice the process.

So far, we have discussed teacher feedback on error and addressed ways in which learners can and should draw on both explicit and implicit linguistic knowledge sources as they write and as they respond to teacher feedback. The teacher is not the only potential source of feedback on error. What about consulting peers? What role can peer response play in increasing linguistic accuracy? Teachers differ in their opinions on this topic. Some advocate the use of peer response for linguistic accuracy as well as for content and organization, especially by advanced learners. My own view is that the use of peer response for grammatical issues should be limited and closely monitored, and not everyone should do it. In low-proficiency classes, this job is best left to the teacher. In higher proficiency classes, peer editing should be restricted to the kinds of errors that the teacher is sure her students can recognize and correct. This basically means that peer editing (vs. peer response) should be limited to proofreading, in which classmates correct errors that writers probably could have caught on their own. Because most writers have trouble catching their own mistakes, automatically filling in missing words or glossing over misspellings, classmates who are unfamiliar with the text may be better at catching these low-level errors as they read.

Self-Correction and Editing Strategies

In the previous section, we concentrated on the teacher's role in helping learners move toward greater linguistic accuracy in their writing. Ultimately, however, it will be the responsibility of the writers themselves to ensure that their texts are grammatically correct as well as rhetorically effective. Therefore, learners must develop autonomy in this aspect of their writing. *Editing strategies* are one essential way to develop this autonomy. They can be used in combination with feedback to address different kinds of learner needs.

All writers need to edit their work; L2 writers are no exception. However, because of the strong emphasis many writing teachers place on ideas and topic development, L2 writers often give accuracy a low priority. This is

162

CHAPTER 7
The Effects of
Production,
Instruction, and
Feedback on
L2 Writing

probably more typical of ESL than FL classes. Yet it is clear from numerous studies of readers'—especially teachers'—responses to error-filled writing that linguistic accuracy is very important. Readers may make assumptions about writers' abilities, educational level, or even intelligence based on the type and number of errors in a text. Feedback can help catch some of these errors, but learners also need to develop self-correcting and editing strategies. This may be an unfamiliar process for L2 writers, and they require instruction on how to edit. It is not enough for teachers to simply tell their students to check over their papers for errors. Students need a plan, a strategy for doing so. The following is a set of guidelines teachers can use to help their students develop effective editing strategies. In the rest of the chapter, we look at them in detail.

1. Demonstrate the consequences of inaccuracy.
2. Provide practice in editing.
3. Begin with what students know.
4. Borrow native-speaker editing strategies.
5. Be flexible; be selective.
6. Use editing in combination with feedback.
7. Expect development and change.
8. Teach students to make editing a habit.
9. Model the use of reference materials.
10. Make learners accountable.

Demonstrate the Consequences of Inaccuracy

Linguistic errors stigmatize the writer. This is particularly true if the text contains obvious cases of ungrammaticality, for example, *Elle a tombé de la balançoire* (She fell off the swing), a sentence that contains major errors in auxiliary and gender agreement. Writers who make these kinds of errors will have difficulty in their academic and professional careers, but this is not the only potential negative result. Linguistic inaccuracy can also affect the communication of meaning. Miscommunication is more likely when the structure is grammatically correct but does not express the intended meaning. For example, many L2 learners of English mix up *he* and *she*. Using *he* where *she* is required will not result in an ungrammatical sentence, but it may well be confusing. The consequences of inaccuracy extend beyond the sentence to the discourse level. For instance, an unexpected tense shift may alter the way an entire paragraph is interpreted. Examples like this, in which meaning is obscured, may help convince learners of the importance of careful editing.

Provide Practice in Editing

The goal of learning to edit, of course, is to self-edit. However, as we have noted, it is often difficult for learners to find their own mistakes. It is also difficult to predict the kinds of errors that will emerge in their own writing. Therefore, many teachers begin with texts by other writers or texts that are specifically created as editing practice activities.

- Model the practice. Teachers can demonstrate how they edit a text by talking through the practice aloud, using a text on an overhead or on a computer screen.

- Move from guided exercises, to authentic activities, to learners' own texts. Many writing texts and handbooks contain error correction activities. When students begin learning this process, it may be helpful to use these specifically targeted texts, that is, texts that contain many instances of one type of error, in order to raise learners' awareness of problems with a particular structure. Practice should then move to more authentic texts, in which there is a variety of problems they must identify and correct. Finally, and most importantly, the knowledge and practice they have gained in these activities must be applied to their own writing.
- Build in time for editing. In the beginning stages, it will probably be necessary to build in time for editing in class. Writers need to see that the process is time consuming and often laborious; editing cannot be dashed off in the few minutes before class.

Begin With What Students Know

Learners need a clear way to identify errors and apply rules to editing practice essays and, ultimately, to their own writing. For each grammar problem, they need to develop a strategy to find and correct errors. Editing strategies will succeed only if the students have the knowledge to find and correct their errors. To develop strategies for finding and identifying errors, learners need a "way in." For example, to find tense errors, a learner needs to be able to identify finite verbs. The crucial element of a successful error correction strategy is that it must provide writers with a point of entry to the text. They must begin the process with something they *can* do and then move systematically from there to what they need to find and change. An error correction strategy can consist of a relatively simple list of steps. For example, for work on tense shifting on unmarked verbs, the steps would be quite basic:

a. Find all the finite verbs and highlight them.
b. For each one, ask, Is the action or event in the present or the past?

- If the action or event is in the present, have you used a present tense verb? If not, change the verb to the present tense.
- If the action or event is in the past, have you used a past tense verb? If not, change the verb to the past tense.

The point of entry in this case is the identification of finite verbs. When learners locate the verb, they have also located the point of potential error and can proceed to use the guidelines provided. If this process seems mechanical, it is. Its advantage is that it does not depend on learners' implicit knowledge. It can even be used for structures that learners have not yet fully acquired. For example, many advanced learners of English continue to struggle with article use; they simply have not yet developed sufficient implicit knowledge for correct spontaneous use. In this case, the methodical form of editing can be used in conjunction with reference materials that compensate for lack of knowledge. These steps can help L2 writers bridge the gap between learning rules and applying them in their own writing.

164

CHAPTER 7
The Effects of
Production,
Instruction, and
Feedback on
L2 Writing

Borrow Native-Speaker Editing Strategies

The approach just described appeals to explicit linguistic knowledge, which is often a good approach with FL learners. Some L2 learners, in contrast, may have considerable implicit knowledge of the language. For them, some of the same techniques used with native speakers may be useful. Writers can try reading their work aloud at a slow pace, testing whether each sentence sounds right. High-proficiency learners, especially those with access to lots of input, may also be able to catch errors this way. Another native-speaker editing activity is sentence-combining. Many inexperienced writers write in short, choppy sentences, so their teachers urge them to make their writing more varied and sophisticated by combining shorter sentences. This practice encourages the use of more complex sentences, such as those containing relative clauses or subordination. Reading the following text, a teacher might ask, "What's another way of saying this? How can we put these sentences together?"

(18) I think the course title is appropriate. I would not change anything. I think it is right for our level of knowledge of English. There is nothing wrong with that.

A native speaker could probably offer five or six different ways to rearrange and combine these sentences. It is possible to use this approach with L2 writers as well, but it depends heavily on the level of learners' implicit knowledge. The ability of most L2 writers to manipulate language is far more limited than that of native speakers; they need considerable guidance in how sentences can be combined and linked. A discussion that makes explicit the relationship among these propositions may well be needed (e.g., causality, addition, and so on) before they are able to offer alternatives. In fact, many L2 writers may have the opposite problem, especially if their L1 writing proficiency is good. They may attempt more complex, sophisticated sentence structures before they are able to control them, as in this text:

(19) This is a limit in learning English and disadvantages to foreign students if there are only foreign students in the class that might have different opinions and objectives which can be beneficial because they can learn different cultures, attitudes and manners.

For learners like this writer, "uncombining" may be the better approach to editing. Writers should write each clause separately and then consider what the relationships among them should be. The teacher can offer some initial rules for how many clauses should be combined in a single sentence. The writers can then recombine the clauses in a more coherent manner.

Be Flexible and Be Selective

Not all learners' needs are the same. Their language proficiency and writing ability levels will differ. This demands a flexible approach to teaching editing, one that may change with each class and from one individual student to another.

Learners will not be able to focus on all their grammatical errors when they edit. It is better for them, in consultation with the teacher, to select several on which to concentrate. As the course progresses, they can add to the list of items to consider during editing.

Use Editing in Combination With Feedback

It takes time for learners to acquire new words and forms. However, if the teacher is convinced that a learner has at least partial mastery of a form, and if the teacher has already provided feedback on the form in previous texts, it may be time to pass the responsibility for accurate use of this form to the student.

Expect Development and Change

L2 writers cannot be expected to catch all of their own errors. For one thing, they may not have the knowledge to do so. Teachers must decide, based on prior performance, what kinds of errors learners can be responsible for and what kinds of errors will need continued feedback before learners can be expected to self-correct. This situation is not static, however. As learners' linguistic competence increases, they can be expected to do more for themselves, and the editing-feedback balance will shift. In spite of the uncertainty about the relative impact of direct and indirect feedback strategies, knowledge of L2 acquisition processes suggests an important bridging role for indirect feedback. If a student is able to make changes to a specific feature based on indirect feedback, this may indicate that she is ready to take on this feature for self-editing.

Teach Students to Make Editing a Habit

We have already stressed that good writers edit throughout the writing process, but they usually also take extra time at the end to ensure that their writing is clear and accurate. L2 writers should be encouraged to edit continuously, lest they be left with a daunting accumulation of errors on their final drafts. If they find it distracting to stop the writing process and make changes, they can simply make a note in the text to return to that spot and reread it. If there are many errors in the final draft, it will be difficult for learners to focus on all of them. Finding errors takes concentration, so if the piece is short, it may make sense to edit in cycles. For example, the first reading could be for tense errors, a second reading for noun errors, a third reading for sentence connectors, and so on. For longer pieces, however, this process would probably be too tedious, so learners will also have to learn to focus on several different error types during a single editing cycle.

Model the Use of Reference Materials

One way that teachers can help learners move toward autonomy in their writing, especially in regard to linguistic accuracy, is to make them aware of reference materials and to show them how to use them. As with so many other aspects of the writing process, the use of reference tools should be modeled. Though it may seem obvious how to use a dictionary, in fact, it is not, especially for L2 writers. Unless someone shows them how it can be a useful resource, it is likely to sit in a locker or desk, or perhaps worse, be used incorrectly. There are four major types of reference materials that L2 writers may want to consult as they edit their work: editing workbooks, handbooks, learner dictionaries, and teacher-made reference sheets.

Editing Workbooks Commercially produced editing textbooks are usually organized around specific grammar points that cause learners difficulty. Most

166

CHAPTER 7
*The Effects of
Production,
Instruction, and
Feedback on
L2 Writing*

contain brief prose or graphic explanations, editing exercises for practice, and checklists. Good ones also offer authentic texts that contain different kinds of errors and make clear connections between editing exercises and students' writing. Most of the available books are for learners of English, because English learners represent the largest market. FL instructors, who may have to make their own exercises and guidelines, can use these books as models. Many ESL instructors do this anyway.

Handbooks Just about every publisher of college textbooks has a handbook for written English. Also available, though with less choice and briefer coverage, are similar volumes for other (widely taught) languages. Most of these books are written with a native-speaker audience in mind, although many English handbooks now contain sections or notes for L2 writers. Handbooks generally provide both rules (e.g., "Use only *estar*, not *ser*, with the present participle") and examples of correct and incorrect usage (e.g., **L'homme vous voyez est mon oncle → L'homme* que *vous voyez est mon oncle—The man* that *you see is my uncle*). Handbooks may also include exercises, in which learners can practice using the knowledge they have gained from the rule provision portion of the material. The problem is that if all it took to write correctly were knowledge of rules, accuracy would not be a problem in students' writing. L2 acquisition research suggests that the process is far more complex. If teachers simply refer learners to the handbook when they have grammatical errors in their writing, the handbook will probably offer little in the way of benefit. If learners are having problems with tense choice because they do not know the distinctions among relevant tenses (and are perhaps not ready to learn them), telling them to consult pages 66 to 69 in the handbook is likely to have little impact on accuracy. It is also unlikely to be much help on rules such as subject-verb agreement in English. Learners "know" this rule; they don't need to look it up—they need to gain control of this knowledge during writing.

Nevertheless, there are some occasions when learners may find a handbook helpful as a reference tool. It is a good resource when learners know a rule but need a quick reminder on details. It may also be useful if learners are aware that they have a problem with a structure, perhaps an indication that they have begun to acquire it. For example, a learner may know that a verb she has written must be followed by either a gerund or an infinitive complement (*She avoided going/to go down that street*) but is unsure which is correct. Most handbooks have accessible charts, lists, and tables to consult on these matters.

Learner Dictionaries Teachers often have strong views about what type of dictionary their students should be using. Many believe that bilingual dictionaries should be avoided, first because they can mislead users and second because they encourage writers to continue thinking in the L1 and then translate. Yet it is unrealistic to expect some learners, particularly low-proficiency learners, to use L2-only dictionaries at the outset. In contrast, it is important for more advanced learners to learn how to use L2-only dictionaries. One way to break into the practice is to use *learner dictionaries*, which, again, are available primarily in English. These dictionaries provide resources that regular dictionaries do not. For example, an English learner dictionary would contain information about whether a noun is countable or not (*book* vs. *information*). This is information that native speakers would not need because it is part of their linguistic competence. Learner dictionaries might also include collocation information, such as that the verb *depend* requires the preposition *on*. They give advice on idioms, levels of formality, and potential pitfalls and mix-ups among similar words (e.g., *famous, infamous, notorious, well-known*). All of this information can be very useful for L2 writers.

Pause to consider...

the use of learner dictionaries. In the language that you teach, what sort of information could a learner dictionary provide that would not be found in a bilingual or native-speaker dictionary?

Most learner dictionaries are now available on CD-ROM, which makes information easily accessible in a variety of formats, including pictures, sound, and video. Technology has changed the way dictionaries are made and used. Most now use massive corpora that show how words are actually used by real speakers and writers. Dictionaries have also been developed for specific purposes. We usually think of dictionaries as reference books to use when we come across a word we don't know while listening or reading. In contrast, some dictionaries have been developed (again in English) specifically for writers.[3] Users begin with a common word, such as *thin*. The dictionary provides the core meaning and then offers synonyms and other linguistic information, such as how synonyms differ, perhaps as applied to animate or inanimate referents; how to intensify or soften the meaning; which are derogatory expressions; and so on. Familiarity with such tools can make learners more active users of the L2.

Some dictionaries come with study guides or workbooks to familiarize users with their features. It is crucial that teachers either have students use these guides or develop other activities that create contexts for natural use in order to show learners how to use these references effectively and to reinforce the idea that such use is a normal part of the writing process. Once learners become familiar with the more obvious uses of the dictionary, they can be introduced to other benefits. For example, one consistent problem of L2 writers is choosing the correct word form (e.g., *difficult, difficulty; gesund, Gesundheit*). If teacher feedback indicates that this is a problem on the draft, writers can look up the correct form in the dictionary. In this way, feedback is linked to editing strategies and to good writing practices.

Teacher-Made Reference Sheets or Guides Sometimes even good reference materials can be overwhelming, especially for beginning writers. In these cases, the teacher may have to select among options and prepare more accessible reference materials. Students can be referred to these guides instead of handbooks or dictionaries as they edit their texts. For example, one area of considerable difficulty in English is the use of logical connectors between

168

CHAPTER 7
*The Effects of
Production,
Instruction, and
Feedback on
L2 Writing*

clauses. They are difficult because the writer must consider not only their meaning but also their grammatical role, distribution, and register. Thus, although a writer might understand that *and* and *moreover* are both additive connectors and *although* and *however* are both contrastive connectors, in neither case are the two interchangeable. Yet textbooks often provide long lists of these connectors as if they were. Teachers may want to prepare a list of a limited set of connectors, with appropriate explanations, that they wish their students to use as they write. The list might exclude connectors like *moreover,* which is relatively rare, formal, and probably unnecessary for most writers, and *nevertheless,* which, as we saw in Chapter 3, has a somewhat restricted meaning that may be difficult for beginning learners to grasp. Teacher-made materials can help students avoid errors until they are ready to learn these more difficult and less frequent forms.

Make Learners Accountable

Whatever combination of strategies a teacher chooses, an essential goal in teaching editing skills is to gradually transfer responsibility for accuracy to students, as their linguistic proficiency permits. Soon enough, they will be in classes in which the teacher expects targetlike accuracy. In ESL situations, L2 teachers give way to composition teachers and content area teachers, none of whom may provide formal feedback. They may also have little patience for L2 learner errors. FL majors, too, will soon enter classes in which the focus of their reading and writing is on meaning and content, with linguistic accuracy no longer a focus of daily classes. Writers will be expected to have mastered this aspect of the language. Thus, learners must develop their own methods for increasing and maintaining accuracy in their writing.

Two ways of assisting learners toward this goal of autonomy are establishing a personal record of problematic structures and developing a formal system of accountability for responding to feedback and using it in future writing assignments. For example, if a student knows she has had difficulty with use of the subjunctive in Spanish, she might make a note of this in a personal error log. The entry might contain instructions on how to check texts for subjunctive forms as well as notations about which structures are typically associated with errors. For example, the log might list contrary-to-fact statements containing *si* (*if*), specific adverb clauses (*a menos que, en caso que, sin que,* etc.), relative clauses with indefinite or negative referents (e.g., *Busqua a una maestra bilingüe que . . .*). Or the log entry could be quite simple, such as one for plural:

1. Grammar point that I plan to work on:
   <u>Noun marking on plurals</u>
2. Strategy for improving my performance:
   <u>Put in a √ mark next to each noun as I go through my draft to remind myself to check if it is singular or plural.</u>

Notes like this serve as a memory aid for writers as they edit their final drafts. Because it is often difficult to focus on all potential errors at once, this record can help them to look for structures that have caused them problems in the past. Such records can also be helpful in evaluating progress at the end of a course.

The personal error log works best with students who are motivated and handle autonomy well. Not all students fit this profile, and sometimes it is useful to take a more teacher-directed approach, at least initially. Some teachers favor a written "contract" with their students, in which writers promise that they have checked their drafts for specific items on which they have already received feedback, structures that both they and their teacher think they are ready to control. Students might be asked to attach a checklist with their drafts, stating which structures they have checked. The structures should be chosen in advance by the student in consultation with the teacher. For both the personal logs and the contracts, the structures must be ones that writers know and that are readily identifiable. Inflectional morphology, for example, makes a better choice than complex syntax.

As we noted back in Chapter 1, L2 acquisition is a long and complex process. It is unrealistic to expect that any of the steps outlined here will result in immediate changes in writers' ILs. Gradually, as they write more, learners will incorporate what they have learned into their writing more automatically. Beyond this gradual increase in linguistic proficiency, realistic goals for L2 writers are the efficient application of their current explicit and implicit linguistic knowledge and the ability to find answers when they do not have the requisite knowledge.

SUMMARY

Good writing requires linguistic accuracy. Writing instructors need to facilitate both L2 development and writing development. The two are intertwined but not the same. In exploring their relationship, we ask, What is the effect of output activities, such as writing, on language acquisition? Research suggests that several kinds of activities, which are often part of the writing curriculum, may be helpful. Preparatory activities, such as collaborative tasks, in which learners interact and negotiate meaning, may facilitate language development by tailoring input and pushing learners toward more targetlike output. Some studies even suggest that dialogue among learners can result in creation of new linguistic knowledge. The writing process itself may also indirectly assist language learning. It permits hypothesis testing, encourages feedback, forces syntactic processing, and consolidates linguistic knowledge. It can also help learners notice gaps in their knowledge, which may in turn foster their awareness of relevant forms in subsequent input.

Many teachers assume the best way to increase linguistic accuracy is through direct instruction in grammar and vocabulary. Current research suggests that drawing learner attention to form is indeed important, but it is not clear how explicit such instruction must be. There are a variety of approaches that permit less obtrusive focus on form.

One major form of teacher intervention is feedback. The efficacy of feedback on linguistic accuracy in writing remains controversial. Although most students can increase their accuracy following teacher feedback on a specific piece of writing, it is not clear if the feedback has any long-term impact. Providing feedback on error is not a simple process. One important decision for

170

CHAPTER 7
*The Effects of
Production,
Instruction, and
Feedback on L2
Writing*

teachers is the level of directness of their response. Although many L2 professionals believe indirect feedback is most beneficial because it allows learners to discover their own errors, there is little solid evidence that level of directness makes much difference. Decisions about feedback must also take into account the error in question. Two considerations in this regard are the learner's developmental readiness and the formal complexity of the form in error. Learners are most likely to be ready to process feedback on a form that they use inconsistently. This shows they have partial mastery of the form.

Editing strategies are another valuable tool in promoting linguistic accuracy. These work best for forms that learners know but have trouble controlling, that is, errors that learners can correct on their own, given time and guidance. As with other activities, the editing process should be modeled and practiced. Finally, it is important for teachers to establish a system that holds learners accountable for the linguistic accuracy of their writing.

CHAPTER NOTES

1. *Developing Composition Skills*, by M. Reuttan, 1997, Boston: Heinle.
2. "The Interaction of Pedagogy and Natural Sequences in the Acquisition of Tense and Aspect," by K. Bardovi-Harlig, in *Second Language Acquisition Theory and Pedagogy*, ed. by F. Eckman et al., 1995, Mahwah, NJ: Erlbaum.
3. For example, the *Longman Language Activator*, 2nd ed., 2002, Essex, UK: Harlow.

READ MORE ABOUT IT

The Role of Output in L2 Acquisition

Izumi, S., & Bigelow, M. (2000). Does output promote noticing and second language acquisition? *TESOL Quarterly, 34*, 239–278.

Shehadeh, A. (2002). Comprehensible output, from occurrence to acquisition: An agenda for acquisitional research. *Language Learning, 52*, 647–697.

Swain, M. (1995). Three functions of output in second language learning. In G. Cook & B. Seidlhoffer (Eds.), *Principles and practice in applied linguistics* (pp. 125–157). Oxford: Oxford University Press.

Swain, M., & Lapkin, S. (1995). Problems in output and the cognitive processes they generate: A step towards second language learning. *Applied Linguistics, 16*, 371–391.

Effect of Form-Focused Language Instruction

*Brinton, D., & Holten, C. (2001). Does the emperor have no clothes? A re-examination of grammar in content-based instruction. In J. Flowerdew & M. Peacock (Eds.), *Research perspectives on English for academic purposes* (pp. 239–251). Cambridge: Cambridge University Press.

Doughty, C., & Williams, J. (1998). Pedagogical choices in focus on form. In C. Doughty & J. Williams (Eds.), *Focus on form in classroom second language acquisition* (pp. 197–261). Cambridge: Cambridge University Press.

Ellis, R. (2002). The place of grammar in the second/foreign language curriculum. In E. Hinkel & S. Fotos (Eds.), *New perspectives on grammar teaching in second language classrooms* (pp. 17–34). Mahwah, NJ: Erlbaum.

Mitchell, R. (2000). Applied linguistics and evidence-based classroom practice: The case of foreign language grammar pedagogy. *Applied Linguistics, 21,* 281–303.

*Spada, N. (1997). Form-focussed instruction and second language acquisition: A review of classroom and laboratory research. *Language Teaching Abstracts, 30,* 73–87.

Truscott, J. (1996). The case against grammar in L2 writing classes. *Language Learning, 46,* 327–369.

Interaction in L2 Acquisition

Ellis, R. (1999). (Ed.) *Learning a second language through interaction.* Amsterdam: John Benjamins.

Gass, S. (1997). *Input, interaction and the second language learner.* Mahwah, NJ: Erlbaum.

Collaborative Activities in L2 Writing

Swain, M. (2000). The output hypothesis and beyond: Mediating acquisition through collaborative dialogue. In J. Lantolf (Ed.), *Sociocultural theory and second language learning* (pp. 97–114). Oxford: Oxford University Press.

Swain, M., Brooks, L., & Tocalli-Beller, A. (2002). Peer-peer dialogue as a means of second language learning. *Annual Review of Applied Linguistics, 22,* 171–185.

Feedback in L2 Writing

Ayoun, D. (2001). The role of positive and negative feedback in the second language acquisition of the *passé composé* and *imparfait. Modern Language Journal, 85,* 226–243.

*Ferris, D. (2002). *Treatment of error in second language student writing.* Ann Arbor, MI: University of Michigan Press.

Ferris, D., & Roberts, B. (2001). Error feedback in L2 writing classes: How explicit does it need to be? *Journal of Second Language Writing, 10,* 161–184

Editing Strategies

*Cogie, J., Strain, K., & Lorinskas, S. (1999). Avoiding the proofreading trap: The value of error correction strategies. *Writing Center Journal, 19,* 19–39.

*Ferris, D. (1995). Teaching students to self-edit. *TESOL Journal, 4,* 18–22.

*Shih, M. (1998) ESL writers' editing strategies. *College ESL, 8,* 64–86.

*Williams, J., & Evans, J. (2001). How useful are handbooks for second language writers? *Writing Program Administration, 25,* 59–75.

*Accessible readings for beginning students

CHAPTER 8

Program Options for Second Language Writing Instruction

Many L2/FL instructors see writing instruction primarily as an extension of structure-based or communicative language teaching. The curricular option that is most familiar is one in which instruction moves from sentence to paragraph to essay, with a consistent focus on linguistic accuracy. This somewhat traditional view of L2 writing does not preclude many of the ideas that have been outlined thus far in this book. In this chapter, however, we address some other curricular options in teaching L2 writing.

TRADITIONAL APPROACHES TO WRITING IN THE L2 CLASSROOM

As language teachers, many L2 writing teachers see their job as facilitating language acquisition. This is an entirely appropriate perspective. In the teaching of writing, as we have noted, we are responsible not only for helping learners develop their L2 competence but also for helping them develop their writing skill. Although these goals need not be at odds, it is sometimes difficult to maximize attention to both goals simultaneously. Therefore, most L2 writing classes focus on a combination of language development and skill practice. Pedagogical approaches may focus variously on structural patterns, functions of writing, or the writing process itself. What follows is a brief outline of the characteristics of a traditional approach to teaching L2 writing.

A Focus on Structural and Rhetorical Patterns

The label *traditional* should not be taken in an exclusively negative light. Indeed, we have drawn on some elements of the traditional approach in this volume. Despite the usefulness of some aspects of this approach, however, it is not a position adopted here. For example, some teachers emphasize mastery of units of writing, that is, the sentence and then the paragraph, before assigning longer, multiparagraph writing. Because it is important for writers to consider the whole developing text, requiring accurate paragraph production as a prerequisite to composing longer texts seems counterproductive. Paragraphs take on meaning as a part of a complete text; they are difficult to write and evaluate on their own. Linguistic accuracy grows with time and skill, and it can improve in longer pieces as quickly as in shorter ones.

This structural approach also favors the traditional five-paragraph essay, with its predictable elements of an introduction, complete with thesis statement and road map for the rest of the essay; three supporting paragraphs, each introduced with a topic sentence; and a final concluding paragraph, which restates the thesis and offers some evaluation. Although this approach has been criticized as a "cookbook" approach that stifles students' imagination and critical thinking, it does contain elements that can be helpful to students and teacher alike. Its very predictability can be an asset for new writers. For example, beginning writers need to understand that every piece of writing needs a main point and that readers expect to be informed of it early in a text. Similarly, readers expect that each paragraph will focus primarily on one idea and that one or two sentences in that paragraph will say what that idea is. On the other hand, we would like to avoid slavish devotion to this formula to the exclusion of any meaningful ideas. Writing teachers generally do not respond positively to essays that begin, "There are many reasons for X," followed by three paragraphs, each beginning with, "The first (second, third) reason is . . . ," and ending with a paragraph that begins, "In conclusion, there are many reasons for X." Such essays usually end up saying very little of substance.

A third characteristic of this approach is that it often stresses the importance of rhetorical patterns. For example, writers might be asked to write an essay that uses a compare-and-contrast pattern, a cause-and-effect pattern, or a pattern that describes a process. All of these patterns are indeed useful in academic writing. In Chapter 3, we looked at an assignment that required learners to make comparisons. These patterns also provide a useful context for introducing and practicing vocabulary and structural elements that express the rhetorical function being taught. The problem that many educators have with this approach is the emphasis on rhetorical form over message. It is quite odd to begin a writing task with a form or pattern like the following:

> Think of two things, people, or places to compare and contrast. Use the point-by-point or block format to compare them. Use transitions and connectors from the list.

Life just doesn't happen like that. Rather, we begin with an idea, and then we consider the format that would best express it. Beginning with the form and then searching for a message to fit the form is simply language/skill practice; it is not writing. If the goal is to have students learn ways to express comparisons or contrasts, the course content should suggest the rhetorical form, such as a comparison of two points of view expressed in class readings. The structural/rhetorical pattern approach stresses the form of student texts; their content is almost entirely irrelevant. Nevertheless, like the five-paragraph essay, this approach contains useful elements that we can still use.

Pause to consider...

which elements of the traditional approach to teaching writing might be beneficial for your students and which might better be abandoned.

A Focus on Writing Purpose and Writing Process

Dissatisfied with the overemphasis on form and patterns in more traditional approaches, many teachers turned to alternative ways to organize their instruction, beginning with writing purpose. Why do writers write? Some examples are writing to inform, to persuade, to entertain, or to solve a problem. This approach reversed the order of decision making outlined in the previous section. Now writers would begin with a purpose and only then decide which forms of organization would work best, taking into account audience and genre. What do the readers know, and what does the writer need to tell them? What different kinds of writing are generally used for different purposes? How does a letter to the editor differ from an abstract for an academic article or a note to a friend?

As we noted in Chapter 2, there was also a shift from a focus on the written product to a focus on the writing process. Although process writing may be relatively new in FL classes, most native speaker and ESL writing classes today, from elementary school to college, include elements of process writing. Teachers encourage their students to discover their own writing processes and to make them more effective. Learners find ways of generating ideas on a topic, focusing their ideas, and putting them into writing. The recursive nature of the process is stressed, including the expectation that most writing will have to go through multiple drafts before it arrives at a final product. In process writing classes, the focus is often on expression of meaning rather than on grammatical accuracy. In order to prevent writers from getting stuck on sentence-level accuracy, teachers may tell students not to worry about grammar, advice that may be counterproductive for many L2 writers. Somewhat ironically for an approach that places such value on meaning, *what* students write about in process writing may actually be relatively unimportant. Content is a vehicle for learning about writing; it is not central to instruction or evaluation.

We have incorporated many of the aspects of these approaches into the suggestions offered in Chapters 3 and 4. Some elements may be found in several different approaches, including the ones we examine in this chapter. These next two approaches—task-based instruction and content-based instruction—offer alternatives to the more familiar approaches.

TASK-BASED INSTRUCTION AND LANGUAGE LEARNING FOR ACADEMIC PURPOSES

Task-based instruction (TBI) is an instructional approach that attempts to incorporate what is known about L2 learning into classroom activities, namely, that language is best learned in the exchange of meaningful messages. It is an approach to both syllabus design and teaching methodology that uses information-gathering/analysis and problem-solving tasks as an organizing principle for language teaching and learning. One way of implementing TBI is to have learners work toward a goal outside of the language domain. *Tasks* have been variously defined but are usually considered to be goal-oriented activities that are relevant to school or life needs. A task is something one does outside of the language classroom; it has little to do with language learning or practice. Some researchers have argued that real life is the best place to begin planning a language course. Teachers need to establish what learners will need to do with the language after their studies are over and then work the results into course planning. This approach has a number of advantages:

- It has high face validity; in other words, learners can immediately see the utility of these tasks.
- Authentic tasks are more likely to engage learners than language practice that requires little thought.
- It allows a dual focus on language and content.
- It places the control of communication in the hands of the learner.
- It may better accommodate learners' sequence of acquisition than pre-sequenced, grammar-based teaching.
- Tasks can be manipulated in terms of cognitive and linguistic complexity.

Sequencing and Manipulating Tasks

Clearly, it is not possible for most learners to tackle a target task immediately. For this reason, it is often necessary to design pedagogical tasks that successively approximate real-life tasks in terms of cognitive complexity and linguistic difficulty. One problem with TBI is that because it emphasizes authentic situations, learners often depend on lexically based communication in completing tasks, trying to convey their message with whatever limited resources they have. Although this strategy may permit task completion or communicative success, it does not always promote the goal of facilitating language acquisition. Therefore, some educators advocate that tasks be "seeded," that is, that they be planned so that learners are likely to use a form being taught, though use can never be guaranteed. For example, a report on past events would be expected to require the use of past tenses.

It is also possible for the teacher to sequence or manipulate tasks to stress different aspects of language development, such as fluency, complexity, and accuracy. One way of doing this is to control the amount of time or planning opportunity that learners have to complete a task. Greater opportunity to plan generally increases the complexity of production, because learners can try out forms or words at the leading edge of their IL development. Tasks that draw learners' attention to form are likely to result in more accurate production. Tasks that involve familiar material or processes will also permit greater attention to accuracy and/or greater fluency, because content does not demand as much attention.

Most examples of TBI are found in settings in which students are learning all skills. For writing in postsecondary settings, most examples of TBI are found in Language for Academic Purposes (LAP) courses. Writing tasks are of the type described in Chapter 3: book reviews, bibliographies, reports, essays, exam questions, and so on. These are all genres that students are likely to encounter in their academic careers. But what do we really mean when we talk about authentic writing tasks in LAP? Much of the exploration of this question has been in ESL, particularly focusing on the articulation between the writing that is done in ESL classes and the writing that is required in mainstream college classes. We may draw parallels between these experiences and the articulation between writing tasks in upper-level basic FL classes and the writing required of FL majors.

Two Approaches to TBI in L2 Writing Instruction

Research suggests that there is an important difference between writing tasks in L2/FL classes and writing tasks in mainstream content classes. Many language classes require primarily personal writing—narratives, opinion pieces, descriptions—and responses to a written or visual stimulus—an article, story, or film. Examples of the first type are

Describe your favorite place.

Write about an important decision in your life.

Examples of the second type include

Explain the theme of the film and describe your favorite part.

What was the importance of event X in this article? Has anything similar ever happened to you?

These kinds of writing tasks provide output practice and may begin to approximate or contain elements of academic writing tasks. They are of low cognitive complexity: They draw on the learners' own experience or require relatively little interaction with the source text beyond comprehension. Content is of minimal importance; intellectual challenge is also often low. Yet such tasks can be useful stepping stones. If the objective is to have learners focus on vocabulary acquisition or linguistic accuracy, the familiarity and straightforward nature of these tasks/texts can be part of a sound pedagogical plan. In classes in which mastery of the language is the goal, these kinds of tasks make sense. Such tasks can also be shaped to include some attention to audience and purpose:

Describe your favorite place in Chicago to an exchange student who is coming to your university for a semester.

In order to prepare learners adequately for future academic work, however, teachers need to include pedagogical tasks that more closely approximate the authentic target tasks. Specifically, learners will have to attempt more *text-responsible* writing assignments. In such writing, students are expected not simply to write from experience or respond to a text; rather, they must demonstrate their understanding of the text and transform this knowledge into a new product. They may have to present an analysis or critique of the argument contained in the text, a synthesis and comparison of several texts, an evaluation of causes of events presented in data they have collected, or some other quite complex task. Very rarely are students asked to offer their own experience or opinions in such tasks. Any task-based academic writing course should culminate in these kinds of activities if learners are to gain maximum benefit. That said, the jump from experiential and response-to-text writing to text-responsible writing can be a big one. Teachers may have to provide intermediate tasks between these kinds of writing. For example, teachers may assign tasks that involve data collection and analysis yet do not require engagement with difficult texts. Instead, learners gather information from more familiar sources, such as peers or visual media. (I described some tasks of this type in Chapters 3 and 4.) In working on such tasks, learners can practice the same critical and analytical skills required of more complex writing assignments but on more accessible material.

> ## Pause to consider...
> the kinds of bridging tasks between experiential and academic writing that would be appropriate for your learners. How much do you know about their target writing tasks?

Designing a course with pedagogical tasks that successively approximate target tasks is one approach to TBI. Another is to begin with tasks that more closely simulate what learners will encounter in the future but to scaffold the tasks so that learners are initially provided with considerable support as they attempt them. Learners who are not yet ready to take on these tasks independently may be successful under the guidance of an expert. Support may be provided in a number of ways. Most academic writing tasks begin with gathering and analyzing information from readings or other sources. In mainstream content courses, learners are expected to do this on their own, but inexperienced writers may not know how to find information or what to do with it once they find it. The process includes several stages: finding sources, evaluating and analyzing information from those sources, synthesizing the information, and turning it into a draft. In task-based L2 writing courses, support can be provided at each stage of the process.

The first stage—gathering information—is used here as an example. Assume the assignment was as follows:

> You will write a 5–6 page paper on the following topic: What was the impact of the arrival of the Spanish on the indigenous cultures of Mexico? Compare the life of ordinary people before and after the arrival of Cortez. What was the effect on religious practices, the arts, health, agriculture, and other forms of work? On administrative and government structures?

Examples of the kinds of support that can be provided, from maximum teacher support and guidance to minimum teacher support/maximum learner autonomy, are shown in Table 8.1.

Once students have identified information sources, teachers can provide assistance in the form of questions to guide critical reading, instructions for note taking, and previews of academic or discipline-specific vocabulary. Scaffolding for later stages in the process might include the use of graphic organizers or outlines after the first draft and teacher feedback once the writing

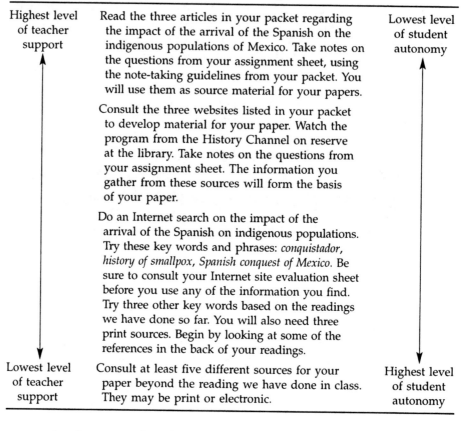

TABLE 8.1 Levels of Support in Academic Writing Tasks

Highest level of teacher support	Read the three articles in your packet regarding the impact of the arrival of the Spanish on the indigenous populations of Mexico. Take notes on the questions from your assignment sheet, using the note-taking guidelines from your packet. You will use them as source material for your papers.	Lowest level of student autonomy
	Consult the three websites listed in your packet to develop material for your paper. Watch the program from the History Channel on reserve at the library. Take notes on the questions from your assignment sheet. The information you gather from these sources will form the basis of your paper.	
	Do an Internet search on the impact of the arrival of the Spanish on indigenous populations. Try these key words and phrases: *conquistador, history of smallpox, Spanish conquest of Mexico.* Be sure to consult your Internet site evaluation sheet before you use any of the information you find. Try three other key words based on the readings we have done so far. You will also need three print sources. Begin by looking at some of the references in the back of your readings.	
Lowest level of teacher support	Consult at least five different sources for your paper beyond the reading we have done in class. They may be print or electronic.	Highest level of student autonomy

process has begun, as described in Chapter 4. All of these forms of support can be manipulated throughout the writing process and the course in order to progressively increase learner autonomy.

Pause to consider...

different levels of teacher support for writing tasks. Table 8.1 shows a continuum of decreasing teacher support for the information-gathering stage of a writing task. Describe a similar continuum for the information-analysis phase.

In summary, there are two basic ways to implement TBI in the L2 writing class. In one, the curriculum includes sequence tasks that build in cognitive complexity and linguistic difficulty and gradually move toward target academic tasks. In the other, the curriculum begins with pedagogical tasks that already closely approximate target tasks but includes considerable support for the reading, research, and writing processes. The support is greatest at the beginning of the course and is gradually withdrawn as learners become more able to work independently. Of course, it is also possible to meld the two approaches and include elements of each. Indeed, it is likely that even in the first approach, learners will need support in specific aspects of the writing process.

CONTENT-BASED INSTRUCTION

Content-based instruction (CBI) is an approach to language teaching that finds its roots in schools rather than colleges or universities. It combines L2 instruction with instruction in mainstream courses such as math or social studies; that is, the course content is taught in and through the L2. In post-secondary settings, CBI is available primarily for advanced learners. It offers a variety of advantages:

- It provides instruction in two subjects at once. Because the L2 is taught through content instruction, CBI is considered "value-added" instruction.
- It provides cognitively and intellectually challenging material that may be missing in language courses.
- It provides cultural orientation and an introduction to the new discourse community that learners will soon enter. At the college level, it can bring a sense of being part of the academic community.
- It provides an authentic context for L2 learning. Acquisition is enhanced when the focus is on communication in real settings.
- Although its focus is on content, it takes into account the fact that learners are not native speakers, accommodating and providing support for their limited L2 proficiency.
- It provides realistic academic preparation for mainstream education. Research suggests that not only does L2 proficiency improve, but overall academic performance benefits as well.

CBI's advantages are also its drawbacks. Because content is the instructional focus and, in some settings, the focus of assessment as well, language acquisition may be neglected. Studies of content-based classrooms indicate that both teachers and students are more concerned with the acquisition of content knowledge than the acquisition of linguistic knowledge. Interaction takes place around the exchange of ideas, often leaving little room for attention to the formal aspects of language. Success is seen in terms of content understanding and writing comprehensibility, not language learning. Learners are more likely to receive feedback on the factual accuracy or insightfulness of their answers than their form. Although this can be an appropriate strategy, language acquisition may stagnate if learners are never asked to attend to the accuracy of their production.

For these reasons language-centered activities should be included in any content-based classroom. If the teaching of content is an effective vehicle for teaching language, then it is a good pedagogical choice. If content learning takes place at the expense of language acquisition, it is time to modify the course and the approach. In CBI writing courses, teachers need to direct learners' attention to linguistic accuracy as well as to course content.

It is worth noting again the distinction between L2 and FL settings. The lack of focus on language may be of particular significance in FL settings. In these classrooms, in spite of the teachers' and administration's efforts to create an authentic language learning context, there is often little contact with native speakers and the L2 culture. An exclusive focus on content can exacerbate the tendency for the students in these classes to develop classroom "dialects" that may make it more difficult for them to progress toward target-like accuracy in the L2.

CBI is more a philosophy than a unified method or approach. In fact, various approaches fall under the rubric of CBI, including immersion, sheltered instruction, adjunct courses, and sustained content language teaching. Each has somewhat different characteristics that make it appropriate for specific settings.

Immersion

The purest form of CBI is *immersion*. It is found primarily at the primary and secondary levels but has been tried in some FL and EFL settings as well. In these programs, the language of instruction for a significant part of the school day is in the L2. The goal of these programs is to graduate students with advanced competence in both the L1 and the L2, along with content knowledge and skills (e.g., in math, science) equivalent to the knowledge and skills of their counterparts who have received their education exclusively in their L1. This approach has been adopted in settings with societal bilingualism, in those with large immigrant populations, and even in those where the parents of children whose L1 is the dominant language want their children to acquire an L2. It is also used in countries outside of North America in which students must prepare for postsecondary education in a language of wider communication, such as French in Morocco or English in Ethiopia. Because full-fledged immersion programs are relatively rare in higher education in North America, we focus here on more common forms of CBI.

Sheltered Instruction

Sheltered instruction is frequently used as a transition program for L2 students in postsecondary education. These students are not quite ready to take on regular content courses in the L2 or, in the case of FLs, upper-level courses for majors. Yet in order to advance academically, they need to begin to experience actual college courses. In sheltered instruction, separate, parallel classes are created for L2 students. Teachers present the same content as in mainstream classes but scaffold the material and the concepts so they are more accessible to learners. In FL settings, sheltered classes can be found in Language Across the Curriculum (LAC) programs, in which students take content courses in the FL, for example, French history in French. (See http://www.cortland.edu/flteach/lac/ for some examples of LAC in higher education.)

Like all models of CBI, sheltered classes provide students with a rich and authentic context for learning and writing. Writing tasks are the same as those required of native speakers, though there may be fewer assignments. What makes sheltered instruction programs somewhat different from other approaches to language teaching is that the teaching is done by content faculty, not language teachers. Not all mainstream teachers are willing or able to make the changes to their courses necessary to make these classes accessible. They may need to change their delivery style, offer more supporting material, or provide material that is more explicit and guided. Professors must also be prepared to cope with writing that may contain more errors than that of their native-speaker students. Studies of sheltered instruction at both the school and college levels generally report positive results for both content mastery and improvement in language proficiency. The main drawback of such programs is the difficulty of finding faculty who are both willing and able to deliver appropriate instruction. A second drawback, at least at the college level, is that the number of students who have sufficient proficiency to benefit from such courses is small compared to the total number of L2 writers at any given institution. Sheltered instruction is generally feasible only for ESL and for FLs with large enrollments, such as Spanish.

Adjunct Courses

In sheltered courses, instruction is provided by content teachers rather than language teachers. In *adjunct courses*, at least some of the instruction is delivered by language teachers; therefore, this type of instruction is more likely to be encountered by L2 writing teachers. In adjunct programs, students enroll in two courses: The first is a regular content course, and the second is a language course specifically designed to support learning in the content course. This model is most common in higher education settings in which an ESL or FL class is linked with an introductory general education class. The advantages and disadvantages of adjunct instruction compared to sheltered instruction are shown in Table 8.2.

Like sheltered instruction, adjunct courses generally involve all skills: listening to lectures, reading texts, taking notes, writing papers, and so on. The writing support in the language component will generally have to include guidance on reading authentic texts; assistance with academic and discipline vocabulary; help in deconstructing assignments, which may not be transparent to L2 writers; and as always, support for research and writing tasks. Reading loads are often particularly problematic for students beginning academic courses. They have difficulty making choices about what material to read first and how closely they need to read. They read slowly, in part because of their limited vocabulary. They may need more direct instruction on the meaning and use of new words, particularly vocabulary that is crucial to understanding the readings, and on producing text-responsible assignments. Thus, although the main focus of a content-based writing course may well be on the writing component, it is essential to include instruction on critical reading and vocabulary building.

Sustained Content Language Teaching

Content-based instruction has been an effective approach in many settings, particularly those in which learners are held responsible for mastery of content. However, because of the importance of content learning in CBI, some in

TABLE 8.2 Advantages and Disadvantages of Adjunct Programs Compared to Sheltered Programs

---

Advantages of Adjunct Programs Over Sheltered Instruction

- Because L2 students are enrolled in the same class as native speakers, adjunct programs create an opportunity for interaction and acquisition and end the segregation of L2 students from native speakers.
- Regular content classes provide an authentic setting and materials for students about to enter the academic discourse community.
- The opportunity to enroll in content classes eases the transition from LAP classes, particularly for minority and foreign students entering North American university programs.
- L2 students can often get credit for the content course, an element frequently missing from LAP classes, at least in English. This may increase student motivation.
- Research suggests that students progress in both content learning and language acquisition.

Disadvantages of Adjunct Programs Compared to Sheltered Instruction

- It can be expensive. Two instructors are required for what may appear to be a single course to both students and administration.
- The language instructor may not have sufficient knowledge of the content to explain it fully to students.
- Students may pay little attention to the content instructor and simply wait for the language teacher to digest the material and present it to them in a more accessible way.

---

the field believe that L2 learning may often be sacrificed. The content emphasis is understandable, given that learners, particularly primary and secondary school learners, are likely to be assessed on content knowledge rather than linguistic performance. This emphasis may be counterproductive for older L2 writers' linguistic development. Research conducted in CBI classes suggests that teachers often pay little attention to linguistic accuracy, either in feedback or in instruction. Teachers respond to student contributions on the basis of factual accuracy, creativity, and so on, not on the basis of linguistic form. Communication continues and is considered successful as long as participants can understand one another. Thus, despite the many advantages of these "purer" forms of CBI, some of their drawbacks have led educators to develop a new strand of CBI, called **sustained content language teaching (SCLT)**.

SCLT courses are taught by language faculty. A sustained content course explores a single topic or content area in depth from a variety of perspectives. It usually includes development in all skills, though some courses may concentrate on reading and writing. Because course content is introductory, even the more technical material is readily accessible to most language teachers. Although the hope is that learners will find the topic engaging and learn from the readings and activities, they are not held responsible for the content material in the same way that they would be in a true CBI course. The main characteristic that differentiates SCLT from other forms of CBI is that it includes a significant focus on the teaching and learning of the L2, both in instruction and in assessment. Language instruction occurs through the content but remains an important component of the course, with learners held accountable for the form as well as the content of their contributions.

The advantages of SCLT in the teaching of L2 writing are similar to those of other approaches to CBI. The most important advantage is that learners develop expertise in a topic during the course, exploring a variety of perspectives and gathering information from multiple sources. This contrasts with thematically based L2 writing courses in which learners may go through four or five unrelated topics in a term (e.g., gender roles, homelessness, personal identity). This smorgasbord approach tends to be less intellectually satisfying than courses with a single theme. The sustained treatment of a single topic allows students to explore it more deeply. They can begin to access and explain the same subject and sometimes even the same material in different ways, an approach that allows them to develop the critical reading and thinking skills they will need in future academic courses. The teacher can spend less time explaining the content of readings, because the ideas in them are recycled in successive readings and assignments. Knowledge builds rather than being discarded in favor of the next theme. Reading becomes easier, not because texts become easier but because they become more accessible. Students develop the required background knowledge that will help them to understand subsequent texts on the same topic. This mirrors the kind of academic experience they will have in mainstream content courses. Vocabulary is similarly cycled, so that learners get the multiple exposure to new words in a variety of contexts that is required for acquisition. Learners also have the opportunity to use these words in their own writing, a step that is considered valuable for anchoring them for long-term retention.

L2 writing instructors face several challenges in establishing sustained content courses. They must find a topic and sources that will engage their students, that will be accessible, and that, at best, could be useful for their future studies or career. SCLT course design and topics may be as varied as the contexts in which they are situated. For FL classes, topics related to the culture, geography, and history of countries in which the language is spoken are a natural choice. It may also be easier to locate materials on these topics in the FL than on more generic topics. The Internet has a wealth of both authentic and pedagogical sources of such materials, particularly in more commonly taught languages (see, for instance, http://www.cortland .edu/flteach/flteach-res.html).

Sustained content courses, like other forms of CBI, are most frequently offered to learners with high proficiency in the L2. However, unlike adjunct and sheltered courses, SCLT may also be offered to somewhat lower proficiency learners, who can also benefit from a sustained focus on a specific topic. Realistically, learners have to be at an intermediate level to benefit from SCLT. The key is to find source materials that will be accessible. Several possibilities have been suggested. If learners have good oral/aural skills, films may make good source material. Teachers may want to use several films on a similar topic, such as ethnicity and identity (*Mississippi Masala, Stand and Deliver, Joy Luck Club*, etc.). Films are universally popular and are a rich source of information about culture, history, politics, and attitudes. Analysis of source material invites comparison to students' own lives and experiences.

Literature is another source of material. Texts written for younger native speakers, both fiction and nonfiction, may work well in sustained content classes. Many ESL teachers use children's or young adult literature in their classes. One potential problem is that these books may contain themes that are inappropriate for L2 students or language that is so culturally or historically embedded that the content becomes difficult for learners to access. For this reason, texts should be screened carefully. Timeless classics that are not set in specific places or historic periods such as *The Giver* by Lois Lowry for ESL, are a good choice. Textbooks for native-speaker children and teens are also a good resource for topics like national history or geography. An example is *Geografía*,[1] a geographic portrait of Latin America produced in Argentina and used in college Spanish classes. In general, these books are conceptually and linguistically simpler than those produced for adult learners. Again, they need to be screened for possible bias.

Teachers can also use sourcebooks—collections of authentic writings and materials from which writers can draw as they research a specific topic.[2] Sourcebooks were popular in the mid-20th century for composition classes in American universities. They provide a fairly thorough treatment of a specific topic through the use of multiple sources that offer different perspectives. They work well because the same material is available to the whole class and learners can concentrate on reading, analyzing, and composing rather than on locating appropriate material. Teachers are also better able to provide guidance, because they are familiar with the material that students are using. Unfortunately, sourcebooks are no longer commercially available and have to be developed in-house. Creating a sourcebook can be a daunting prospect for individual teachers, but large programs can develop files of materials that can be shared by teachers and assembled and reassembled for a variety of purposes. Such material is more flexible than commercial publications; it can be tailored to student interests, with sources added and subtracted as classes try them out and as different needs arise. Four of the curricular alternatives discussed in this chapter—TBI, sheltered, adjunct, and sustained content—are compared in Table 8.3.

All of the program options we have discussed offer the L2 writing instructor alternatives for course development that are consistent with what we know about L2 learning and the teaching of writing. They provide a consistent focus on communication and the expression of meaning, but they also allow integration of instruction on language acquisition with skill development. They are well suited for academic learners who need to make the transition from L2 courses to courses in other disciplines or, in the case of FL majors, to more challenging upper division courses. They are especially appropriate for students learning to write in an L2, a skill that requires linguistic facility and accuracy as well as knowledge of academic genres.

TABLE 8.3 Comparison of Curricular Alternatives in L2 Writing

	Program Type			
	Task-based	Sheltered	Adjunct	Sustained content
Possible target population	ESL, FL, 1.5, heritage	ESL, 1.5, FL	ESL, 1.5	ESL, FL, 1.5, heritage
Who teaches	L2 instructor	Content instructor	L2 instructor	L2 instructor
Primary instructional focus	Writing and language	Content	Content	Writing and language

---

> ## *Pause to consider...*
>
> **which curricular options would work best in your program. How could you adapt them to engage your learners?**

SUMMARY

Traditional approaches to teaching L2 writing have focused on language rules, vocabulary use, and rhetorical patterns. Process approaches shifted the emphasis to audience and purpose. In neither case has the content of the writing been paramount. Some alternative approaches to teaching L2 writing place more importance on mastering content.

Task-based instruction (TBI) is often found in academic language programs. The organizing principle in TBI is the task—one that has importance outside of the language classroom. In academic writing programs, tasks include essays, reports, critiques, and so on. Because it is based on the real-world needs of the learners, TBI may be more likely to engage learners. Activities are authentic or at least derived from authentic activities. The curriculum is organized around these tasks rather than linguistic forms and is generally sequenced in terms of the cognitive complexity of the tasks. Using various forms of scaffolding and other guidance, teachers can help learners gradually tackle the kinds of tasks they will encounter outside of the language classroom.

Content-based instruction (CBI) stresses mastery of content in a specific discipline. There are several CBI program designs. In immersion programs, usually found in secondary school classrooms, students learn academic content through the L2. In sheltered instruction, learners prepare for entry into mainstream academic programs by taking a transition course in which content material is adapted for their proficiency level. Classes are taught by content instructors. In adjunct programs, students enroll in two classes, one mainstream content class and one support class, in which an L2 professional helps learners access and process the material in the content class. Critics of CBI maintain that the focus on content can result in neglect of language development. In a slightly different version of CBI, sustained content language teaching (SCLT), classes are taught by L2 instructors rather than content professionals. Although content remains central, there is consistent emphasis on language development, both in instruction and in assessment.

CHAPTER NOTES

1. *Geografía,* by R. Bertoncello, H. Castro, M. A. Casaís, and I. Thisted, 2001, Buenos Aires: Santillana.
2. "Sourcebooks in a Sustained-Content Curriculum," by B. Powell and R. Ponder, 2001, *TESOL Journal, 10,* 18–22.

READ MORE ABOUT IT

LAP and Task-Based Instruction

Carson, J. (2001). Reading and writing for academic purposes. In M. Pally (Ed.), *Sustained content teaching in academic ESL/EFL* (pp. 19–34). Boston: Houghton Mifflin.

Carson, J., Taylor, J., & Laureen, F. (1997). The role of content in task-based EAP instruction. In M. Snow & D. Brinton (Eds.), *The content-based classroom* (pp. 367–376). New York: Longman.

*Moulton, M., & Holmes, V. (2000). The ESL capstone course: Integrating research tools, techniques and technology. *TESOL Journal, 9,* 23–29.

*Williams, J. (2001). A task-based composition course for resident L2 writers. In I. Leki (Ed.), *Academic writing programs* (pp. 111–120). Washington, DC: TESOL.

Content-Based Instruction

*Brinton, D., & Master, P. (Eds.). (1997). *New ways in content-based instruction.* Arlington, VA: TESOL.

Brinton, D., Snow, M., & Wesche, M. (1989). *Content-based second language instruction.* Boston: Heinle.

Kasper, L. (Ed.). (2000). *Content-based college ESL instruction.* Mahwah, NJ: Erlbaum.

Kreuger, M., & Ryan, F. (1993). *Language and content: Discipline and content-based approaches to language study.* Lexington, MA: D. C. Heath.

Stoller, F., & Grabe, W. (1997). A six-T's approach to content-based instruction. In M. Snow & D. Brinton (Eds.), *The content-based classroom.* (pp. 5–21). New York: Longman.

Stryker, S., & Leaver, B. (Eds.). (1997). *Content-based instruction in foreign language education.* Washington, D.C.: Georgetown University Press.

Adjunct Models

*Andrade, M., & Makaafi, J. (2001). Guidelines for establishing adjunct courses at the university level. *TESOL Journal, 10,* 34–39.

Sustained Content Language Teaching

*Murphy, J., & Stoller, F. (2001). Sustained content language teaching: An emerging definition. *TESOL Journal, 10,* 3–5.

Pally, M. (1997). Critical thinking in ESL: An argument for sustained content. *Journal of Second Language Writing, 6,* 293–311.

*Powell, B., & Ponder, R. (2001). Sourcebooks in a sustained-content curriculum. *TESOL Journal, 10,* 18–22.

*Accessible readings for beginning students

Draft Texts for Practice Response

ENGLISH

This text was written by a student in response to the Robert Frost poem "The Road Not Taken." Students were asked to say what they thought the poet was trying to express in the poem and to relate it to their own experience.

The poem was written by Robert Frost. It is about a traveler who encounters two roads that lead to two different directions. He chose the way which he thought was a better claim. As he walks by the road he then wanders what if he chose the other road. Would it make a difference?

As we grow older we are force to face life's complexities and one of this is decision making. Everyday we decide on minor and major things and these decision somehow effect our lives. Decisions are particularly hard to make especially when we are face with two good options. Usually our choices are based on what we thought is good. The results are often satisfying but sometimes it is frustrating. But what if we chose the other option? Would it probably make our life much better? I believe that it is not a question of whether life would be better but how this decision taught us to become better persons. It is true that we experience hardships as a result of wrong decision but we can never change or bring back yesterday we only have now and a future to make. We need to move on and to look forward to good possibilities and new beginnings.

This poem personally touched me because there have been several instances in my life were I have to choose and make the best decision. I just earned my degree and got my license to practice when I left my country. In fact, before I left for the States, there were many job offers from small and big pharmacy companies. I do not accept the offers because I have better future plans and besides all my family is finally migrating here. It was a hard decision to make and I felt that there isn't much choice but come here in the 'Land of the Opportunities.' Sometimes I wonder what if I accepted one of the job offers. I should be in the middle of my career now and probably slowly making a name for myself. Was it worth leave my home, my friends, my dogs? Until now I don't know if it was a right decision. I only have faith, I only have a hope, that someday I will know what was the right road.

FRENCH

In this assignment, students were to assume the identity of Napoleon and write a persuasive letter to a government official.

Monsieur:

Je vous prie de faire attention a cette lettre. Excusez-moi s'il ya des petites fautes. J'ai écrit tellement milliers de lettres. Alors, laisser donner des détails a propos de mes reformes. Écouter soigneusement s'il vous plait. Premièrement, il faut que vous sachez ma stratégie militaire. Quand on commence une bataille, je lui demande d'avoir beaucoup de soutiens. Après, on doit chercher la partie la plus faible de vos ennemies. Ensuite, attaquez au bon moment! Veuillez faire avec cette stratégie, bien qu'il soit difficil de le faire, as la différence de moi.

J'ordonne que tous mes suivants fassent tout ce qu'ils peuvent pour fortifier ma réputation militaire. Il est dispensable que j'aie seulement des bons administrateurs. Je pense que vous savez que je suis un administrateur et un législateur excellent. J'ai codifié le droit français. Avec ma surveillance, il y a sept nouveaux codes de droit. Je suis sur que vous le savoir, et aussi que le meilleur connu est mon "Code Napoleon." Je veux que vous sachez ces codes et que vous les estimiez parce qu'ils entraînent des libertés. Par example, l'abolition de servage et la tolérance de religion. J'espère aussi que vous sachez que j'ai centralisé le gouvernement de France par administrater des départements avec des prefects.

J'insiste que vous sachez la nécessité d'avoir les sentiments de nationalisme et d'être en communication avec l'opinion du public. Bien qu'il soit très important d'avoir le bien-être. Ça c'est la raison pour les sénatories que j'ai creé. Il est essential d'employer des sénateurs seulement pour des investigations. Ces investigations doivent être conduites en secret pour des territoires spécifiques. Elles aident de donner au gouvernement les idées et les besoins du public, et aussi d'aider le public de savoir "la véritable pensée du gouvernement."

Mon gouvernement doit être fondé sur la Révolution française et ce fait est extrémement important pour l'existence de mon régime.

GERMAN

In this assignment, students were asked to write an analysis of the film *Run, Lola, Run* and interpret the director's intentions.

Ein neues Märchen

Man muß laufen. Oder zumindest denkt Lola so, denn sie will Mannis Leben retten. Lola is der Star im Film "Lola rennt." Und Manni ist ihre Freund.

Anfangs hat Manni ein Problem. Er arbeitet für einen Autoscheiber. Mannis Job? Sien Boss Geld von einem kummen Geschäft bringen. Aber als Manni mit dem U-bahn fuhr, hat er das Geld (100.000 Mark) verliet. Jetzt muß er etwas machen für das Geld wiederzulangen und seinem Boss es zu geben.

Aber was war passiert? Warum hat Manni das geld verliet? Also, der Plan war daß Lola Manni mit dem Motorrad abholen sollte. Aber also Lola Zigarreten kaufte, hat jemand seiner Motorrad gestohlen und konnte sie Manni nicht abholen. Also, sie ist zu Hause gekommen an dann hat Manni sie angerufen. Manni erklärt was passiert ist. Er sagt sie auch daß er die 100.000 Mark in zwanzig Minuten haben muß oder seinem Boss ihm toten wurde.

Was dann muß oder kann Lola machen? Sie sagt Manni, daß er dort aus die Telefonzelle bleiben soll und nichts machen. Lola denkt wo und von wem kann sie das Geld erreichen. Sie erinnert sich viele Leute und dann entscheidt sie sich zu ihren Vater zu gehen.

Das Schiksal hat drei Geschichte in "Lola rennt." In der ersten, Lola ist tot, in der zweiten, Manni stirbt, und in die dritten, Lolas Vater und sein Freund, Herr Meyer, sterben. Der Regisseur hat mit diesem Thema sehr gut arbeitet. Er spielt mit dem philosophishen Them, daß sagt was Menschenleben bestimmt ist. Er macht das dreimal.

"Lola rennt" is ein kompliziertes Film und man soll ausführlich sie studieren. Aber wie ich ehrlich sein, dan muß ich sagen, daß ich gut Essay über "Lola rennt" auf Deutsch nicht schreiben kann. Über "Lola rennt" kann ich nur sagen, daß sie ein talles Film ist. Ich denke, daß der Regisseur hat ein gut Arbeit gemacht hat. Die Geschichte daß er geschreiben hat ist nicht neu. Das was er gemacht hat, ist die Rolle von Mann und Frau umgekehrt. Der Prinz erlöst die Prinzessin von dem Schloss und von die böse Hexe nicht mehr; jetzt muß die Frau ihrem Mann von dem städtishe Dracher erlösen. Lola, dann, ist eine moderne Heldin.

Endlich, obwohl "Lola rennt" von eine alten Tradition kommt, ist sie eine neuere Geschichte weil, überalles, "Lola rennt" eine Liebegeschichte ist.

SPANISH

In this assignment, students were asked to write a review of the film *Fresa y Chocolate* describing the plot and commenting on the effectiveness of the film.

Fresa y chocolate

La película, *Fresa y Chocolate,* es de dos personas oppositas que se encuentran intercambiando ideas y formando una amistad incomun. Uno prefiero el helado de fresa y el otro el helado de chocolate. David es un joven cubano que cree fuertemente en los ideales de la revolución. Diego es una persona muy intelligente y cultural. Infortunadamente es homosexual y una persona con opiniones muy fuertes. Esto resulta en muchos problema para Diego. La película nos enseña que todas personas nos pueden enseñar algo importante. Los efectos negativos de un gobierno comunista se hacen aparente.

Los actores actúan el guión honestamente, representan sus partes respectivas de una manera inteligente y con mucha compasión. Los directores encuentran una manera de contarnos la historia simplemente sin necesidad de extravagancias. La ciudad de Havana es muy bella. Los directores hacen bueno uso del ambiente cubano. El guión de la película es maravilloso, escrito con una ternura que es muy rara. Verdaderamente se ve el amor y el apoyo entre Diego, David, y Nancy. La película provoca cólera por las injusticias que deben sufrie los personajes. Nos enseña que todas las personas forman parte de una comunidad aunque no sean estimados. *Fresa y chocolate* se la recomiendo a cualquiera persona que busque una película entretenida y honesta.

Assessment Guidelines for FL Writing

1. ADVANCED PLACEMENT GERMAN — COMPOSITION

Scoring Guideline for Question 2 — Composition

Below is the 2002 scoring guideline used for compositions:

9–8 Demonstrates superiority through outstanding control of the language with regard to structure, syntax, idiomatic usage, and vocabulary. The student makes few significant errors and demonstrates a broad command of the language and obvious fluency. An 8 is less impressive with regard to structure and syntax, or range in idiomatic usage and vocabulary.

7 Demonstrates strong command of the language with, however, some grammatical inaccuracies and errors, and some awkwardness of expression. Shows very good, although not always accurate, use of vocabulary and idioms. Errors do not detract from the generally clear demonstration of competence and control.

6–5 Demonstrates good to acceptable use of the language. The student is basically competent in the language although less impressive with regard to structure and syntax or range in idiomatic usage and vocabulary. Occasional serious errors. Occasional signs of fluency. Recurring questions about sustained control of the language lower the score to a 5.

4–3 Suggests weak use of the language. The student has less than adequate language skills. Numerous errors and frequent use of non-German syntax and language patterns. Contains sentences that paraphrase or repeat what has essentially been stated earlier or sentences that force interpretation. The lack of occasional redeeming features, such as correct advanced grammatical constructions or range of vocabulary, lowers the score to a 3. Note: Occasional grammatically correct simple sentences are not redeeming features.

2–1 Demonstrates incompetence in the language. The student has little or no sense of syntax and few vocabulary resources. A response that is essentially a Germanized version of another language or gobbledy-gook lowers the score to a 1.

0 Responses that are entirely blank, consist of fewer than 50 words, do not attempt to address the topic, are written in a language other than German, appear to be compositions prepared ahead of time, or that contain the following: obscenities, nonsense, poetry, drawings, etc.

2. ACTFL PRELIMINARY PROFICIENCY GUIDELINES—WRITING, REVISED 2001

Summary Highlights

Superior	Advanced	Intermediate	Novice
Superior-level writers are characterized by the ability to:	Advanced-level writers are characterized by the ability to:	Intermediate-level writers are characterized by the ability to:	Novice-level writers are characterized by the ability to:
• express themselves effectively in most informal and formal writing on practical social and professional topics treated abstractly and concretely. • present well-developed ideas, opinions, arguments, and hypotheses through extended discourse. • control structures, e.g., general and specialized/ professional vocabulary, spelling and symbol production, punctuation, diacritical marks, cohesive devices, and other aspects of written forms and organization with no pattern of error that distracts the reader.	• write routine informal and some formal correspondence, narratives, descriptions, and summaries of a factual nature. • narrate and describe major time frames, using paraphrase and elaboration to provide clarity, in connected discourse of paragraph length. • express meaning that is comprehensible to those unaccustomed to the writing of non-natives, primarily through generic vocabulary, with good control of the most frequently used structures.	• meet practical writing needs—e.g., simple messages and letters, requests for information, notes—and ask and respond to questions. • create with the language and communicate simple facts and ideas in a loosely connected series of sentences on topics of personal interest and social needs, primarily in the present time frame. • express meaning through vocabulary and basic structures that is comprehensible to those accustomed to the writing of non-natives.	• produce lists and notes and limited formulaic information in simple forms and documents. • recombine practice material supplying isolated words or phrases, transcribe familiar words or phrases, copy letters of the alphabet or syllables of a syllabary, or reproduce basic characters with some accuracy. • communicate basic information.

Note. From *Preliminary Proficiency Guidelines*, American Council on the Teaching of Foreign Languages. http://www.actfl.org/public/ articles/writingguidelines.pdf. Reprinted by permission of the American Council on the Teaching of Foreign Languages. Retrieved December 3, 2003.

GLOSSARY

Analytic scoring an assessment procedure in which the components of writing are analyzed and scored separately

Attention concentration of mental focus

Audience the person or group who is expected to read a text

Composing writing with a communicative purpose

Comprehensible input input that is or has been modified to be better understood by the learner

Computer-assisted language learning (CALL) any approach to language teaching that uses computer or multimedia technology

Concordances computer programs that search corpora to show patterns of occurrence and co-occurrence of specific words and structures

Content-based instruction (CBI) instructional approach in which the subject matter (e.g., math, history) is taught in a second language

Contrastive analysis a method of comparing two languages to establish differences and similarities

Contrastive rhetoric a subfield of applied linguistics that investigates the rhetorical influences of the first language on second language writing

Controlled writing activities in which much of the structure or content of the final product is supplied to the student

Corpus large collection/database of language samples

Discourse a coherent sequence of connected spoken or written text

Discourse community a group of people with their own characteristic genres and lexicon, and rules and conventions for sharing information

Discussion boards electronic forums for discussion among people with common interests

Explicit knowledge conscious knowledge of language rules, generally developed under explicit learning conditions such as direct teaching and practice of forms

Extensive reading an approach to reading instruction in which students do a large amount of reading for general comprehension, often for pleasure and outside of class

First language (L1)   the first language a person learns as a child

Fluency   the ability to produce language with ease and efficiency

Foreign language (FL)   a second language learned and spoken in an environment in which the language is not spoken, for example, English in Japan

Form-focused instruction   instruction that is intended to draw learners' attention to formal aspects of language

Form-meaning connections   situations in which a form encodes referential meaning

Generation 1.5   Language learners whose linguistic and educational experiences have been partly in the first language environment and partly in the second language environment

Genre   a particular type of text, such as a report, memo, or poem, which has a characteristic format, features, and use

Graphic organizers   visual means of displaying thinking processes

Heritage learners   learners of a language that is considered foreign in the larger community but one they speak or hear in their home or local community, for example, Latinos learning Spanish in New York

Holistic scoring   scoring procedure in which student texts are assessed as a whole

Implicit knowledge   unconscious knowledge of a language system, including rules and vocabulary

Input   language that a learner reads or hears in the process of communication of meaning

Input enhancement   input that has been modified with the goal of bringing formal features to the attention of the reader or listener

Intake   linguistic data held in memory and available for further processing

Intensive reading   an approach to reading in which learners read shorter and fewer texts but do so to develop specific skills, such as connecting ideas and finding supporting details, and to build linguistic knowledge

Interlanguage (IL)   the linguistic system of second language learners

Invention techniques   strategies for generating or expanding ideas for writing

Item learning   the accumulation of linguistic forms, stored separately and only loosely connected with one another

Language Threshold Hypothesis   regarding reading skill in a second language: Learners must have sufficient second language knowledge to access their first language reading skills

Logical connectors   transitional expressions that link clauses, phrases, and sentences (e.g., *in spite of, afterwards, because*); also called *transition words*

Metalinguistic knowledge   knowledge about language, for example, English does not allow initial consonant clusters that have *b, d,* or *g* as their second element (e.g., **sgup*)

Metatalk   Talk about language (e.g., *This verb takes the dative case*)

Modified output   learner production that has been changed (usually in the direction of the target language) in response to interactional feedback from another speaker or reader

Monitoring   the use of explicit knowledge to edit output

MOO   A virtual environment in which participants interact with other participants and objects on-line (from Multi-User Domain [MUD], object oriented)

Needs analysis   procedure for collecting information about learner needs

Negative evidence   information about what is not possible in the L2

Negotiation   conversational work that is necessary to achieve mutual comprehension

Network-based language learning   language learning that involves the use of computers linked in a local or global network

Other-regulation   Guidance in executing a task by someone with greater expertise

Output   language that the learner produces orally or in writing to communicate meaning

Peer response   process in which learners respond to one anothers' texts during the writing process

Portfolio   a collection of student writing that demonstrates ability, achievement, and progress, often used for assessment purposes

Practice   repeated engagement in the behavior to be learned, provided that the activity involves the communication of meaning

Process approach   approach to writing instruction that views composing as a multi-staged recursive activity

Prompt   the instructions for writing an essay test or assignment

Reading to learn   reading with the purpose of gaining extensive content knowledge

Rubric   description of guidelines or rules attached to scoring levels on writing assessment instruments

Scaffolding   temporary instructional support that allows learners to perform tasks that would otherwise be too challenging

Second language (L2)   (1) any language that is not the native language. (2) A non-native language used in an environment in which it is spoken by others as a native language (e.g., ESL in the United States)

Self-regulation   task execution and problem solving without the assistance or guidance of others

Skill   the ability to perform an activity or task

Structured input   input that pushes learners away from nonoptimal processing strategies

Sustained content language teaching (SCLT)   instructional approach with a balanced focus on content and language teaching

System learning   rule-based learning yielding a network of connected forms

Task   goal-oriented work or activities that are relevant to school or life needs; what a writer is expected to do

Task-based instruction (TBI)   instructional approach in which the focus is on successful accomplishment of tasks rather than directly on language acquisition; based on the belief that language is best learned during meaningful communication

Transition words   see *Logical connectors*

Treatable error   error that can be explained with recourse to rules

Washback effect   the effect of testing on instruction

Zone of proximal development   level at which learners can perform tasks under the guidance of someone with greater expertise

INDEX